Abbott and Costello
on the Home Front

Abbott and Costello on the Home Front

A Critical Study of the Wartime Films

SCOTT ALLEN NOLLEN

McFarland & Company, Inc., Publishers
Jefferson, North Carolina, and London

Frontispiece

Keep 'Em Flying (1941). Bud Abbott and Lou Costello, in Army Air Corps flight gear, happily cavort with Carol Bruce. Who wouldn't?

LIBRARY OF CONGRESS CATALOGUING-IN-PUBLICATION DATA

Nollen, Scott Allen.
Abbott and Costello on the home front : a critical study of the wartime films / Scott Allen Nollen.
p.   cm.
Includes bibliographical references and index.

ISBN 978-0-7864-3521-0
illustrated case : 50# alkaline paper ∞

1. Abbott, Bud, 1895–1974.   2. Costello, Lou.   3. World War, 1939–1945—Motion pictures and the war.   4. War films—United States—History and criticism.   5. Comedy films—United States—History and criticism.   I. Title.
PN2287.A217N65   2009   791.43'75—dc22   2008053634

British Library cataloguing data are available

Cover photograph: Lou Costello and Bud Abbott in *In the Navy*, 1941 (Photofest); Porthole ©2009 Shutterstock

Manufactured in the United States of America

McFarland & Company, Inc., Publishers
Box 611, Jefferson, North Carolina 28640
www.mcfarlandpub.com

For Dad

TABLE OF CONTENTS

Foreword
by Chris Costello

My dad was always a giver and loved being able to help those less fortunate. During World War II, he and Bud performed at many locations, big and small, to raise money for war bonds. One story has it that they performed in the backyard of a family's home after a small boy approached them at a rally and said he had some change to give if they would perform. Both Dad and Bud visited the boy at his home, performed some routines in the backyard for neighbors, and never took the child's money. That's what Bud and Lou were all about.

When Dad was at the height of his success, both he and Bud paid for many operations (and for people they didn't even know). Dad especially was a champion supporter for young kids who had rheumatic fever. Like himself, he encouraged bed rest and taking their medications while convalescing. If he heard of anyone in need, especially a child, he was right there to help. He loved children and being able to use his success to make their lives brighter and a bit better.

Dad never returned to his hometown of Paterson without bringing in truckloads of baseball gear for the Little League, and he always made sure that their films were first premiered at the neighborhood Fabian Theatre, which he had frequented as a child.

The Lou Costello Jr. Youth Center opened its doors to the kids of East L.A. (Boyle Heights district) in May 1947. It was his dream to build a memorial to his son, Lou, Jr. ("Butch"), who tragically drowned in the family pool just three days before his first birthday. To promote funds to build the center, Dad and Bud launched a nationwide tour. Bud was Lou, Jr.'s godfather and was devastated when the baby died. As Dad did, he wanted a place for kids less fortunate, where they could enjoy baseball, an Olympic-size swimming pool (a lifeguard and lessons were offered for free), machine shop, day care center, basketball, woodshop, soda fountain, and theater.

During the early 1950s, when stars who had promised donations to the center began to falter on their commitments, Dad was forced to turn the center over to the City of Los Angeles' Parks and Recreation Department, but under two conditions: that the name of the center remain the Lou Costello, Jr., Youth Center; and that the portrait of Lou, Jr., hanging in the main foyer of the center remain in full view at all times.

In the 1980s, after a major renovation was completed, the portrait, which had been temporarily stored until it could be re-hung, disappeared. When the family learned of this, the decision was made to donate the only other portrait in existence to the center, where it remains to this day.

My congratulations to Scott Allen Nollen on this book. I hope it achieves great success!

PREFACE

My father, Harold N. Nollen, is ultimately responsible for this book. An Abbott and Costello fan since the beginning—1941—he first introduced me to Bud and Lou on a Sunday afternoon during the early 1970s, when their best films were broadcast by the local NBC affiliate in Omaha, Nebraska. Growing up during the Great Depression and World War II, he, early on, discovered that "laughter is the best medicine." For him, Bud Abbott and Lou Costello delivered it when most needed—from 1941 through 1947, when their characters were in the cinematic U.S. Army—then, through the timelessness of their talent, on television and video. Harry Nollen laughs when just *thinking* of Abbott and Costello.

What a cultural treasure I discovered while watching those first few films, laughing myself to the floor while witnessing perhaps the best verbal comic timing ever filmed and simply smashing Big Band music that heavily influenced me from that day forward. *Buck Privates*, *In the Navy* and *Hold That Ghost* offered not only Abbott and Costello, but also the incomparable Andrews Sisters.

After being broadcast on local TV Sunday matinees during the mid–1970s, Bud and Lou's 1943 Universal film *It Ain't Hay* disappeared from the airwaves. According to Costello's daughter, Chris, this particular film was tied up in a copyright dispute with the estate of writer Damon Runyon.[1] Fortunately I was able to locate an excellent video copy from a Bud and Lou enthusiast. (The film is now included in the *Abbott and Costello: The Complete Universal Pictures Collection* DVD box set.)

While researching my book *Boris Karloff: A Gentleman's Life* in southern California during the autumn of 1996, my father and I shared a memorable Abbott and Costello moment. While driving from Palm Springs to Los Angeles with Boris' daughter, Sara Jane, and her husband, William "Sparky" Sparkman, Dad and I launched into our own rendition of a key scene from one of our favorite A&C films, the vastly underrated *Little Giant* (1946), in which Lou Costello's character, Benny Miller, attempts to aid a farmer, Mr. Perkins, in moving his stubborn mule, Ashtabula. (In the film, Lou travels from Cucamonga to Los Angeles to Stockton, then back.) My Costello impression—after several "Ashtabula!" shouts from the back seat of the Karloff convertible—began to wear thin on Sara's patience.

"Can you put an end to that *nonsense*?" she asked. (I can imagine her father asking the same question during the shooting of his two films with Bud and Lou.)

I was having entirely too much A&C–inspired fun. "I can't help it," I replied.

"Oh, I think you *can*," Sara suggested. (That was the end of our *Little Giant* sojourn.)

For fans and collectors of vintage movie memorabilia, this book is illustrated exclusively with original, studio-produced Abbott and Costello photo stills and lobby cards from my extensive personal collection compiled over several decades. Several images represent out-takes or deleted scenes previously unpublished.

Bud and Lou pose to promote the innovative *Little Giant* (1946).

I would especially like to thank Chris Costello for writing the very personal foreword. She has done much to keep her father's legacy of laughter alive since the publication of her book *Lou's on First* in 1982. In her foreword, she focuses on Lou's career-long charitable efforts, always magnanimously supported by his partner, Bud. Chris continues to provide access to her dad's comic genius via rare films and footage on DVD available at the *www.abbott andcostellocollectibles.com* website.

I also offer a tip of the fedora to the following individuals: Todd "Dane" Jacobsen, Harriet Jenkins, John "The Slack" Jensen, Mark Louis, Shirley A. Nollen and Tom A. Pennock.

For some reason, even the propaganda-fueled, World War II–era films of Bud and Lou will never really become dated. Herein are provided some plausible ideas about why they'll *always* be funny.

INTRODUCTION

Although viewed as "low-brow" comics by the critics, Abbott and Costello, along with the Marx Brothers, were among the first comedians to use wordplay, instead of slapstick, as a comic vehicle. The obvious example is their "Who's on First?" skit. This type of comedy is timeless and classic in form. Not exactly low-brow.

—Mark Louis

Film fans often assume that Bud Abbott and Lou Costello were not the critical darlings of their day: To "high-brow" reviewers who lauded Charles Chaplin, Buster Keaton and—begrudgingly—Stan Laurel and Oliver Hardy, Abbott and Costello couldn't be taken seriously because their roots were in the "low" comedy of vaudeville. The truth is that their *films*, produced on modest "B" budgets, were rarely given serious consideration; but Bud and Lou—during the early 1940s—often were praised for their comic talents. In time, their reliance on tried-and-true burlesque material—something that Lou Costello insisted on—led critics to blame the boys for the stale formula repeatedly used in their Universal films.

Of course, there were elitist commentators who confoundedly couldn't understand why people *laughed* at Abbott and Costello, but these attitudes didn't faze the American working class. Bud and Lou were loved by millions of everyday filmgoers for whom laughter provided an essential balm for the sorrows of the Great Depression and World War II, which swept away so many family members and friends.

Even in recent decades, film professors pontificating from their academic ivory towers, have equated Bud and Lou with the Bowery Boys. So wrapped up in their ever-pretentious search for social significance, these pedagogues don't realize that Universal—a studio saved from bankruptcy by the popularity of Abbott and Costello's films—was *not* on Hollywood's Poverty Row of the 1940s. In their day, Bud and Lou had a more widespread effect on American society than did Chaplin's self-important *The Great Dictator* (1940).

Nonetheless, major critics labeled them as low comedians, although Lou Costello always insisted on avoiding "blue" humor like the plague. Today, the innocent antics of Abbott and Costello can rest on the highest rung of the comic ladder when compared to the often disgusting gutter slop the current generation hails as "comedy": jokes and actions increasingly centered on sex, flatulence and bowel movements.

Most critics were consistently contradictory. The same journalists who complained that the boys were always saddled with the same tired, romantic-plot-with-music formula also wrote negative reviews each time the team tried something new. *Who Done It?*, *Little Giant* and *The Time of Their Lives* were all panned in their day, but now can be viewed as underrated "experimental" gems that, in particular, show the range of Lou Costello's comic genius.

My father, H. N. Nollen, who was 11 years old when *Buck Privates* was released, remembered:

Living on a farm outside a small town, I would redeem pop bottles, do just about anything, to get enough money to go to the latest Abbott and Costello movie on the weekend. There were two shows, an early and a late show; and, at each one, people were lined
up around the corner and down the block. Everyone loved Abbott and Costello, and
they brought a lot of joy to people during the war. They also did a lot for recruiting, in
Buck Privates, *In the Navy* and *Keep 'Em Flying*, maybe more than any other American
entertainers.

Photographs showing long lines surrounding theaters across the nation bear witness to
my father's remarks. And a few earlier writers on Abbott and Costello—including Stephen
Cox and John Lofflin—also have eruditely pointed out their impact on American culture:

> The common wisdom ... is that their mindless humor was a gentle respite from the oth-
> erwise hard times of the war years. That's really inarguable. But it's not the whole story.
> The audiences of that era must also have desperately needed affirmation—they pro-
> duced it for themselves ad nauseam in every art form during that time— affirmation
> that virtue lies with the unwashed, the unimperial, the sons and daughters of Will Rogers,
> Mark Twain, and even Teddy Roosevelt. It was a powerful mythological notion, so pow-
> erful that Harry Truman won an improbable campaign for the presidency at the height
> of Abbott and Costello's popularity. It may sound crazy to talk of their films as "mes-
> sage" movies, but perhaps in popular culture of their times they were. They represented
> the triumph of the American underdog so often that the audience waited patiently for
> the tonic chord, for Lou to win, knowing that no matter what abuse was heaped upon
> him he'd survive.[1]

Cox and Lofflin also provide the perfect summation of why the comedy of Abbott and
Costello will always be timeless—why their films can be watched over and over again, never
becoming ones to stash away for long on the video shelf of today *and* tomorrow:

> Lou ... was a guy we fell in love with. He had the ability to make us care about him....
> Despite his clowning, we see a real, lovable human being in a real human drama, and
> that sets Abbott and Costello pictures apart from the antics of the Three Stooges, Lau-
> rel and Hardy, or even the Marx Brothers. In his ability to make us care, Lou Costello
> has much more in common with his hero Charlie Chaplin and, today, with Woody Allen.
>   There are few unhip comics today. Lewis and Martin [sic] followed Abbott and
> Costello in their unhip style. Red Skelton kept the tradition alive even longer. Art Car-
> ney and Jackie Gleason in *The Honeymooners* are an example from early television. That
> Gleason, as a hapless, besieged bus driver, simply took Costello into the 1950s is pretty
> obvious. But hip has ruled, from Mort Sahl and Bob Newhart to Whoopi Goldberg and
> Eddie Murphy.[2]

Indeed, literal scores of "hip" comics have proliferated since this assessment was written, and the great majority of them will ultimately be forgotten, while Abbott and Costello—
like their fellow timeless comics Chaplin, Keaton, Laurel and Hardy, the Marx Brothers,
Martin and Lewis, and Woody Allen—will continue to provide essential laughter for the
masses.

And those who do praise the team usually focus on Costello, which is initially under-
standable. Perhaps his daughter Chris explained it best, alternately praising her Pop and his
partner:

> Dad was a notorious ad-libber and often would get completely away from the script. When
> he did, Bud would bring him right back in and nobody knew the difference, except
> those familiar with the original script. Usually his innovations were better than the orig-
> inal scripting, because he could play the scene more comfortably in his own words.[3]

1

New Jersey Boys Make Good

Bud: "Did you ever go to school, Stupid?"
Lou: "Yeah, and I come out the same way."

Abbott and Costello were New Jersey boys. William Alexander "Bud" Abbott, the son of Barnum and Bailey Circus folks, supposedly wisecracked his way into life in Asbury Park on October 2, 1895. (However, the Bureau of Vital Statistics in Asbury Park lists his birth date as October 6, 1897.) Bud inherited the gift of gab from his father, Harry Abbott, Sr., who was an advance man for the circus. His mother, Rae Fisher Abbott, excelled in athletics, performing as a bareback rider. The allure of show business was too much for all four Abbott children: Harry, Jr., Olive, Florence ("Babe"), and young Bud, who, after the fourth grade, dropped out of school to take a job at Coney Island, where the family had moved during his infancy. He worked as a candy butcher and a shill, luring customers into the amusement park's House of Mirrors, where he offered to lead them out for 10 cents each.

In 1911—with some pull from his Pop—Bud landed in the box office of Brooklyn's Casino Burlesque Theatre. As assistant treasurer, he was entrusted with paying such major burlesque stars as William Claude Dukenfield (W. C. Fields), Fanny Brice, Bert Lahr and Sophie Tucker. Whenever he could, he watched the performers from backstage and began to develop his own keen sense of comic timing.

In 1918 Bud was working as the treasurer at the National Theater burlesque house in Washington, D.C., where he met Jenny Mae Pratt, a dancer and comic who used the stage name "Betty Smith." One week later, they were married at the courthouse in Alexandria, Virginia. Soon after, they headed for Cleveland, where Bud had landed the manager job and Betty worked as a soubrette.

Fortunately Bud had an uncle with a position at Tammany Hall who was just crazy enough to loan him $1500. Cash in hand, he used the dough to produce his own touring show, *Broadway Flashes*, which featured a comedy team, two singers, and 10 chorus girls. Bud quickly realized that he could save money by assuming the role of the straight man.

When the company landed in Detroit, he settled in at the National Theater as producer for the next three years, staging a new show every week. It was during this period that he learned all the major burlesque routines from the greatest comics in the business, including his cousin, Al Golden, who coached him on technique while downplaying flamboyant, costume-oriented characters in favor of a straightforward approach: a fast-talker in a business suit.

Louis Francis Cristillo made his initial pratfall in Paterson about a decade after Bud, on March 3, 1906, the son of an Italian father, Anthony Sebastian Cristillo, who had emigrated from Caserta, and a mother, Helen Rege, of French and Irish descent. Sebastian had followed two older brothers, Phillip (who had settled in Paterson) and Joseph. A fourth (female) sibling had decided to enter a cloister, the Sisters of Sorrow.

Lou joined an older brother, Anthony ("Pat"), and the brothers later had to share the roost with a sister, Marie. Like Bud Abbott, Lou Cristillo was no scholar, but he loved performing; by 1918, he had decided he wanted to be a movie star. His talent for physical comedy was apparent when he entered a Charles Chaplin Halloween contest at the Paterson Armory, where he won first prize. He also became an impressive athlete, playing basketball at Central High School and with a team called the Armory Five. Later, he played an exhibition basketball game with the Boston Celtics, and boxed as an amateur under the name "Lou King"—until his mother found out.

In 1927 Lou and a friend, Gene Coogan, rode the rails, slept in cars, worked on labor gangs, and subsisted on poached fruit to try their luck in Hollywood. (They attempted to save $200 donated by Lou's old man as long as they possibly could.) Lou managed to land a few jobs as an extra and stuntman at MGM, where he actually doubled for Dolores Del Rio in *The Trail of '98* (1928). He also can be glimpsed briefly as a spectator during a boxing match in the Laurel and Hardy classic two-reeler *The Battle of the Century* (1927).

In 1930 Lou and Gene began hitchhiking back to the East Coast. In Lawrence, Kansas, they stayed with some of Coogan's relatives, who continued to support Gene while Lou moved on to St. Joseph, Missouri, where he found a job as a "Dutch comic" at the Lyceum, a local burlesque theater. He raised enough dough to make it back to New York, where, using the name "Costello" (first appropriated by his musician brother, Pat), he became steadily employed in burlesque. Girls were the main attraction at burlesque houses, with comedians filling in between dance acts. While working in a show together, Lou and Anne Battler, a lovely young chorus girl who had emigrated with her parents from Glasgow, Scotland, fell for each other and were married in 1934.

Now considered the top straight man in the business, Bud currently was performing with Harold Minsky's shows, pulling in $250 per week. During the summer of 1936—awaiting the birth of his daughter, Paddy (who arrived on September 28)—Lou was working with another comic, Joe Lyons, at the Eltinge burlesque theater on West 42nd Street in New York. Bud enjoyed Lou's work, and soon the two comics were running through classic routines backstage, then out front, when Lyons couldn't make the gig. They developed an unprecedented sense of timing, and when Abbott and Evanson parted company, there was only one choice for his replacement: Costello.

The following year, they announced a formal partnership, with Bud as the devious straight man and Lou as the hapless, childlike dimwit. The financial take wasn't evenly split, however. While Abbott grabbed 60 percent, Lou was relegated to 40 (a tradition that reflected the importance of the straight man in burlesque comedy).

On May 3, 1937, burlesque was officially outlawed by Mayor Fiorello La Guardia, who considered the material too blue for public consumption. Bud and Lou had been touring in the show *Life Begins at Minskys*, continuing to hone their respective personae and the relationship between them. They never resorted to risqué material, relying on a straight man named John Grant to adapt the old routines for a "family" audience. While performing in Philadelphia, they signed on with Edward ("Eddie") Sherman, a manager who moved them into vaudeville, including a 10-week run at the Steel Pier in Atlantic City. Tying together the old shtick with inspired improvisation, they never did the same show twice.

Their New Jersey engagement was popular enough to land them additional gigs in Baltimore and Philadelphia. At first, the pay was ridiculously low, but a meeting with Sherman grabbed them more money at better venues, including Fay's Theater in Philly and the Hippodrome in Baltimore. They hit the big time when they were signed to play the Loew's State Theatre in New York, where they broke all attendance records. At this point, Lou told Sherman that they were ready for radio and films, using Laurel and Hardy as the measure of success.

Polishing one of their sketches (not "Who's on First?" as is often reported), they were very nervous about making their radio debut on the February 3, 1938, *Kate Smith Hour*, the first time they were *heard* by a national audience. Ted Collins, Smith's producer, initially was concerned about the equally visual nature of their comedy, but decided to give them a one-shot chance. The team received enough applause to land a return engagement that became a two-year stretch, when they were asked to replace Henny Youngman, who had accepted an offer from Paramount in Hollywood. The development of Costello's boisterous and somewhat high-pitched voice was a direct result of the radio broadcast. His and Abbott's rapid-fire, Jersey-accented deliveries were so similar that listeners initially had difficulty telling them apart.

Their initial 10-minute performance earned them $350. Less than two months later, on March 24, they were a smash hit with "Who's on First?" and audiences couldn't get enough of them. Abbott insisted that Collins put John Grant on the payroll, and the laughs increased even more. (Grant would remain with the team until the end of their partnership in 1956.) By the end of their *Kate Smith* run (on June 28, 1940), they were being paid $1,250 per week. Their success on the show led to a featured spot in the 1939 Broadway revue, *The Streets of Paris*, starring the comedy team of Olsen and Johnson, though the applause they received paled to that generated by Bud and Lou, who performed the classic routines "Hole in the Wall," "Lemon Bit" and "Crazy House" every night. Raves from critics, including Ed Sullivan, bolstered their new status as the Toast of the Town. While appearing in the stage production, they were interviewed during *This Is New York*, a 15-minute experimental television program broadcast by NBC to a limited regional audience.

On December 23, 1939, Lou and Anne's second daughter, Carole Lou (named after Christmas and her Poppa), was born. The *Streets of Paris* closed after 274 performances at the Broadhurst Theater on February 10, 1940, then went on tour, including a date in Washington, D.C., where President Roosevelt invited Bud and Lou to perform for his White House dinner guests on March 16. When the road company began to venture too far away from New York, the boys, who now could grab $3,500 per week playing movie theaters, left the tour. Michael Todd, who had purchased the rights to the Broadway show, signed them for another prestigious engagement, the 1940 World's Fair, where they co-starred with Gypsy Rose Lee in four shows a day, combining these with three at Manhattan's Roxy and a midnight gig at a Times Square nightclub.

Louis B. Mayer was the first Hollywood mogul to make an offer to Abbott and Costello, but Lou didn't want to accept less than $20,000 for them to appear as a supporting act to MGM's powerhouse musical stars. While awaiting a possible counteroffer, Eddie Sherman was contacted by Matty Fox, an executive in Universal's New York office, who offered the team $35,000 to appear in a musical, "Riviera," as a supporting, but featured, act.

The Costello family promptly made plans to move to Beverly Hills; but before leaving for California, Bud and Lou were filmed attending the July 18, 1940, New York premiere of Universal's current release *The Boys from Syracuse*, starring Allan Jones and Martha Raye. Considered their motion picture debut, the footage was included in the July 23 installment of the *News of the Day* newsreel series.

Universal re-titled "Riviera" to "Caribbean Holiday" and "Moonlight in the Tropics" before finally settling on *One Night in the Tropics*, based on the novel *Love Insurance* by Charlie Chan creator Earl Derr Biggers, after the location was switched to "San Marcos," an island off the coast of South America. Composer Jerome Kern objected to Bud and Lou appearing in the film, as did producer Leonard Spigelglass, who thought the film better suited to Clark Gable and Carole Lombard but accepted the job purely for the paycheck. Spigelglass conferred with star Allan Jones (whose contract gave him approval of story, cast and director) and screenwriters Gertrude Purcell and Charles Grayson to devise a rationale for the two comics to appear in the film. Jones didn't mind the presence of Bud and Lou, as long as their scenes did not detract from the romantic plot involving his character, "love insurance" salesman Jim Moore.

A. Edward Sutherland (who had directed Jones in *The Boys from Syracuse*) began shooting on August 26, 1940, with Jones and Nancy Kelly in the leads, and Bud and Lou sharing third billing, above Robert Cummings. During the first day on the set, they were understandably nervous, but developed a warm rapport with their costars, particularly Jones, who recalled, "Lou was a lot of fun on that picture."[1]

Jones had personally chosen Sutherland, who had worked in Hollywood films since 1914,

One Night in the Tropics (1940). Lou and Bud indulge a favorite pastime—gambling—in their first feature-film appearance.

first as a stuntman, then as an actor in Mack Sennett's Keystone comedies. After serving as Chaplin's assistant director on *A Woman of Paris* (1923), he helmed several memorable comedy features, working with W. C. Fields, Mae West, and Laurel and Hardy.

Bud and Lou weren't accustomed to performing without an audience, so Spigelglass explained that they indeed had one—the crew—but some of them laughed loud enough to spoil several takes. Making a smooth transition from radio to film, the boys are *heard* before they are seen. Walking into the club Roscoe, William Frawley tells Jones, "It's about time you met up with the boys."

"C'mon, Costello," Bud is heard to say.

"Okay, Abbott," Lou replies in a high-pitched voice. "Oh, I'm a baaaad boy!" In their first scene on film, they are shown gambling, one of their favorite real-life pastimes.

Moore, who claims he can insure anything, invents "love insurance" to safeguard Cummings' upcoming marriage to Kelly, although his old flame, Mickey Fitzgerald (Peggy Moran), is still in hot pursuit.

Bud and Lou perform some of their most popular routines, including "Two Tens for a Five," "Jonah and the Whale" and "Mustard." Just before boarding the ship, while standing next to a taxi, they rip through an abbreviated version of "Who's on First?" featuring cutaway close-ups to the poker-faced cabbie. Throughout their career, they performed flawless arithmetic shtick, here including the "365 Days" routine, wherein Lou speaks of his earning $1 per day for a year. By the time Bud is through with his con man spiel, Lou has only a single dollar left, which a waiter then grabs from his hand as a tip.

Some indirect references to Laurel and Hardy distinguish their film debut. Hal Roach regular Charlie Hall plays the ship's steward, and Costello—already demonstrating highly accomplished nonverbal acting—does a smooth double-take combining a slight movement of the head with a Stan Laurel-like "eye take." The team also gets the last shot in the film, with Costello's famous line, "A husband is what's left of a sweetheart after the nerve has been killed."

Universal chose the Los Angeles suburb of Huntington Park as the location for the film's premiere, which they hoped would be attended by "average moviegoers." Indeed, the film's story and score were lambasted by critics. A tedious, absurd romantic farce, *One Night in the Tropics* is only tolerable when Bud and Lou are on screen. The audience laughed loud and long at their routines, and they easily stole the show away from the principals. According to Chris Costello, Lou told her mother, "The picture should have been scripted as an Abbott and Costello film. We should've been the stars. In order to showcase us, Universal screwed up Allan's movie. That bothers me because he's a nice guy."[2]

During the shoot, Bud and Lou moonlighted as summer replacements for Fred Allen on his Wednesday night radio program, which they had moved from New York to Hollywood, where their final show was broadcast on September 25, 1940. *Tropics* stars Allan Jones and Robert Cummings were guests on the August 21 broadcast. After the film's premiere, the boys began a 10-week vaudeville tour on October 12, playing to packed houses from Los Angeles to New York. Universal, realizing that Bud and Lou were largely responsible for the success of *One Night in the Tropics*, opened new contract negotiations.

2

ON THE LAND AND ON THE SEA

Buck Privates (1941) and *In the Navy* (1941)

With Abbott and Costello dropping gags once a minute and the Andrews Sisters crooning patriotic boogie-woogie airs, well, it's going to be a merry war, folks.—New York Times, February 14, 1941[1]

The practice of using the cinema as a nationalistic propaganda tool is as old as the medium itself. Beginning in 1896, in both the United States and Great Britain, one-reel subjects consisting of "actuality" footage were exhibited by traveling showmen. In the U.S., fabricated "events" from the 1898 Spanish-American War (toy boats were floated in a bathtub) were used in an attempt to sway public opinion; while, in England, dramatic narratives such as *The Call to Arms* (1902) were intended to gain support for the nation's aims during the Boer War in South Africa.

From 1914 to 1919, American society experienced and participated in one of the first mass propaganda campaigns of the 20th Century. Leaders in Europe and the United States, utilizing the burgeoning news, entertainment and advertising media, attempted to rally the support of the American people behind the Allied war effort. The infant film industry, which had just begun to develop the format of the feature film and its simplistic, stereotyped conventions, became the ideal medium for this campaign. American film producers, originally depicting war-related themes to increase ticket sales, were influenced by those who presented positive views of preparedness.

Prior to any official government propaganda policy (which began to be articulated in April 1917, when President Woodrow Wilson, backed by the U.S. Congress, declared war on Germany) feature films "prepared" many Americans in embracing attitudes that were needed to create support for the war effort. Titles such as *The Brand of Cowardice* and *The Deserter* (both 1916) told of American males who became like treacherous "foreigners" and spies when they refused to enlist in the U.S. armed forces.

Shortly after Wilson delivered his war address on April 2, 1917, the administration created its official propaganda apparatus, the Committee on Public Information, which included the War Co-operating Committee, a department that dealt directly with film producers. The control that the CPI exerted over the fiction film industry was far more important than actual "documentary" films being produced. Titles such as *The Unbeliever* and *Tony America* (both 1918) were actually rousing moviegoers to action, rather than merely providing images they wished to see in a theater. A new sub-genre (the "anti-slacker" film) encouraged popular support against any attitudes promoting anti-violence and peace, views that were not tolerated by the federal government, as reflected by the CPI, and the Espionage and Sedition Acts.

Prior to President Franklin D. Roosevelt's establishment of the Office of War Information on June 13, 1942, the most extensive involvement of the federal government in the production of Hollywood films was embodied in the Department of Publicity for the Fourth Liberty Loan Drive in 1918. Having been criticized for his pacifism and failure to become an American citizen, Charles Chaplin "did his part" by touring in support of the Third Liberty Loan (1917) and producing a short film for the Fourth Loan Drive. He then combined propaganda with comedy in *Shoulder Arms*, which began shooting in May 1918. (A lifelong Chaplin admirer, Lou Costello went to see this "Little Tramp" classic several times.)

Slapstick also was used to encourage home front support and satirize "un–American" attitudes and activities. The new Soviet state was spoofed in *Bullin' the Bullsheviki* (1919), and "Broncho Billy" Anderson's short, *The Lucky Dog* (1919), the first film to feature both Stan Laurel and Oliver Hardy, which showed Americans being menaced by "Bolsheviki Candy" (dynamite).

The years between 1919 and 1940 included major comic actors starring in military spoofs, invariably set during World War I. Buster Keaton made *Doughboys* (1930) for MGM, the Marx Brothers engaged in warfare in the anarchic *Duck Soup* (1932) for Paramount, Laurel and Hardy made *Pack Up Your Troubles* (1932) and included a war scene to open *Block-Heads* (1938) for Hal Roach, and Chaplin released the anti–Hitler "comedy" *The Great Dictator* (1940) through United Artists.

The idea for *Buck Privates* began at a meeting involving Universal suit Matty Fox, Eddie Sherman, and Bud and Lou, who suggested that the financially strapped studio might make some serious money if they actually constructed a film around their characters. Lou cemented the concept, claiming that a *major* studio had made the team a counter offer—allowing them script approval—that would easily cause them to defect. When Fox asked Lou what kind of script he had in mind, he replied that a "soldier picture" would be perfect for capturing current moviegoers. Then, he and Bud, right there in the office, performed their version of the classic burlesque "drill routine." The result was a four-year contract, guaranteeing them $50,000 per picture, plus 10 percent of the profits—a true Hollywood rarity.

Regardless of where the concept for a "soldier picture" originated, executive producer Milton Feld hired screenwriter Alex Gottlieb to produce a U.S. Army comedy created to capitalize on the Selective Service and Training Act passed by Congress on September 16, 1940, and signed by President Roosevelt. The first peacetime draft in U.S. history, requiring all males aged 21 to 35 to register with local boards, began in October.

To compete with Paramount, who were planning *Caught in the Draft* with Bob Hope, and other Army-bound studios, Universal rushed their military spoof into production. On November 11, Harold Shumate turned in a screenplay tentatively titled "Abbott and Costello Conscription Story," then "Sons o' Guns" and, finally, *Buck Privates*. Bud, Lou and the Andrews Sisters were cast as vaudevillians who befriend a struggling songwriter (actually the proverbial filthy-rich black sheep posing as a commoner).

Gottlieb and Feld disliked the material and replaced Shumate with Arthur T. Horman, who supplied the story—one that retained the subplot involving a playboy, Randolph Parker III (Lee Bowman), who eventually becomes a hero; Bob Martin (Alan Curtis), his ex-chauffeur; and Judy Gray (Jane Frazee), an Army hostess—but the reliable John Grant integrated the comic material certain to make the first real "Abbott and Costello film" a resounding success. The Gottlieb gang also altered the Bud and Lou characters of *One Night in the Tropics* into the more aggressive schemer and the childlike innocent (the cinematic "couple" that soon became familiar—and popular). Another element that guaranteed a box-office bonanza was the inclusion of pop music, namely some great songs performed by the Andrews Sisters. (This blend would become the formula for nearly all the Abbott and Costello films made prior to 1946.)

Fans of the three-part harmony of the Boswell Sisters, LaVerne Sophie (1911–1967), Maxene Angelyn (1916–1995) and Patricia Marie ("Patty") Andrews (b. 1918) were talented Minnesota siblings who made their professional singing debut in 1932. They performed on the road while traveling in the family car, with their father at the wheel. Between shows they honed their comic skills while listening to Jack Benny and Fred Allen on the radio. Working with the Vic Schoen Orchestra, they contributed a new sound to Big Band music, taking African American boogie woogie and distilling it for the masses. Their tight harmonies combined with an uncanny sense of collective rhythm made their vocals irresistible. They began to sing on radio with Glenn Miller in 1940, when they also made their film debut in *Argentine Nights* at Universal. By the time they were signed to appear in *Buck Privates*, they were the most popular singing group in the nation. Maxene recalled:

> America was still a year [away] from becoming involved in the war, but we were already concerned about those nations whose people were suffering and dying at the hands of the invading German and Japanese armies.... When the Red Cross appealed for finan-

Buck Privates (1941). Raw recruits Slicker Smith (Bud) and Herbie Brown (Lou) dig the Andrews Sisters (Patty, Laverne and Maxene) as they head off for boot camp in the inaugural Abbott and Costello preparedness picture (original lobby card).

cial help in 1940, an all-star lineup from show business responded with a special benefit program.... LaVerne, Patty and I sang as part of a two-hour radio show which was broadcast simultaneously over every Los Angeles station, plus NBC and CBS, from nine to eleven on a Saturday night.[2]

Maxene also revealed:

> Universal executives were still not sure if Abbott and Costello could carry a picture alone—or whether the Andrews Sisters could either. Universal came to the collective decision that a hot singing group and a fantastic comedy duo just might bring it off. That's how we got signed to do *Buck Privates* with Bud and Lou.[3]

The songwriting team of Don Raye and Hughie Prince, who had written the hits "Rhumboogie" and "Beat Me Daddy, Eight to the Bar" for the trio, were hired to compose four new Sisters songs for the picture.

After the completed screenplay was submitted to the Production Code Administration, Joseph Breen expressed a general concern about a comedy that might incite criticism or even legal action by the War Department. He also had specific objections to situations involving shirtless recruits (when they receive their shots), showing money (during a crap game), the potential for violence (during a boxing match), and the offensiveness of "extreme moves" made by couples doing the jitterbug and Herbie Brown (Costello) kissing Sergeant Mike Collins (Nat Pendleton)!

Allowed a $233,000 budget and a 20-day schedule, B-Western director Arthur Lubin (who had never heard of Bud and Lou) fired up the cameras on December 13. To save money, Universal avoided building new sets by re-dressing old ones, but allowed some minor location work at Provedencia Ranch and Lake Elinor. A second unit was sent to Camp Ord to film some establishing shots. Unsure of Bud and Lou's potential, Lubin instantly became confused by the neophytes' ignorance of film production. Grant hadn't bothered to write out the dialogue for the comic routines. Bud and Lou had all the shtick committed to memory, and preferred to improvise as much as possible, playing to the people on the set rather than the camera. Lubin needed to give them a crash course in cinematic technique, and had them act out a routine so he could devise appropriate camera set-ups. In no time, the director was impressed by their professionalism and fascination with learning the cinematic ropes.

Bud and Lou inaugurated their infamous backstage poker games during the shooting of *Buck Privates*. Though Lou usually restricted visitors, Maxene Andrews somehow slipped into his trailer to observe the high-stakes contests that also involved Alex Gottlieb:

> On one occasion I remember looking at the pot on the table and there must've been close to $30,000 on it! I had never seen that much cash! I was sworn to secrecy, and if they were wanted on the set and somebody asked me where they were, I always acted dumb.[4]

While Universal was promoting military preparedness on the back lot, President Roosevelt delivered his "Arsenal of Democracy" fireside chat on December 29. Coined by French businessman Jean Monnet and appropriated by top presidential advisor Harry Hopkins, the term was first used by FDR when referring to Detroit, where the auto industry was being converted for armaments production. To awaken the American people from two decades of isolationism, Roosevelt called for their support of the European and Asian nations battling the world's fascist powers. The need for *Buck Privates* was obvious, as the actual U.S. Army then consisted of only 250,000 troops.

The film's opening credits include the billing "Special Material for Abbott and Costello by John Grant." Bud and Lou are introduced on the street, as Slicker Smith and Herbie Brown attempt to con passersby into buying cheap neckties. Menaced by beat cop Mike Collins, they hide out in what they *think* is a movie theater, only to discover they've just signed on for a hitch in the U.S. Army. Confident that he weighs too much to be accepted, Herbie relaxes on a radiator, which Slicker cranks up to sweat off enough blubber to insure his pal's induction.

As soon as the men are processed, the propaganda takes over, and the new recruits are graced by beautiful broads offering them cigarettes, apples, chewing gum and even lollypops, all courtesy of their Uncle Sam. "It won't be an ordeal," Major Emerson (Samuel S. Hinds) assures the parents (Douglas Wood, Nella Walker) of playboy Parker. "A year in the Army can do a great deal for any man." Here, the Andrews Sisters make their first appearance, launching into "You're a Lucky Fellow Mr. Smith," a number soon taken up by everyone as they march off to the fantasy land of Camp Greeley.

On the troop train to the base, Slicker organizes a crap game that is soon dominated by Herbie, who claims ignorance of shooting dice, but knows all the jargon as he hauls in the jack. Lou took advantage of the opportunity to improvise, at one point referring to his age by adding, "Startin' Tuesday, I'm goin' out with girls."

"I don't blame you," quipped Bud before continuing with the familiar routine.

Buck Privates (1941). Herbie Brown (Lou) undergoes a grueling U.S. Army regimen of five chocolate milkshakes prepared by Patty Andrews.

Stock footage of a training camp leads to narration about the National Defense effort and images of the American working man, the "taxpayers." The base is a serviceman's dream, replete with a recreation hall, soda fountain (where Herbie enjoys several huge chocolate milk-shakes), full orchestra and, of course, the Andrews Sisters. After only one day in boot camp, Bob is serenaded by Judy (whose father fought in the "Fighting 69th" during World War I) as he writes a "love letter" to send back home, and Herbie pines away for Patty Andrews while enjoying his milkshakes.

More stock footage of infantry training and maneuvers is followed by the Andrews Sisters singing "Apple Blossom Time" to the recruits. This lovely ballad—which became a signature number for the trio—was almost jettisoned when Milton Feld refused to pay the $200 usage fee. Refusing to give in to such penny-pinching nonsense, the singers put up two c-notes themselves.

The following morning, Collins (now an Army sergeant), while attempting to train Slicker, Herbie and two more buck privates, claims, "You four men are the dumbest numb-skulls I've ever had the misfortune of drilling!"

Though he has just arrived in boot camp, Slicker is put in charge of the drill (though this is one of the least fantastic incidents at this Hollywood version of an Army base). After editor Philip Cahn assembled a rough cut of the picture, Alex Gottlieb instantly knew that this was the funniest scene, though it ran a mere 2:30. Screening all the additional footage and outtakes, he ordered Cahn to add several bits of business improvised by Costello, a re-edit that stretched the sequence to five minutes. Arthur Lubin had decided to shoot each scene with two or three cameras, in order to pick up all of Lou's inventions. Lou was pleased that his variations on an old stage routine were retained, and he began to pay closer attention to cinematic technique from then on. (Unbelievably, Arthur Horman originally had adapted the drill for Pendleton and Costello.)

Another classic sequence resulted from John Grant's inclusion of the "Go Ahead and Sing" gag, here adapted for Slicker's insistence that Herbie play the radio in their tent, much to the dismay of Collins. On another occasion, after accidentally tossing a bucket of water on the sergeant, Herbie attempts the climb the tent wall, unleashing the famous Costello phrase, "I'm a baaaaaad boy!"

Assigned to KP, Herbie peels onions as another soldier (Frank Cook) furiously plays a guitar and harmonica. Once and future Stooge Shemp Howard appears as a cook, joining in during Lou's performance of "When Private Brown Becomes a Captain." Herbie's musical effort is followed by an athletic one, after he is tricked into a boxing match by seeing a "pushover" (Frank Grandetta) in the ring. In reality, he is forced to box a big bruiser (Al Billings), but not until the Andrews Sisters have finished their rousing rendition of "Boogie Woogie Bugle Boy."

This dynamic sequence begins as Herbie dresses in the locker room. Patty Andrews takes a solo in the middle of the number as her two sisters harmonize flawlessly behind her, and the trio wraps up this classic (the first boogie woogie number to hit the mainstream airwaves) just as Herbie emerges for the big fight. Following a parade of Costello's improvised ineptitude, Herbie's opponent slams his head into a stool, and the "little, fat guy" falls from the ring to the floor.

Maxene Andrews recalled the preparations for filming the number at the tight-fisted, nearly bankrupt Universal:

> When Don and Hughie wrote "Boogie Woogie Bugle Boy" for us, we had to learn the dance routines at night. We were busy shooting during the daytime, and we were not

allowed to learn dancing on Universal's time. We begged the executives to bring in Nick Castle from Twentieth Century–Fox to choreograph that song for the film. Universal didn't want a choreographer. So, in spite of the studio, we all made *Buck Privates* big."[5]

A lengthy section combining stock footage with a "sham" battle during which two opposing teams compete to blow up a blockhouse rounds out the film's plot, such as it is. Having let down his comrades by ducking out of a previous rifle contest, Parker saves Martin's life while climbing a rocky cliff, then creates a diversion while Bob detonates the objective. This tedious sequence is followed by a memorable swing number, "Bounce Me, Brother, with a Solid Four," featuring several furiously jitterbugging couples and Herbie (Costello's brief "dance" is a highlight) on the floor as the Andrews Sisters inject another dose of rhythmic harmony.

The film ends with an extended version of "You're a Lucky Fellow, Mr. Smith." As more stock footage of workers is included, all the buck privates on screen (and potential ones in 1941 audiences) are reminded what a paradise their upcoming military service will be. After all, Uncle Sam was really beginning to gear up for a wonderful war.

Running just four days over schedule and $12,000 over budget, *Buck Privates* raked in nearly 20 times its cost: $4.7 million on a $245,000 investment (50 Gs of which went to Bud and Lou), out-grossing such heavyweight films as *How Green Was My Valley*, *Sergeant York*

Buck Privates (1941). Herbie Brown (Lou) and Slicker Smith (Bud) jitterbug with Judy Gray (Jane Frazee).

and *Citizen Kane* to become the number-two box office champ to date (just behind the monumental *Gone with the Wind*, released two years earlier). Unleashed nationwide on January 31, 1941, it was the first Hollywood film to depict the U.S. rookie Army following the institution of the peacetime draft. Alex Gottlieb recalled Milton Feld's reaction after the January 28 preview at the Alexander Theater in Inglewood:

> Feld ran up to me in the lobby and practically screamed, "You son of a bitch! You were right! They're going to be the biggest stars this studio has ever had!" When I finally caught my breath, I said to Milton, "Costello will be a big star. Abbott will be what he needs to work with." That was never meant to be a malicious statement. I think the facts bear me out. [6]

The studio had been in serious financial trouble, and the front office now realized that more Abbott and Costello comedies might pull them out of the red. Arthur Lubin was awarded a $5,000 bonus and retained as Bud and Lou's official director—and Gottlieb began making a list of successful comedies starring previous comedy teams to use as a springboard for future projects.

The Andrews Sisters also benefited substantially, especially after they recorded a commercial version of "Boogie Woogie Bugle Boy" with the Vic Schoen Orchestra for the Decca label. The cinematic version of the song was nominated for an Academy Award, as was Charles Previn's rousing score.

Buck Privates (1941). Maxene, Lou, Patty, Bud and Laverne.

After working on one picture with the boys, Patty Andrews was particularly impressed with Bud's talent: "Bud Abbott was the greatest straight man that ever lived. I mean, to be able to keep it all together with Lou, when you never knew what Lou was going to do. Bud was fantastic."[7]

At the suggestion of John Grant, Universal chose to blend the comedy of Abbott and Costello with elements of their successful horror genre in "Oh, Charlie," which was in production when *Buck Privates* was released. But the solid box-office returns from the service picture induced the front office to put the haunted house spoof on the back burner, in favor of a follow-up military comedy, a possibility foreseen by Alex Gottlieb, who had been writing an outline while *Buck Privates* was in post-production.

On March 11, 1941, FDR took the United States another step closer to involvement in the European war by signing the Lend-Lease Act, which allowed the President to provide "defense articles" to any government whose protection was considered vital to U.S. security. Within six months, $1 billion in aid was approved for Great Britain. Eventually, Lend-Lease (extended to France, China and the Soviet Union) would become a crucial component in the victory of the Allies over the Axis forces, even after the U.S. entered the war.

An Abbott and Costello preparedness picture was much cheaper. Originally titled "Hello, Sailor," *In the Navy* was budgeted at $335,000 and filmed, again under Arthur Lubin's direction, from April 8 to May 9, 1941. Repeating their *Buck Privates* partnership, Grant and Arthur Horman collaborated on the screenplay. Universal worked closely with the U.S. Navy Department to insure that everything in the film was above deck, including the filming of location footage at San Pedro and San Diego; but when a completed print was sent to Washington, D.C., to receive the stamp of approval, the Navy brass were *not* amused by the climactic sequence in which Pomeroy Watson (Costello) wrought maritime havoc after taking control of the U.S.S. *Alabama*. Universal quickly scheduled a re-shoot, adding a framing story about Watson dreaming the whole affair after being slipped a mickey, and the Navy approved the film.

In the Navy opens with an instrumental version of "You're a Lucky Fellow, Mr. Smith," as Bud and Lou raise two signal flags: the first reads, "Bud Abbott and Lou Costello," but the second promotes, "in Buck Privates." Of course, Lou receives a brisk slap from Bud. Retrieving the incorrect banner, they then hoist "and Dick Powell" and "In the Navy," and all is shipshape.

Dick Powell had been a major star at Warner Bros. during the mid–1930s, headlining such Busby Berkeley musical masterpieces as *42nd Street* (1933), *Footlight Parade* (1933) and *Dames* (1934). By the end of the decade, he was trying his luck at various Hollywood studios, eventually winding up as second banana to Abbott and Costello at Universal (where he was hired for four weeks at $6,000 per). A major subplot involving Russ Raymond, a popular crooner who tries to escape stardom by joining the military under his real name, Thomas Halstead, opens *In the Navy*.

Ordered to deliver a letter, Pomeroy Watson and Smokey Adams arrive at the address in the back of a small dump truck. Immediately they tangle with the law. "Every time you open *my* mouth, I get in trouble," "Pommy" tells Smokey. When Chief Petty Officer "Dynamite" Dugan (Dick Foran) drops a money roll on the sidewalk, Pomeroy tries to give it back, but the CPO thinks it's a bribe. Pommy pockets the dough, telling Smokey that he's going to "buy every record the Andrews Sisters ever made."

Costello's two-year-old daughter, Carole, appears in the scene as a baby who grabs the letter from Pomeroy, who takes it back, causing her to cry. The child's mother arrives and calls for the police. Dynamite jerks Pommy around, and the baby stops crying; but when he lays off, the child wails away again.

They deliver the letter to Tommy Halstead, and then loiter in the hall while Dorothy Roberts (Claire Dodd), a newspaper reporter, poses as a chambermaid to snap a photo of the incognito Russ Raymond. Eventually they break in to discover Tommy spanking the intrepid journalist and yanking a string tied to the camera's shutter release. No one can believe that "America's Singing Heartthrob" would give up a $100,000-per-year job for a $21-per-month sailor's life.

At the naval base, the Andrews Sisters arrive to salute new recruits ready to ship out for the first time. The Commander (Edward Fielding) delivers a rousing propaganda speech to the men just before the sisters, decked out in snappy uniforms, sing "We're Off to See the World," assuring the sailors, "You'll earn your promotions but quick." As in *Buck Privates*, everyone joins in the performance of the song, the men joyously carrying their bed rolls down the wharf to their ship.

The storyline of *In the Navy* is an improvement on *Buck Privates*, with the Andrews Sisters actually included *as* characters who directly affect the action. In fact, their presence at the base is a result of a letter sent to Patty Andrews by "a hunk of stuff named Pomeroy Watson." Describing himself as "tall, dark, and then some," Pommy can't wait to "crush [Patty]

In the Navy (1941). "Hunk of stuff" Pomeroy Watson (Lou) "trains" his lifeboat crew (on dry land) in the team's second service picture.

in his arms." Though he's only a baker, Smokey had told him to claim he was an admiral, six-feet-two, with eyes of blue.

"Is he standing in a hole?" Patty asks while observing Pommy drilling some sailors in a lifeboat. Though the craft is on dry land, the very motion of the oars makes him seasick. "The big shot turns out to be a blank cartridge," concludes Patty.

The world of the U.S. Navy is even more of a fantasy land than the Army of *Buck Privates*. Though they're not raw recruits this time (Watson has the stripes of a petty officer, third class, while Adams is PO, second class), the boys enjoy leisure activities most of the time. At a nightclub, they dig the Andrews Sisters swinging "Give Me Some Skin," then Pomeroy tries to dance with Patty while the orchestra plays an instrumental version of "Bounce Me, Brother, with a Solid Four."

"I'm in love. I don't know what I'm doin,'" he tells his would-be girlfriend. When a burly sailor butts in, Patty tells him to "take a poke" at the rude interloper. Pomeroy gets slapped, a full-scale brawl erupts, and he, Smokey and Tommy all land in jail, where he receives a note from Patty, who reveals, "I'm taking the clipper to Hawaii."

"She's going away with a barber," Pomeroy says sadly. Miraculously, all three men are transferred to the battleship U.S.S. *Alabama*, which just happens to be bound for Hawaii.

In the Navy (1941). Pomeroy Watson (Lou) destroys the film from the camera of Dorothy Roberts (Claire Dodd), who attempts to blow the cover of Tommy Halstead, a.k.a. crooner Russ Raymond (Dick Powell) (original lobby card).

The environs of the ship are even more fantastical than the base, with a large band, tap dancing sailors (the Condos Brothers), the "captain's nephews," Butch and Buddy (Billy Lenhart, Kenneth Brown) running amok, and a "tomato in the potato locker," Dorothy Roberts, posing as a sailor while still trying to snap a publishable photo of Russ Raymond. "The only pictures on this ship are tattooed on the men," Smokey reports. When Dugan orders Pomeroy to "dog" the door of the locker, he barks at the handle. (Although the content is preposterous, art director Jack Otterson worked with actual Navy Department blueprints to design an "authentic" ship set.)

A comic highlight involves Pomeroy's attempts to bed down in his hammock for the night. Costello ignored the script, which included an elaborately contrived routine and ad-libbed a much funnier tour de force. After tossing his clothes out a porthole ("I thought it was a little closet," Pomeroy tells Smokey) he makes three valiant attempts to climb into his hanging sleeper. Wearing enormously out-sized boxer shorts, he first makes a conventional attempt, and then saddles it like a horse, petting its "head" before falling to the deck. At one point, he "plays" the strings of the hammock like a harp. Costello's improvisational skills shine throughout this scene, and in another sequence involving his efforts to join the "Sons of Neptune," a ritual that results in having water spit in his face by other sailors.

In the Navy (1941). Tommy Halstead (Dick Powell), Smokey Adams (Bud) and Pomeroy Watson (Lou) receive shipboard orders from Dynamite Dugan (Dick Foran) en route to endless parties in Hawaii (original lobby card).

"Dizzy" (Shemp Howard), a fellow baker, is in charge, asking him what branch of the military he prefers: "the air, the land, or the water?"

"Give me the water!" Pomeroy insists, receiving water blasts from five seamen. Costello's ad-libbing was so effective that Arthur Lubin broke down laughing at one point. Lou also cracked up, spitting a mouthful of water onto the deck. Lubin loved the take so much that he left it in the finished film.

Pre-dating a similar scene in MGM's lavish *Anchors Aweigh* (1945), Dick Powell, backed by the full band, sings "We're in the Navy," and is soon joined by all the officers, proclaiming they are "watchdogs of liberty." The moment the ship reaches Hawaii, all the men relax at a lavish luau, where the Andrews Sisters swing to the beat of "native" drummers as they dance their way through a ridiculous number called "Hula Ba Luau," a play on words that receives another variation when Pomeroy asks Smokey about a photo in his Navy handbook.

"That's a hull of a ship," Smokey replies.

"You're tellin' me!" Pomeroy agrees.

The set for the "Hula Ba Luau" number, a mock-up of the grounds surrounding the Honolulu Royal Palms Hotel, was the largest ever built on a Universal soundstage. The sisters, with flowers in their hair and bongos on their belts, were backed up by a Hawaiian contingent of 60 musicians and 40 dancers.

Other burlesque routines resurrected by John Grant and the boys include the "Lemon Bit," here called "Find the Submarine," during which Smokey pulls the old shell game on Pomeroy by using tin cups and lemons. Bud and Lou also demonstrate "$7 \times 13 = 28$" for the first of several times in their Universal films, a brilliant bit of business during which this equation is proved through multiplication, division and addition. One of their most repeated dialogue exchanges occurs here, with Smokey asking, "Did you ever go to school, Stupid?"

"Yeah," replies Pomeroy, "and I come out the same way."

The dream sequence involving Pomeroy's inept command of the ship begins with Dizzy and the boys preparing breakfast for the Captain. Costello shines during an inspired bit of business when grabbing a piece of toast made by Shemp Howard. "What is this?" asks Pomeroy. "A burnt offering?" He then accidentally drinks a "sleeping solution" in a glass of orange juice. While unconscious, he imagines he has "doped the Captain," then attempts to show off when the Andrews Sisters visit the CO's cabin (even Maxene and Laverne have dialogue in this scene). Footage of sea planes and torpedoes (much of which was shot at Pearl Harbor) is inter-cut with Pomeroy's shenanigans.

As soon as he awakens, yet another party is raging. During "Starlight, Star Bright," Pomeroy loses "his girl" as Patty dances with a sailor who is truly "a hunk of stuff." A rousing reprise of "We're in the Navy" concludes with the two nephews using a giant firecracker to detonate Pomeroy's bass drum.

The cast of *In the Navy* is uniformly excellent, with Bud and Lou ably supported by Dick Powell, arguably the best actor to play a romantic lead in their films. Dick Foran is his usual reliable self, contributing his singing cowboy voice on "Oh, for the Life of a Sailor," a duet with Costello. Patty Andrews provides a bubbly element in a likeable and humorous performance, combined with her quota of trademark comical facial expressions during the musical numbers. "Patty was the fun one of the group," wrote Maxene, "the clown who kept us laughing."[8]

Lubin ran three days over schedule, wrapping the film at a cost of $379,207. But the Navy Department's objection to the battleship sequence necessitated an additional rewrite by Gottlieb on May 17. Lubin shot the retakes with Bud and Lou the following day, and Philip

In the Navy (1941). "Captain" Watson (Lou) entertains the Andrews Sisters (Maxene, Patty and Laverne) in "his" cabin.

Cahn re-cut on the 19th. Maurice Pivar, head of the editing department, personally delivered a print to Washington, D.C., and the Navy passed the picture "100 percent" on May 21. Giving another boost to the morale of recent draftees and the American public, *In the Navy* was an even bigger hit than *Buck Privates*, sailing to the 6th spot on the list of top grossing films of 1941. The picture broke box office records at Loew's Criterion in New York, where Bud and Lou made two personal appearances at the premiere on June 11. During the first week, 49,000 patrons packed the theater.

Three days later, even bigger financial matters concerned President Roosevelt, who ordered a freeze on all German and Italian assets in the United States. On June 22, the Nazis invaded the Soviet Union, and FDR responded by extending Lend-Lease to the Russians. His official policy was now "all aid short of war," which included providing Naval escorts (and firepower, if necessary) to Allied convoys across the Atlantic. U.S. Navy aircraft carriers had also begun transporting British fighter planes to the Mediterranean.

Meanwhile, Universal's cinematic Navy continued to attract attention at home. In his *New York Times* article "Low Comedy of a High Order," Bosley Crowther pointed out that the boys were superior to their material:

> Frankly, one might wish a more auspicious occasion than this...the film is not one of the best and the boys are not at their best in it. After all, what could they do except be

themselves and salvage what they can in a picture which gives the Andrews Sisters and Dick Powell too much prominence? ...For our money Abbott and Costello are the best and most promising clowns to hit the screen in ten years. ...Costello is a truly lovable character... Right now the screen can use a couple of new and adroit funny men. Abbott and Costello are the boys, provided they get the proper support.[9]

Inspired by the success of the Abbott and Costello service sub-genre, 20th Century–Fox rushed their "new" discovery—Stan Laurel and Oliver Hardy, retaining little of their classic Hal Roach personae—into *Great Guns*, which filmed from July 11 until early August 1941. The studio suits spent as much on a huge advertising campaign, announcing "The Return of Laurel and Hardy," as they did on this B-film about two dimwits who, regardless of their age and physical condition, are drafted into the U.S. Army. While the duo had worn facial makeup that made them look younger in their Roach films (1927–1940), Twentieth Century–Fox "normalized" their appearance, which also included reining in their well-known exaggerated gestures, to bring them in line with other current screen comics. By transforming them into actual "adult" characters, Fox robbed "Mr. Laurel" and "Mr. Hardy" of the essential *childlike* qualities that had made them so appealing. Now, when they did something stupid, it *was stupid*.

The original script for *Great Guns* actually made a direct reference to *Buck Privates*, though the bit wasn't included in the final cut. Ollie was supposed to stop Stan from tossing the water from a wash basin out the barracks doorway; claiming that the sergeant (Edmund MacDonald) would walk right into it; he then added that the incident already had been used in it, the Abbott and Costello film.

A scene that *did* make it into the final cut of *Great Guns* involves Stan and Ollie being bombarded by flour sacks during maneuvers, another bit used in *Buck Privates*. However, it has been reported—by none other than Laurel's daughter, Lois—that Stan actually had mentioned the bit to Bud and Lou during a dinner that occurred prior to the release of the Universal film. This is certainly possible, since Stan and Lou were friends who occasionally visited at Laurel's home, and it is no secret that Abbott and Costello "borrowed" Laurel and Hardy material on several occasions. (Like great jazz musicians, first-rate comics often improvise variations on the riffs of others.)

While Stan and Ollie were toiling away at Twentieth Century–Fox—a Hollywood "major"—Bud and Lou were the new boys on the lot at a "minor" studio. Witnessing the star treatment given to Deanna Durbin at Universal, Costello commanded the same treatment, namely separate trailer dressing rooms, for him and his partner. Ultimately, Universal capitulated—but it didn't stem the tide of Lou's squalls.

3

Money in a Moose Head

Hold That Ghost (1941)

I remember being in the projection room, looking at this dance scene, and it's hysterical. Literally. And from the back of the room we hear a voice that is obviously Costello's saying, "Who's the star of this film?" He felt he was being upstaged by Joan Davis. But what he didn't realize yet was that, when he had a good comedienne to play off, it made him funnier, too.

—Robert Lees[1]

Originally titled "Don't Look Now," then "Oh, Charlie," *Hold That Ghost*, filmed from January 21 to February 24, 1941, was in the can before production began on *In the Navy*. However, after the military farce was completed, Universal—responding to the comments of a preview audience—began shooting retakes, featuring the Andrews Sisters and bandleader Ted Lewis, for the new "haunted house" film. Patty Andrews remembered, "[T]he producers got a lot of resentment that we were originally excluded. Then they called us in from New York, and they stuck us in at the end of *Hold That Ghost*."[2]

The musical numbers have nothing to do with the plot, so a scene introducing Chuck Murray (Bud) and Ferdie Jones (Lou) as "relief waiters" at the Chez Glamour nightclub was quickly written. The original budget for this exceptional Abbott and Costello romp had been a mere $190,000, but the additional scenes quickly doubled the studio's investment.

After playing themselves as characters in *In the Navy*, the Andrews Sisters are merely relegated to vocalizing in *Hold That Ghost*, the last of their trio of films with Bud and Lou. Maxene Andrews recalled:

> LaVerne, Patty, and I made three movies with Abbott and Costello, and because of Lou, they were easily the most fun of the seventeen films the Andrews Sisters made. He was a delight, and one of the hardest workers imaginable. Lou wanted to succeed more than anyone I think I've ever known, and not just in comedy. He always wanted to move beyond comedy into serious acting roles, but his fate was to remain a comedy actor— albeit a good one.[3]

Robert Lees and Frederic Rinaldo had completed the screenplay on January 14, soon after *Buck Privates* wrapped. The screenwriters wanted to move Bud and Lou beyond playing supporting roles in a romantic plot with music. For *Hold That Ghost*, they developed real characters who do much more than perform patter routines, the main reason that this film is one the team's finest.

Clever animated titles, featuring Bud and Lou in cartoon form menaced by a ghost, open the film. The action begins at the Chez Glamour, where the camera tilts up to a neon image of Ted Lewis above the entrance to the swingin' joint. A dissolve introduces the real Lewis on stage, while the maître d' (Mischa Auer) frets over the two relief waiters sent by an employment agency. In fine Abbott and Costello style, Chuck and Ferdie are shooting craps in the kitchen.

Ferdie is excited about an appearance by the Andrews Sisters, who sing "Serenade" following a performance of "Me and My Shadow" by Lewis and an African American sidekick. Costello mugs his way through a hilarious scene as Ferdie attempts to sell some soup to Alderman Birch (Thurston Hall), a "respectable" middle-aged customer out on the town with a pretty young woman whom the naïve waiter first assumes is his daughter. Birch doesn't want any soup, suggesting that the chef eat it himself. "The chef is all souped up now!" Ferdie replies.

An entertaining gangster subplot involving Sidney "Moose" Matson (William B. Davidson) and Charlie Smith (Marc Lawrence) creates a mood for *Hold That Ghost* totally unlike anything in Abbott and Costello's first three films. Meeting with his lawyer at the club, Matson reveals, "The hiding place for my money is in my head."

Back at their day job as service station attendants, Chuck and Ferdie wait on Matson, who is in no mood for anything except filling his car with gas: eight gallons for one dollar. (After searching in vain for a suitable service station, Universal built one on the back lot for $2,500.) While "dusting" the interior of Matson's car, Ferdie finds a stash of pistols hidden in an armrest. Pointing one of them at his right temple, he pulls the trigger but nothing happens. He then points the gun away from his head and blasts off a round. An exciting chase erupts as the police attempt to run him down. Ferdie—who has no driver's license—takes the wheel as the Moose battles with the bulls. When Matson is hit, Ferdie pulls over, and the mobster pulls his last will and testament from his pocket just before he expires.

The scene of the lawyer's reading of Matson's will features some amusing gangland lingo, including the mob boss' bequeathal of his fortune "to those who stick by me when, in that final moment, the coppers dim my lights." Told that the Moose always said he kept his money "in his head," they are awarded the Forrester's Club, an old, abandoned roadhouse in the country. Charlie Smith offers to supervise the entire affair, telling them, "It's going to be a pleasure to take you boys for a ride."

After barely escaping a hit by Smith's gang, Chuck and Ferdie wait to board a private bus (actually a sedan) the following morning. Against orders, the driver, Harry Hoskins (Milton Parsons), has accepted additional passengers: Dr. Jackson (Richard Carlson), Norma Lind (Evelyn Ankers) and Camille Brewster (Joan Davis). In a hilarious entrance, Joan Davis, one of the most gifted and funny female comics in Hollywood history, runs down the sidewalk, slamming head-on into Costello. Camille then demonstrates her talent as a radio "actress": She screams, sending Ferdie flying into the arms of Chuck. In the film's only (indirect) reference to military preparedness, Ferdie, pretending it's an air-raid, makes siren and machine-gun noises and gestures as Chuck cradles him like a baby!

At a nearby soda fountain, the jerk (Shemp Howard) tries to pass off hour-old orange juice as "fresh squeezed" on the doctor, who informs him about the short life of optimum vitamin C content. Norma is immediately smitten with the handsome egghead, but his "scientific" nature precludes any reciprocation on his part. After Ferdie accidentally tosses Chuck's suitcase onto the roof of a passing bus, all the passengers pile into the car, and Hoskins, with a crazed look on his face, drives them into the country.

It is pitch dark, with the weather worsening by the minute, when they arrive at the roadhouse. When Hoskins speeds off with all their luggage, Smith comments, "That's the oldest

Hold That Ghost (1941). Publicity photo of Lou and Bud with the incomparable Joan Davis.

chisel in the world—the wildcat bus racket." Intending to break into the joint like a "barricading ram," Ferdie runs through the entrance as the door swings open and slams into the wall at the far end of the room. Fumbling around in the dark, Chuck reports, "I feel a damp opening."

"You've got your hand in my mouth!" announces Ferdie.

Several candles are lit, and Ferdie is ordered outside in the rain to fetch some water from the pump. He doesn't want to go alone, and needs someone to talk to.

"Why don't you talk to yourself?" asks Chuck.

"I get too many stupid answers," Ferdie replies.

Charlie descends the stairs into the cellar to "rustle up" some heat, and is strangled by a gloved killer who emerges from the furnace. The survivors prepare some soup with the water from the pump and sit down at the dining table. The scene is peppered with classic bits of Abbott and Costello dialogue. Giving Ferdie suggestions on etiquette, Chuck asks him, "You've got a tongue, haven't you?"

"Yes," Ferdie replies, "but I can reach much farther with my hands."

Tasting the soup, Camille declares, "Just like mother used to make. It *stinks*." When Chuck mentions that the water "might be poison," Ferdie is chosen as food taster, and (in a bit of classic Costello shtick) he uses his necktie to hoist the glass to his mouth.

Joan Davis' dry wit is followed by her participation in one of the funniest sequences ever filmed, a "ballet" that was scripted but greatly improved by her improvisations with Costello during rehearsals. Joan was so good, in fact, that Lou began to complain that he was being upstaged. Chuck plays a Johann Strauss record and "conducts" the orchestra while Ferdie and Camille trip the light fantastic. The others, watching from the dining table, somehow manage to keep straight faces as Ferdie slips and falls down in a pool of water, where the two "dancers" then splash each other in infantile fashion. At one point, Camille's choreography consists of her pummeling Ferdie in the head with her elbows. The dance ends as she shimmies away with her rear end stuck in a metal bucket, which Ferdie plays to the strains of a Latin beat.

While searching through the creepy house, Chuck tells the women to stay behind. Ferdie wants to remain with them, admitting, "When I was a little boy, I used to play with dolls." He is frightened by the hidden assailant, and Chuck tells him that it's only the wind. "Since when does the wind eat garlic?" Ferdie asks.

Cinematographer Elwood Bredell contributed some atmospheric images to the film, including a stunning expressionistic shot, combining depth of focus with lighting that casts elongated shadows down the hallway as the intrepid group explores the upper floor. Preparing to retire for the evening, Camille tells Norma, "Looks like we're going to sleep together." Thinking the comment was directed at him, Ferdie unleashes a wolf whistle (this was Costello's most oft-used response to many situations).

For the first of many times in the Abbott and Costello films, a dead body suddenly turns up as Charlie Smith's bound and gagged corpse falls out from behind some curtains onto the floor. "He's been strangled," observes the doctor.

"Is that serious?" asks Ferdie. When some "cops" (actually gangsters) arrive, the body has disappeared.

Ferdie then gets ready for bed in a room that unexpectedly transforms into a gambling casino whenever he hangs an article of clothing on the coat tree. Of course, Chuck never sees what Ferdie does, sarcastically stating, "I like roulette tables. I like to sleep on 'em." When the script was submitted for approval, the Production Code Administration had expressed concern over possible "vulgarity" in this scene. Costello avoided any such overtones by wearing pajamas under his street clothes.

Composer Hans J. Salter, who provided the score for the film, integrated melodies from some of his recent Universal horror films, including *Black Friday* (1940) and *The Wolf Man* (1941), into this scene. (This "recycling" was common practice at the studio, and the same themes can be heard in many other horror and mystery films, including the Sherlock Holmes series of 1942–46.)

As always, Abbott is the perfect straight man throughout *Hold That Ghost*, but Costello really shines, particularly in his constant use of non-verbal gestures and expressions. Though the team is known for its consistently clever verbal comedy, here Lou's *silent* acting puts him on a par with Chaplin and Stan Laurel. For the only time, Lou was paired with an equally brilliant female comic, and it seems a shame that Joan Davis didn't appear in more Abbott and Costello films. *Hold That Ghost* gave Lou the opportunity to be part of two comedy teams, as he shares an equal number of scenes with Bud and Joan.

A memorable routine (one that would be resurrected famously for *Abbott and Costello Meet Frankenstein* seven years later) involves Ferdie being struck speechless by two moving candles that aren't seen by either Camille or Chuck. "Oh, Chuck!" Ferdie yells when first left alone with a road map. After his pal darts back into the room, Ferdie scolds, "I called forty-two 'Oh, Chucks,'" telling him to "get in here on the '*Oh*'" the next time.

Hold That Ghost (1941). Chuck Murray (Bud), Doctor Jackson (Richard Carlson), Ferdinand Jones (Lou), Camille Brewster (Joan Davis) and Norma Lind (Evelyn Ankers) cautiously explore the "haunted" road house (original lobby card).

Referring to the moving candle business, Chuck observes, "This is all nonsense."

If he is frightened again, Ferdie tells Camille, "I'll get out of here so fast, the suction will carry you along with me." Menaced by one of the mobsters wearing a linen sheet, Ferdie and Camille think it's a ghost. When the candles go out, Ferdie lifts a "sheet" in the darkness and receives a wallop from Camille in return.

Ferdie, noticing a "horse with a hat rack on its head," climbs up and reaches into its snout. Costello improvised the dialogue. "I'm going to put my hand in your mouth," Ferdie tells the stuffed head. "*Don't* bite it. This one's going in. This is the one I eat with." The animal doesn't bite him, but his hand temporarily becomes stuck on some sort of throat obstruction. "The moose's tongue is peeling," he says as "thousands of ten-dollar bills" waft down to the floor.

"Ferdie, I love you!" declares Chuck. One of the wiseguys reappears, claiming that he's sought the Moose's moola for 15 years. A wild chase ensues, with Ferdie running around the house with the satchel of money, punching out the mugs as he goes. Finally, he imitates a police siren, scaring them off the property.

Hold That Ghost concludes with Ferdie and Chuck opening a "health resort" nightclub. The doctor has discovered that the strange-tasting water has therapeutic qualities. Real-

Hold That Ghost (1941). The Andrews Sisters (Maxene, Patty and Laverne) perform the lively "Aurora" at Chuck and Ferdie's new nightclub in the film's closing production number.

izing his dream of hiring Ted Lewis and the Andrews Sisters, who perform "Aurora," Ferdie is caught by Chuck after stuffing his tuxedo shirt with all the dough from the cash register.

Prior to the addition of the musical sequences, Lubin had filmed a different ending, depicting Chuck and Ferdie opening a high-class sanitarium for the upper crust. Camille appeared as the dietician, but Joan Davis was not brought back to shoot the new closing scene (Camille is merely mentioned as having bought a marriage license, causing Ferdie to take it on the lam). The original scene ended with Charlie Smith's body falling out of a closet.

Beautifully paced by Lubin, *Hold That Ghost* is filled with consistently funny gags and dialogue performed by a sterling cast. The three faultless comics are well supported by Richard Carlson as the naïve scientist who eventually gets a clue about Norma Lind, who, at one point, unleashes a scream that only Evelyn Ankers could manage (she did a great deal of it for Universal in *The Wolf Man* that same year, and in *The Ghost of Frankenstein* in 1942). Released on August 6, 1941, *Hold That Ghost* was the third big hit of the year for Abbott and Costello. Universal had renewed their contract, guaranteeing them $35,000, plus 10 percent of the profits, per film.

The Andrews Sisters accompanied Bud and Lou on the publicity tour. While appearing at the Steel Pier in Atlantic City, they recalled having met for the first time while playing the boardwalk three years earlier. Though *Hold That Ghost* would be their last cinematic collaboration, the boys and the sisters reunited several times on radio and maintained a close relationship throughout the 1940s. Lou and Anne Costello often invited the trio and their parents to barbeques and pool parties, at which they all enjoyed the family atmosphere and excellent Italian cuisine.

4

IN THE AIR CORPS

Keep 'Em Flying (1941)

"Why try to explain it? We're doing all right, aren't we?" — Bud Abbott, to Frank S. Nugent, August 1941[1]

For the team's fourth film in a scant 10 months, Universal moved Bud, Lou and Arthur Lubin into yet another genre with *Ride 'Em Cowboy*, filmed from June 30 to August 9, 1941. The film's release, however, was postponed when Uncle Sam again blew reveille for another military extravaganza. After the U.S. War Department announced "Keep 'Em Flying Week" to recruit volunteers for the Army Air Corps, pre-production began on "Flying Cadets," a title that previously had been assigned to a preparedness picture starring Freddie Bartholomew and Jackie Cooper. Realizing that the Abbott and Costello picture was more important, Universal re-titled the Freddie and Jackie project *Keep 'Em Flying*; but, by the time Lubin began working with the team on September 5, the titles had been switched.

In July, President Roosevelt had ordered Secretary of State Henry L. Stimson to begin preparing for U.S. military involvement in the war. The following month, FDR had met with British Prime Minister Winston Churchill during the Atlantic Conference, held aboard warships at Naval Station Argentia in Newfoundland. On August 14, the two leaders issued the Atlantic Charter, a nine-point joint declaration of their vision for the post–World War II world. The points covered pledges from the U.S. and Britain not to seek territorial gains, the right of all people to self-determination, the lowering of trade barriers, global economic cooperation and the advancement of social welfare, freedom from want and fear, freedom of the seas, disarmament and—most importantly—the defeat of the Axis powers.

On September 24, these policies received unanimous support from the governments of Belgium, Czechoslovakia, Greece, Luxembourg, the Netherlands, Norway, Poland, the U.S.S.R., and Yugoslavia. Free French representatives of General Charles de Gaulle also voiced their approval. As a direct result, the Japanese began to take a more aggressive stance against the U.S. and Great Britain.

As Bud and Lou continued to "do their part" by gearing up for their third service picture, critic and screenwriter Frank S. Nugent attempted to explain their popularity with the American people:

> [I]t may be that the pundits have the right theory: which is that Bud and Lou are war babies. In times of stress and pother—the experts maintain—the average man drops the thin mantle of pseudo-sophistication he had worn during the soft years and trustingly bundles himself in the mental burberry of his forefathers. Hence the churches are crowded again, heads are unembarrassed to be bared to the flag, and real property

becomes more desirable than a bundle of prettily engraved stock certificates. Hence the average man wants to be reassured of the Eternal Verity of comedy—said verity being that nothing is more reliably funny than a fat man falling on his— well, there you have it. Costello's falls always have been resounding.[7]

Extensive training scenes for *Keep 'Em Flying* were filmed with actual recruits at the nation's largest Air Corps facility, Cal-Aero, near Ontario, California, one of 28 flying schools that had been contracted by the War Department. Universal allowed Lubin to shoot on location for 12 days with a cast and crew of 150.

Arthur T. Horman, who had penned the scripts for *Buck Privates* and *In the Navy*, was out this time around. To make *Keep 'Em Flying* a more "serious" look at military training (never fear, John Grant was still there to inject *plenty* of prime gags for the boys), True Boardman and Nat Perrin, for the most part, avoided the outlandish party atmosphere of the two previous films, but still included enough USO material and scenes set outside the base to please comedy and musical fans.

The United Service Organization was the result of FDR's call for the provision of morale and recreational services to U.S. military personnel. Six civilian agencies—the Salvation Army, YMCA, YWCA, National Catholic Community Service (NCCS), National Travelers Aid Association (NTTA) and the National Jewish Welfare Board (NJWB)—responded, and the USO was formed in New York on February 4, 1941. Delegates decided that the USO would be funded, not by the federal government, but with contributions from the American people.

Prior to the premiere of *Keep 'Em Flying* on November 28, 1941—just nine days before the Japanese aerial attack on Pearl Harbor—Universal released a nine-minute trailer titled "The Army Air Corps Presents Bud Abbott and Lou Costello in 'Life with the Flying Cadets.'" Itself a recruiting film combining footage shot at Cal-Aero with some of Bud and Lou's funniest scenes, the trailer trumpeted "the world's finest air fleet" as providing "a promising career" for recruits—not only those who made it into the blue, but also non-fly boys who became members of the essential ground crews.

The film opens at a carnival, where daredevil stunt flyer Jinx Roberts (Dick Foran) has three girls—and their families—waiting for him on the ground. He wants his "two pals" to get rid of them, but Blackie (Bud) and Heathcliff (Lou) are too busy with their respective jobs. (Lou, impressed with Laurence Olivier's unforgettable performance in William Wyler's *Wuthering Heights* [1939], had inspired the "Heathcliff" name.) Gonigal (William B. Davidson) has hired Blackie as the funhouse barker, while his "nitwit partner" is pushed around to perform any number of dangerous functions.

At the "Hit the Umpire" attraction—which Blackie refers to as "Kill the Umpire!"— Heathcliff, of course, becomes *the umpire*. As the sucker unfortunate enough to assume the position stands behind a "protective" umpire's outfit, participants attempt to hit him in the head as a second employee pushes a button under the counter to swing a baseball bat held by the player at the plate. After Heathcliff is hammered in the head several times, he tosses a ball that hits the button, causing the bat to whack Gonigal in the skull. The carny fires them both, and then receives another head slam savage enough to split the bat in half!

At a local nightclub, Jinx persuades his pals to join him in getting a "real job."

"Buck Privates?" asks Heathcliff.

"No ... the Air Corps," he replies.

Inside, Linda Joyce (Carol Bruce) performs "I'm Getting Sentimental Over You" (Tommy Dorsey's theme song). Heathcliff wants to keep Jinx away from the opposite sex, so he and Blackie form the "Women Hater's Union," but the inveterate wolf still takes to the

Keep 'Em Flying (1941). Lou, Bud, William Gargan, Carol Bruce, Dick Foran and Martha Raye celebrate the U.S. Army Air Corps flying cadets in the third Abbott and Costello military opus (original title lobby card).

floor with the luscious dame. Heathcliff—maintaining his loyalty to the newly established union—ends the terpsichorean affair by cutting in to slow dance with—*Jinx!*

At Cal-Aero, Blackie and Heathcliff, looking for the administration building, instead stumble across the USO hall. Outside the entrance, Bud nobly imparts some patriotic propaganda as Blackie attempts to stem his pal's confusion over the organization's acronym:

> "United Service Organization. You see, this building is donated by the government and supported by unselfish Americans. This building here provides for these boys' entertainment and refreshments and books. In other words, everything to make it a home away from home."

Inside, while waiting for Jinx, Blackie decides to spend their bankroll of 25 cents on a turkey sandwich, saying he'll split it with Heathcliff, who is told *not* to order any food himself. Martha Raye, a gifted comic heavily influenced by Stan Laurel, plays twin sisters, Barbara and Gloria, who—unbeknownst to the boys—both work as waitresses at the lunch counter. The two women look identical, but Raye wisely played them with opposing personalities: Barbara is a sweetheart, while Gloria suffers no nonsense.

Heathcliff declines to order, but Blackie continually coaxes him, then slaps him in the face when he gives in. This routine, an improvisation added by the team, is hilarious, but

Keep 'Em Flying (1941). Heathcliff (Lou) and Blackie Benson (Bud) confound Gloria Phelps (mighty Martha Raye, who plays twins) with the "Go Ahead, Order Something" routine.

hardly a cinematic innovation. Bud and Lou may have played it numerous times in burlesque, but variations on the scene were used several times previously by Laurel and Hardy, most notably in their 1929 short *Men o' War*, in which Stan and Ollie stretch the non-ordering shtick to *half* the film's 20-minute running time.

In a reprise of their *Buck Privates* induction, the boys accidentally get in line with a busload of recruits, and then frantically run onto a lawn, engaging a fleet of sprinklers. Heathcliff's pants fall down, he hits the ground, and then attempts to *swim* across the sodden turf. This mayhem is followed by an informational speech by an Army officer who describes the flyers and their ground crews—"the backbone of the corps"—before he is interrupted by Jinx, who buzzes the field and the formation with his plane. (This scene is a parody of what, in 1941, was already a cliché scene in aviation sagas. James Cagney had performed the same maneuver in Warner Bros.' *Devil Dogs of the Air* [1935], and soon would repeat it in the preparedness picture *Captains of the Clouds* [1942].)

Jinx struggles with military discipline, but his pals are denied a place in the service. In a scene featuring Costello's first opportunity to display his dramatic abilities, Heathcliff patriotically appeals to Major Barstow (Loring Smith) to allow him and his partner to "do their part":

> There are thousands and thousands of guys like Blackie and I who want to do something to serve our country. We can't help it if we have flat feet or we got poor eyesight.

Keep 'Em Flying (1941). How in the Wild Blue Yonder did the likes of Blackie (Bud) and "Heathy" (Lou) make it into the Air Corps? (original lobby card).

> Maybe we haven't got training, but we're willing to try. Honest we will, and we'll try hard, too. It all don't mean nothin' if you don't give us this chance. After all, our hearts are in the right places.
>
> Look, Major, when I was a little bit of a kid, I was too fat to play on the baseball team, so they made me the bat boy. And, then, when the football season came around, I couldn't run fast enough to make the football team, so they made me the water boy. And, now, Major, when you're training the biggest team that we ever had, there surely must be a place for Blackie and I, maybe as a water boy or a bat boy. Won't you, Major, give us a chance? Please, Major?

Barstow agrees to send them to the chief mechanic for a job, and Heathcliff offers to "sneak him into the Women Hater's Union!" Ordered to "mop up the field," the two new recruits ineptly appear on the runway, mops and buckets in hand, ready to apply their janitorial skills.

In another reprise of *Buck Privates* material, Martha Raye (capably aping Patty Andrews' style and phrasing) sings the boogie-woogie number "Pig-Foot Pete." Outside the USO hall, Gloria kisses Heathcliff, instantly toasting the sandwich he's holding in his hand! To give Jinx a chance with Linda, "Heathy" then draws flight instructor Craig Morrison (William Gargan) away by staging a bogus phone call (allowing Costello to perform the team's familiar "I Ain't Gonna Be There" gag, in which he comically refuses to fight his aggravated opponent).

The film reaches its patriotic apex during a sequence in which Jinx sings "Keep 'Em Flying" as he and other cadets are shown enthusiastically responding to "Reveille," happily thrusting themselves out of bed, showering, dressing and performing calisthenics. "We're an all–American team," warbles Dick Foran. In 1941, this fantastical scene may have roused audiences to action, but now it's embarrassingly hokey. Fortunately, this over-the-top patriotism is balanced by some equally energetic comedy when Heathcliff attempts his own demonstration of the "aerial-type torpedo" for Gloria.

"Hi, ya, Heathy. What's cookin'?" she asks the smitten ground crewman.

Heathcliff pulls the pin and then rides the torpedo during a lengthy chase scene. Of course, Blackie winds up sharing the ride, which culminates with their being knocked off before the torpedo blows up a local junk barn. Tires fly through the air, conveniently encasing both of the boys. Lou's brother, Pat, appears in the long shots, while unconvincing rear-projection is used in the closer shots of Heathcliff. Pat, who abandoned his musical career to join Lou in Hollywood, was put on the Universal payroll. While he rode on the outside of the torpedo, a driver, lying facedown, piloted the craft from the inside. Unfortunately, the driver was inexperienced, and kept turning the torpedo, causing Pat to fall off numerous times. Finally, Lubin hired a professional stunt man to replace the driver; and, although the antics still proved dangerous, Pat participated in some usable takes.

Keep 'Em Flying features fewer outlandish scenes than *Buck Privates* and *In the Navy*, but does include a major non-military sequence in mid-film, set at the carnival. At this point, Blackie and Heathcliff still don't know that they are involved with twins; and the confusion caused by Barbara and Gloria is compounded by the sisters' own apparent obliviousness to *each other*. While wandering through the haunted house attraction (a scene recalling *Hold That Ghost* that also foreshadows the team's later horror spoofs), the boys finally see both girls; and when Heathcliff attempts to kiss Gloria, he lands one on the lips of an ape (Emil Van Horn in the classic Hollywood "gorilla suit"). The two couples then relax in some "duck boats" that float into the tunnel of love. Carol Bruce and Martha Raye sing "The Boy with the Wistful Eyes" and Heathcliff and Blackie cozy up to the twins (Lou unleashes his little-boy playfulness, placing his hat on the duck's head, as Heathy woos Gloria).

Back at the base, Blackie tries to teach Heathcliff how to fly in a plane "without an engine." Jinx continues to irritate his superiors, including Craig Morrison, with whom he has worked in the past. He also tangles with Linda's young brother, Jim (Charles Lang), a cadet who is afraid to attempt a solo flight. Though Morrison reports that Roberts is "the best flier that ever hit the blue," Jinx mistakenly believes that his old nemesis had his case reviewed by the brass. Intending to spark Jim into a solo effort, he takes the kid up into the air, then bails out. Following a satisfactory flight, Jim crashes the plane onto its nose when trying to land, and Jinx is washed out of the service.

During a second lesson in the "engine-less" plane, Blackie and Heathcliff take to the air (in a distinct improvement on a similar scene featuring Laurel and Hardy in *The Flying Deuces*, made for RKO two years earlier). Heathy falls out, slides to the end of the wing and tumbles head-first into the cockpit, before Blackie "turns it over." The plane dives several times and the wheels fall off before they actually manage to land. Scampering out of the cockpit, Heathcliff kisses the ground.

The comic flight is followed by a final preparedness demonstration of "one of the finest groups of cadets ever turned out." Carol Bruce reprises "Keep 'Em Flying" and the new fly

Keep 'Em Flying (1941). The boys in one of their most memorable and hilarious action scenes (original lobby card).

boys hit the blue, as a long crane shot shows the remaining men standing at attention in a "V" formation in front of an impressive lineup of aircraft. Jinx is preparing to leave with his two pals when Morrison's parachute becomes stuck on the fuselage of his plane. Jinx takes off in his own "ship" to rescue the imperiled instructor, wins back his wings and lands Linda.

Meanwhile, Blackie and Heathcliff attempt some heroics of their own by taking to the sky with another pilot. When the plane's motor apparently "conks out," they bail, and Heathcliff lands on top of his partner's parachute, pulls out a pocket knife, and cuts his way through. Blackie manages to pull the rip cord on Heathy's chute and they land safely, to be greeted by Barbara and Gloria. However, Heathcliff is pulled back into the air by another plane. Pointing to his rear end, he exclaims, "It's got me!"

"Where?" asks Blackie, and the words "THE END" emanate from Heathy's posterior.

Two major scenes were cut before *Keep 'Em Flying* could be released. One featured a USO show during which the team performed a magic act, with Heathcliff revealing all of Blackie's "secrets." Another was set at a roller rink, with Heathy spending more time on the floor than on his feet. (Bud and Lou would later resurrect the former scene for *Lost in a Harem* and the latter for *Hit the Ice*.)

Carol Bruce—arguably the most stunning female in the history of Bud and Lou—was appearing in her second film, after being signed by Universal. Initially nervous about performing with the team, she was calmed by Lubin's professionalism and Lou's shenanigans. She later described two scenes of edited footage, actually requested by Costello, which attests to his growing power at the studio:

> I recorded two songs for the picture: "You Don't Know What Love Is" and "I'll Remember April." Lou didn't think they fit and had them cut out of the picture. I felt a lot of rejection and trauma when I viewed the picture the first time and found them missing. I was young and it took a long time before I realized that Lou knew what was best for the film. It was Abbott and Costello who'd get credit for the success or failure of the picture—not Carol Bruce.[3]

Not surprisingly, Bruce was pursued by Dick Foran, who fashioned himself quite the ladies' man; but when he invited her to his dressing room, he added, "We'll play jacks." Intrigued by this nonsense, she accepted his offer. She revealed, "I went back to his dressing room and, son of a bitch, he got the jacks out!"[4] Bruce later went on to a successful multi-decade singing and acting career on Broadway and television.

Keep 'Em Flying premiered in Detroit on November 19, 1941. Bud, Lou and Carol Bruce, who had been touring to promote the film, made a personal appearance at the theater, and then moved on to Chicago, Cleveland, New York, Washington, D.C., and Baltimore. Released nationwide on November 28, the film was another box-office success for Universal. Critics, though panning the standard romantic subplot, praised Bud, Lou and especially Martha Raye, referring to their scenes together as the funniest since Chaplin during his heyday. (In 1947, Chaplin would cast Raye as one of his doomed wives in his dark comedy *Monsieur Verdoux*.)

5

B Western Bunk

Ride 'Em Cowboy (1942)

Yippee! Abbott and Costello are cowboys now ... and even the cows are laughing. —Ride *'Em Cowboy* trailer

The completion of *Keep 'Em Flying* allowed Universal to shift back to Bud and Lou's singing cowboy picture set primarily on the "Lazy-S" ranch in Arizona. Robert Lees and Frederic Rinaldo's original treatment included some funny incidents retained by Alex Gottlieb and Milton Feld, but a rewrite was assigned to Edmund Hartmann, who added the major plot involving a celebrity "cowboy" who'd never actually been on a horse. Harold Shumate fleshed out the story, and the final screenplay was written by True Boardman and John Grant.

Location scenes were shot at two California dude ranches, the B-Bar A near Newhall and Rancho Chihuahua in Solemint Canyon. To save money, Universal bussed the company back and forth every day, rather than allowing them to stay on location. Additional B-Western atmosphere was provided by the casting of Johnny Mack Brown (a personal favorite of Costello, who loved low-budget oaters), while the requisite musical numbers were contributed by the Merry Macs and Ella Fitzgerald—"that sensational sepia songstress," according to the trailer—in her film debut.

Ride 'Em Cowboy features less plot than all the previous Abbott and Costello films, and is badly dated by the consistent insensitive portrayals of Native Americans, particularly in the casting of British character actor Douglas Dumbrille as Jake Rainwater, an "Indian" who dresses up in traditional chief's garb to sell stereotypical trinkets to tourists at Gower Gulch. Typical period shtick involves Willoughby (Costello) immediately proposing violence when spotting some "Indians," and Rainwater's insistence that the fool marry "eligible squaw" Moonbeam (Jody Gilbert) after he accidentally shoots an arrow through a heart on her teepee. Willoughby and Duke (Abbott) run off and hop on the back bumper of a bus bound for the Lazy-S, as Rainwater tells Moonbeam, "Don't worry, little sister. We'll have a bow-and-arrow wedding!" Later, Willoughby vows, "I'll get those dirty redskins!"

The film opens at a charity rodeo on Long Island, where "Broncho Bob" Mitchell (Dick Foran), a famous Western novelist, sings cowboy songs for the spectators, including columnist Martin Manning (Charles Lane), who has written an expose on "Bunco Bob," who hasn't "been west of the Hudson River." In the arena, Mitchell is on horseback for the first time in his life. When a steer runs wild, Bob is thrown and the animal is bulldogged by Anne Shaw (Anne Gwynne, Universal's most unique-looking contract actress, with eyes larger than those of Bette Davis), a young student rider.

Costello is first seen, *apparently* riding, as the camera pulls back to reveal Willoughby

Ride 'Em, Cowboy (1941). Lou and Bud enjoy an ice cream sundae break during production.

in a saddle atop a wooden frame. After a mule walks past, Duke asks his fellow hot-dog vendor, "Did you ever ride a jackass?"

"No," Willoughby replies.

"Well, you ought to get onto yourself," advises Duke.

As Anne strides by, Willoughby repeats Duke's question: "Did you ever ride a jackass?"

"No," she responds.

"No?" says Willoughby. "Jump on my back!"

Anne injures her leg during her valiant wrestling match with the steer, losing out on a $10,000 cash prize. Bob gives her a check made out to "Cash," but she tosses it away. Willoughby then finds it, but tears it to shreds, thinking only the person named "Cash" may claim it. Anne decides to return to her father's dude ranch in Arizona, and is followed by Bob, while Willoughby and Duke attempt to hide out from their angry boss (a repeat of the same shtick at the carnival in *Keep 'Em Flying*).

Willoughby suggests they escape into a "black tunnel," actually a cattle car, where they hold themselves above the entering animals. As the steers' horns poke Willoughby, Lubin includes a daring, hilarious close-up of Costello's rear end. Aboard the caboose, the boys join a poker game with some cowpokes led by ubiquitous character actor Harry Cording. In a tip of the cowboy hat to *Buck Privates*, Willoughby asks, "Is this anything like dice?"

Ride 'Em, Cowboy (1941). Willoughby (Lou) and Duke (Bud), perhaps the most incompetent vendors in rodeo history.

"Well, yes," replies Duke, inspiring the familiar Costello wolf whistle from Willoughby. (This content reflected the real gambling occurring on the set: When they weren't on camera, Bud and Lou spearheaded a continuous poker game, having "stashed thousands of dollars in cash in [their] trailers.")[1]

By the time the train arrives in Arizona, the cowboys are stripped down to their long underwear and Willoughby walks off with their effects. During the trip from the station to the ranch, the boys again hitch a ride on the back of the bus. In the back, Ella Fitzgerald (as Anne's aide, Ruby) sings "A Tisket, a Tasket," the signature song of her early career, while the Merry Macs, Bud and Lou interject some brief backing vocals.

At the Lazy-S, Willoughby and Duke enjoy the swimming pool *and* the bevy of bathing beauties surrounding it. A scripted gag, involving Willoughby opening a door marked "Men," a female scream, and his remark, "Pardon me, Mister!" was nixed by the Breen Office, concerned over possible "pansy" content. When the team emerges for a swim, Duke wears a modest pair of swim trunks and Willoughby is practically straitjacketed by a vintage 1920s rig, complete with cap.

They are hired as ranch hands, attired in ludicrous variations on 1930s B-Western "dude" outfits. Costello sings a bit of "Bury Me Not on the Lone Prairie" as he emerges from their cabin with a holster buckled around his torso.

Willoughby accidentally fires his shootin' iron and then swallows a bullet that goes off

Ride 'Em, Cowboy (1941). Duke (Bud) and Willoughby (Lou) enjoy a bevy of bathing beauties at the Lazy S dude ranch (original lobby card).

when a horse kicks him in the bum. Universal's tendency to dub-in Costello's laughs and yells is apparent in a scene pitting Willoughby against a horse in the corral. He then is accosted by Jake Rainwater, whose tribe has "moved down for his wedding to Moonbeam." An elaborate musical sequence includes the first appearance of tap-dancing African Americans in the Abbott and Costello films. A later number, "Rockin' and Reelin'," also features the terpsichorean trio, who leave the scene before the Caucasian dancers take over. This cinematic segregation is briefly interrupted by a shot including Ella in the background as the Merry Macs harmonize to the fore. The song is the best Macs performance, including the classic 1940s line, "You swing like a rusty gate."

Willoughby's attempts to milk a cow feature some of Costello's funniest moments. He first tries to perform the chore from the front of the animal, his head thrust between its legs, then switches to manipulating its tail like a water pump. When Duke tells him to place the bucket under the cow's udder, he asks, "The cow's udder *what*?"

A life-size mannequin of a Native American chief is placed in Willoughby's room. Duke assures him not to be afraid, insisting that the "Indian" is made of wood. When Rainwater arrives to take the dummy's place, Willoughby is harried by its lifelike gestures, which, of course, are *not* witnessed by Duke. In a variation on the team's classic "Crazy House" burlesque routine, Willoughby dreams he's a patient at "Dr. Ha Ha's Sanitarium," where *every-*

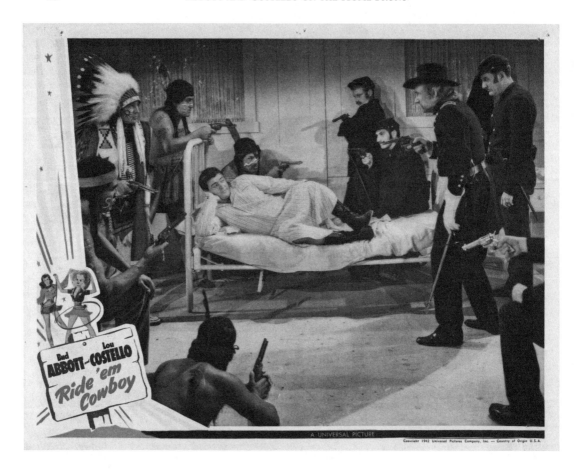

Ride 'Em, Cowboy (1941). Willoughby (Lou) caught between "Sitting Bull" and "General Custer" in the film's dream-sequence reworking of the team's famous "Crazy House" routine (original lobby card).

one is an "Indian." The sequence concludes with a showdown between "General Custer" and "Sitting Bull."

The routine, which had brought down the house during the team's performances in *Streets of Paris*, originally was played as if the events were actually happening; but two factors—the decision to "explain" the craziness by using the dream premise, and interference from the Breen Office—rendered the cinematic version incomprehensible. As always, Breen objected to anything that might be "suggestive" (Moonbeam approaching Willoughby while in his "nightgown"), and Ella Fitzgerald appearing as Ruby dressed like an "Indian" was deemed highly objectionable.

Meanwhile, Anne teaches Broncho Bob how to ride and rope. By the time the "Frontier Day Celebration" rolls around, he's a regular rootin', tootin' cowboy, but the villainous Ace Anderson (Morris Ankrum) places a large bet against the success of the Lazy-S buckaroos, then kidnaps Alabam (Johnny Mack Brown) as gambling insurance.

Before chugging into the desert in an old car, Willoughby unleashes a variation on *the* classic Costello line when he tells Bob, "You're a *bad* boy!" Halted by an apparent rock slide, they are held up by Anderson's gang, who abduct Bob. The B-Western trappings really rise to the fore as the rival cowpokes, garbed in their dude outfits and spewing cliché dialogue, duke it out in badly staged fistfights. Rainwater's tribe rides in to chase the boys, who crash through a barn and house, briefly pushing a sleeping old coot in his bed down a dusty road, *under* a river—where Willoughby gets out to fill a mug with "drinking water"—and into a cave. When the car emerges from the other end, a bear is driving the car. This chase had audiences howling with laughter, so Universal made sure to end each subsequent Abbott and Costello film with a similar comic pursuit.

Bob and Alabam are picked up by the boys, and the former arrives at the celebration just in time to win the contest. (Brief footage of an actual rodeo rider is inter-cut with an unconvincing close-up of Foran "in the saddle.") Of course, Rainwater again appears to chase Willoughby into the film's ending, which concludes with a parade of flag-wavers on horse-back. (This image is the only indirect patriotic reference in this first post–Pearl Harbor Abbott and Costello picture, released on February 20, 1942.)

The nearly plot-less *Ride 'Em Cowboy* features uniformly good performances, though Bud and Lou are less enthusiastic than in the service pictures and *Hold That Ghost*. The effortless energy of the youthful cinematic neophyte Ella Fitzgerald is a treat. Allowed to perform "A Tisket, A Tasket," a 1938 hit which she co-wrote, she also sang "Cow-Cow Boogie," but it was eliminated from the final cut.

Lou compares gams with Marlene Dietrich, who was costarring in Universal's *Pittsburgh* (1942) with John Wayne and Randolph Scott.

Dick Foran's performance of Don Raye and Gene de Paul's lovely "I'll Remember April" is arguably the film's musical high point. The song had been written for Carol Bruce in *Keep 'Em Flying*, but Alex Gottlieb decided that it was more appropriate for a romantic interlude between Dick and Anne. Later, Gene de Paul complained that Gottlieb's choice made no sense:

> [A] midnight horseback ride.... Dick, without taking off his cowboy hat ... begins to sing. The opening words of "I'll Remember April" are "This lovely day will lengthen into evening." Don and I nearly fell out of our chairs. It's midnight and here he is singing about this lovely day. We went to Alex Gottlieb and asked him if he was trying to crucify us.[2]

Actually, Gottlieb's use of the song is totally justified. Clearly marked on a sign displayed at the Lazy S ranch, the *moonlight* ride takes place at *8:30 P.M.*, and Foran opens the song with the lyric, "This lovely day *has lengthened* into evening."

Ride 'Em Cowboy proved Arthur Lubin's Abbott and Costello swansong. He recalled:

> They were becoming difficult to work with. They were bored. They arrived on the set later and later each day. One day Bud was ill and couldn't come to the studio. The next day Lou was ill. And for the first time, they were beginning to complain about the scripts.[3]

Nevertheless, the film ranked number eight on the list of top-grossing films released in 1942. To assure their continued success and the team's own sense of security, Universal (one year in advance) picked up a *two*-year option on Bud and Lou's contract.

Bud and Lou began headlining their own weekly radio series, *The Abbott and Costello Program*, on October 8, 1941. Broadcast by NBC on Thursday nights, the show was sponsored by Camel cigarettes and featured announcer Ken Niles, singer Connie Haines and the Leith Stevens Orchestra. During its six-year run, the program required an enormous amount of comic material, and the boys' classic burlesque routines were complemented by fresh bits written by John Grant, Sid Fields, Leonard Stern, Pat Costello and others. The constant need for new material created an inconsistency in the boys' characterizations, and the "Lou Costello" on radio became a completely different animal than the lovable, childlike cut-up he played on the screen. While his cinematic characters suffered the bossy, sometimes verbally abusive behavior of his partner—thus gaining audience sympathy—his radio persona was brash, often insulting Bud and the weekly guests.

6

THE NAZIS OF MGM

Rio Rita (1942)

*After you've laughed
with our lovable tramps ...
Go out and buy
Defense Bonds and Stamps!*
—*Rio Rita* trailer

Louis B. Mayer was still stinging from Bud and Lou's snubbing of the mighty MGM in favor of a minor studio. Following six quickly produced films, Universal, in order to get Mayer off its back, agreed to loan the team to MGM for one picture per year. Mayer refused to offer a percentage of the profits, but agreed to pay $300,000 per film, half of which would be split between the boys.

Meanwhile, Robert Lees and Frederic Rinaldo were writing another horror-comedy, first titled "By Candlelight" (a title already used at Universal by James Whale in 1934), then renamed "You Hypnotize Me," a script intended to pit Bud and Lou against Basil Rathbone as Dr. Ayoff, the crazed inventor of a machine used to tap into his former clients' brains to obtain information about their intimate relationships and financial assets.

Their first project "away from home," *Rio Rita*, became their one and only direct "anti–Nazi" home-front film of the World War II years. Following the attack on Pearl Harbor, MGM led the pack in its adherence to FDR's mandate for the Hollywood studios to provide cinematic propaganda for the Office of War Information (OWI). As part of its $300,000 payment for Bud and Lou's services, MGM allowed their own Ann Rutherford to replace Miriam Hopkins in Universal's *Badlands of Dakota*.

The Florenz Ziegfeld operetta *Rio Rita* was originally adapted for the screen by RKO in 1929, with Bert Wheeler and Robert Woolsey filling the comic roles. For the MGM remake, producer Pandro S. Berman and director S. Sylvan Simon retained only two songs from the original score, "Rio Rita" and "The Ranger's Song," which is used as a motif throughout the film. One additional number, "Long Before You Came Along," was written for the new version by the legendary team of Harold Arlen and E. Y. "Yip" Harburg. Twenty-year-old Kathryn Grayson, then beginning her career at MGM, received the top vocal honors (and third billing) as Rita Winslow, supported by John Carroll as Latino heartthrob Ricardo Montera.

The *Rio Rita* shoot, which ran from November 10, 1941, to January 14, 1942, marked Costello's return to MGM after having worked at the studio as a property man and stunt performer during the 1920s. John Grant accompanied the boys on their loan-out, adding his "special material for Abbott and Costello" to the screenplay by Richard Connell and Gladys

Lehman, who retained very little of the original plot. Ziegfeld's Mexican bandits were transformed into Nazi spies, who are played primarily by American character actors (headed by Peter Whitney as "Jake") under the command of an Englishman, Maurice Craindall, manager of the Hotel Vista del Rio (Tom Conway, the B-film version of his more famous brother, George Sanders). Due to Breen Office concerns about possible reactions in Latin American countries, the locale was switched from Mexico to Texas.

By December 1941, two-thirds of polled U.S. citizens supported President Roosevelt's "mobilization program." Meanwhile, in Japan, the imperial government, knowing full well that FDR would not allow further expansion in the Pacific, authorized a preventive attack on the U.S. fleet. On December 6, following a final appeal to the Japanese Emperor, FDR and Secretary of State Stimson received a report from U.S. intelligence agencies including a decipher of the first 13 parts of a 14-part coded message, leading them to believe an attack would probably occur somewhere in Southeast Asia.

The following morning, at approximately 9 A.M. EST, the final part of the Japanese transmission was received and decoded. At 1 P.M., the Japanese Embassy was to announce the severing of diplomatic relations with the U.S. An alert was issued for the Pacific fleet at Pearl Harbor, but official radio contact with Hawaii was temporarily unavailable, and the message was sent through a commercial service. By the time the alert arrived, the attack commanded by Admiral Chuichi Nagumo was already well under way.

That afternoon, Bud and Lou had joined composer-conductor David Rose for a USO performance at an Army base outside San Francisco. While they were on stage, the commanding officer interrupted to announce news of the attack. The show ended quickly, and the performers were rushed into a plane bound for Los Angeles, which was difficult for the pilot to find because the runway had been blacked out.

By the next day, when Roosevelt declared war on Japan with his "date that will live in infamy" speech, American support for participation in World War II was nearly unanimous. During the afternoon, Bud and Lou appeared at Grauman's Chinese Theatre to put their hand- and footprints in the cement. "To our pal, Sid," Abbott wrote to the legendary owner, adding "Hi, ya, neighbor," while Costello scrawled, "I'm a bad boy."

Unlike the Universal productions, which open with musical or expository scenes not involving Abbott and Costello, MGM's *Rio Rita* offers an immediate dose of Bud and Lou as "Doc" and "Wishy," employees of the Star of Texas pet shop. The film was *supposed* to begin with a musical number performed by Mexican peones, but any possible offensiveness was avoided by immediately establishing the Texas locale.

Wishy is completely ignorant regarding dog breeds, a fact that leads to some rapid-fire verbal comedy. When Mrs. Pike phones about her Pekingese, Doc orders, "Wishy, go over and get a Peke at Mrs. Pike's."

"Why can't I take a good look?" asks Wishy.

"I want you to get me Pike's Peke!" Doc explains.

"Pike's Peak?" puzzles Wishy. "What do you think I am? A mountain climber?"

Discussing a dog in the shop, Doc asks about the breed: "Spitz?"

"No," replies Wishy, "but it drools a little."

However, while the Universal films blend the comedy of Abbott and Costello with romantic subplots *supported* by musical sequences, *Rio Rita* is a lavishly mounted MGM musical using Bud and Lou as comic relief.

Fired for their incompetence, the boys spot a car pointed east and decide to stow away in the trunk, hoping to wind up back home in New York City. The driver, Ricardo Montera,

Rio Rita (1942). Bud and Lou in their first feature for MGM.

instead heads to Vista del Rio, where the Nazi agents headed by Craindall are in receipt of secret radios hidden inside fake apples! The goons intend to distribute the phony fruit in time for the singing star's "national broadcast."

Still hiding in the trunk, Doc and Wishy are placed in a precarious position when the car is raised on a hoist at the local service station. Perched over a deep canyon, the hoist eventually runs wild, spinning around furiously, and giving Wishy the most dangerous ride of his life. Meanwhile, Rita watches a group of Rangers led by Montera joyously singing in Spanish as they gallop along the Rio Grande.

Doc and Wishy steal a crate of the apples, then toss them away after finding them inedible. Several animals, including a mule and a German Shepherd, quickly swallow them and begin to run amuck. Later, the dog "talks" in the voice of an announcer at a radio station in El Paso!

Several classic Abbott and Costello bits follow. One of Bud's most often used set-ups— "Did you ever go to school, Stupid?"—is followed by Lou's reply, "Yes, sir—and I came out the same way." On this occasion, Costello follows up with an improvisation, when Wishy claims that he went to school, "Kindergarten ... for one year."

The "starving" Doc convinces Wishy that he is seeing "mirages." When two waiters deliver a table loaded with food, Wishy begins to wolf down a roasted chicken. "Hey, Doc," he says. "Come on over and cut yourself a piece of mirage!"

Rio Rita (1942). Doc (Bud), Ricardo Montera (John Carroll), Rita Winslow (Kathryn Grayson) and Wishy (Lou) mugging it up in the "Texas" desert.

Abbott then launches into another familiar bit, "You're Not Here," as Doc tries to filch Wishy's food by proving his pal isn't actually at the table. Referring to the mirage, Wishy adds, "Even the chicken's not here. Nothin's here."

"I'll bet you you're not here," offers Doc, requesting his pal's chicken. "You're not here. You're not in Philadelphia. You're not in Baltimore, and you're not in Washington. Well, if you're not in Philadelphia, Baltimore or Washington, you must be someplace else—and, if you're someplace else, you can't be here, can you?"

"No," replies Wishy as he attempts to grab Doc's plate. "Who took your chicken?" he asks.

"You just took my chicken!" Doc insists.

"I took your chicken?" Wishy asks.

"Yeah!" reiterates Doc.

"Get outta here!" growls Wishy. "I didn't take your chicken! Didn't you say I wasn't in Baltimore? I wasn't in Washington? I wasn't in Philadelphia. Well, if I'm not in Baltimore, Philadelphia or Washington, I must be someplace else."

"You must be someplace else," agrees Doc.

"Well, if I'm someplace else, I can't be here," says Wishy. "If I'm not here, how can I have your chicken?" To cap off this nonsense, the boys are accused of stealing the food by the Nazi agents, prompting the film's first chase involving Jake and Wishy.

In order to help Rita land Ricardo, Doc orders Wishy to sweep rival beauty Lucette Brunswick (Patricia Dane) "right off her feet." Entering the hotel, Doc asks his partner, "Do you know anything about being a detective?"

"You ever heard of Bulldog Drummond?" replies Wishy.

"Sure," says Doc.

"I'm his cousin—Cocker Spaniel," Wishy claims.

Unnoticed by Wishy, Doc then follows a lovely tennis player into a dressing room. Wishy knocks on the door, prompting Doc to answer through the transom. Delivering what is possibly the most extreme double-take of his film career, Costello walks away, pivots and falls face-first to the floor.

At the fiesta, Doc and Wishy sport "Mexican" outfits during Montera's performance of "Rio Rita." The pair then participate in "Double Your Money," a kissing contest in which the emcee, with his back turned, attempts to guess which girl the contestant has smooched. "If I do, you pay me 10 dollars," he explains. If he doesn't, he pays the participant 10, plus a bottle of pulque, the local booze: "Like soda pop," observes Wishy.

Doc claims his friend can perform the same feat, advising Wishy that he'll tap him on the back with a newspaper to indicate the number of the girl kissed by the emcee. First, the boys don't pay attention; then the emcee kisses number "0," but when Wishy kicks Doc in the bum, he exclaims, "Oh!" Wishy grabs the pulque and they run away. The caustic booze then causes Wishy to hallucinate, and he imagines seeing a blonde "taking off her clothes." Doc reaches for the bottle, insisting, "Give me a drink of that stuff!" (This drinking scene was the only comedy bit that survived from the 1929 Wheeler and Woolsey version.)

Brazilian dancer Eros Volusia offers an "authentic native" number, and Kathryn Grayson performs a light opera piece, a scene that became a familiar element in her MGM musicals. Bud and Lou then get deeply involved in the Nazi plot as Doc and Wishy are visited by a member of the "secret police," who gives them a code book before he is gunned down. Acting as a double agent, Lucette informs Montera that she belongs "to the secret service," then tries to steal the book from Wishy, but Ricardo has hidden it.

"Ain't you ashamed...making love to me! I'll call for help!"

Rio Rita (1942). Sultry Lucette Brunswick (Patricia Dane) puts some heavy moves on the defenseless Wishy (Lou) (original lobby card).

The Nazis grab Wishy to "take him for a ride," but he escapes, diving into a laundry cart that is immediately emptied into a chute leading to an enormous washing machine that gives him a thorough "cleaning." The film's comic high point, the scene inspires the classic line, "This is not Saturday night!" from Doc, who stops the machine. Wishy flies out, slams his head through a wall, and receives a good steam pressing for his trouble. Doc extracts him from the plaster and then pulls an entire pair of long underwear from his mouth.

Pat Costello followed his brother on the loan-out, performing the most dangerous portion of the washing-machine maneuver. Unfortunately, several wool blankets became heavily soaked, at one point pulling his head under the water and suds, nearly drowning him. But Lou made sure to procrastinate on the set long enough to insure his beloved brother more than the scale fee for the work ($300–$400). Pat found the less-hectic shooting schedule at MGM a welcome respite from the grind at Universal, but considered the general atmosphere a bit pretentious. "I think we were treated better at Universal," he later said.[1]

The boys are tied up by the Nazis, who have set a TNT time bomb to explode, just as a white mule sticks its head into the room. Having swallowed one of the radios, the jackass speaks in the voice of Adolf Hitler! "Heil, Hitler!" chant the Nazis, raising the fascist salute.

Craindall orders Montera to carry out his nationwide broadcast, then prepares to deliver a propaganda speech, but the macho singer punches him out. Wishy enters with a parade of mules playing "The Ranger's Song" on their swallowed radios. Thinking the Rangers themselves have arrived, the Nazis speed off in their car, but the time bomb is aboard and they are blown to smithereens. Looking straight into the camera, Wishy announces, "11:25." Costello waves to the audience and concludes, "Goodnight, folks." "The End" is accompanied by the pitch, "America needs your money. Buy defense bonds and stamps every pay day."

The scripted ending originally had Wishy pulling off a bad joke during a radio broadcast to the Nazis, whom he ordered to place a piece of ice in an inkwell. "Now, all of you stand up, and tell me what's in the inkwell," he commanded, to which they responded, "Iced ink!"

Wishy's voice over the radio, yelling, "You're telling me!" was to end the film. Neither ending makes much sense, but the version in the finished film is preferable to this hackneyed shtick.

At a studio that depicted even Tarzan battling the Nazis, it was inevitable that Abbott and Costello would "do their part" at MGM. After pitting Bud and Lou against Nazi agents in *Rio Rita*, MGM varied the wartime formula for Laurel and Hardy in *Air Raid Wardens* (1943) and *Nothing But Trouble* (1945). (Fox followed suit by casting Stan and Ollie in *Jitterbugs* [1943], *The Dancing Masters* [1943] and *The Big Noise* [1944].)

Interestingly, after their one MGM battle with the Nazis, Bud and Lou returned to their now-familiar formula of burlesque routines and improvisation mixed with popular music, providing much-needed comic relief for wartime audiences. Their shying away from topical material also gave their films a more timeless quality, while they continued to "do their part" on the weekly radio show, making references to home-front inflation, shortages and rationing.

7

WIDESPREAD COMIC RELIEF

Pardon My Sarong (1942) and *Who Done It?* (1942)

Fundamentally, a chase represents the life struggle of an individual. A chase is therefore the most sure-fire act in the motion picture bag of tricks. The elements haven't changed in 25 years, and they're likely never to change.

—Erle C. Kenton[1]

The MGM deal led to a new contract at Universal, guaranteeing Bud and Lou $150,000, plus 20 percent of the profits, per picture. Costello began demanding a 60 percent cut, and Abbott, to keep the peace, agreed; but the split actually was divided 55–45 on all their future films.

Their first new project, *Pardon My Sarong*, was actually an independent production made for Jules Levy's Mayfair Productions and released through Universal. Veteran director Erle C. Kenton shot the film from March 2 (eight days before MGM released *Rio Rita*) to April 28, 1942. One of their most unusual pictures, it was written by True Boardman and Nat Perrin as "Road to Montezuma," a title obviously "inspired" by the Paramount "Road" films starring Bing Crosby and Bob Hope. Working on his third Abbott and Costello project, Boardman had become used to hashing out a 12-page plot that then was delivered to John Grant, who would reduce the story line to about three pages in order to work in all the gags for Bud and Lou.

Kenton had an extensive comic career which began as one of Mack Sennett's Keystone Kops. By 1919, he had graduated to directing two-reel comedies for Sennett, and his major feature films include the Paramount horror classic *Island of Lost Souls* (1933). He had just completed *The Ghost of Frankenstein* (1942) at Universal when the studio asked him to return to his original specialty: knockabout comedy. *Pardon My Sarong* begins as a contemporary chase comedy with the usual musical sequences; then, roughly at midpoint, *completely* shifts into a South Seas parody a la the "Road" series. But the narrative transition is a smooth one, made possible by the inclusion of playboy Tommy Layton (Robert Paige) and his yacht. Though most of the film was shot on a soundstage, Kenton was able to film some location scenes at Newport Beach and on the Salton Sea, the largest lake in California, situated in the Colorado Desert north of the Imperial Valley.

The opening credits begin with an exploding volcano, the first eruption leading to "Bud Abbott and Lou Costello" and a second blast igniting the title itself. In the Windy City, the managers of the Chicago Municipal Bus Company are attempting to locate cross-town bus number 5111, piloted by the team of Algernon Shawhang (Bud) and Wellington Phlug (Lou). Covering a route that extends only 10 blocks in any direction—and with "no left-hand turns"—the vehicle has disappeared!

At the wheel, "Algy" and Wellington are transporting Tommy Layton and a bevy of young beauties to Los Angeles, where the playboy intends to enter a yacht race. Breathtakingly paced, these early scenes are indicative of Kenton's comic background, and Bud and Lou are back at the top of their game, their beautifully timed gags and one-liners simply flowing across the screen. Working with a new director at Universal was a breath of fresh air for Bud and Lou after the uneven *Ride 'Em Cowboy*. Though Arthur Lubin had faulted the boys for being "bored" during the making of that film, perhaps they had only become tired of *him*. Kenton's pacing and the team's performances are flawless throughout the film, which features an impressive array of incidents packed into an 84-minute running time. In fact, more events occur in *Pardon My Sarong* than in any other Bud and Lou film released prior to *Abbott and Costello Meet Frankenstein* (1948).

During the trip from Chicago to Los Angeles, the bus runs low on gas, so Wellington puts the pedal to the metal, much to Algy's dismay. They reach a service station, where Algy convinces his pal to try the "baseball story," a diversion intended to take the attendant's mind off being paid; but two other customers have just pulled the con. When the grease monkey (Irving Bacon) takes after Wellington with a baseball bat, he jumps aboard the departing bus, but the door closes on his neck!

The entire party reaches the Seaside Yacht Club in L.A. On hand are the Ink Spots, who perform their hit "Do I Worry?" Making their second and last appearance in a feature film (the first was in 20th Century–Fox's *The Great American Broadcast* the previous year), the vocal quartet comprised of Orville "Hoppy" Jones (bass), Charles Fuqua (baritone), Bill Kenney (tenor) and Deek Watson (tenor) provide some of the finest music in an Abbott and Costello film since the trilogy with the Andrews Sisters, a solid return to popular swing and boogie woogie after the operetta style preferred by MGM in *Rio Rita*.

After Wellington consumes an alarming amount of ice cream, the boys attempt to leave the nightclub, but are waylaid by Detective Kendall (William Demarest), a private eye hired by the bus company, who delivers a subpoena and mentions a place in Joliet known as "The Pen." When Algy describes the joint—"They've got men walking all around the walls"—Wellington asks, "They're picketing the place?"

They manage to escape Kendall's clutches, long enough to duck into the backstage dressing room of Marco the Magician (Sig Arno), whom Wellington refers to as "Marco the Magicken." This hilarious scene involves Algy impersonating Marco and Wellington attempting to pass himself off as the magician's "twin brother," although he wasn't born in France like his sibling! As they try every trick in the book to elude the dimwitted detective, the boys expose a number of fakeries used by stage escape artists.

The Ink Spots return for "Shout, Brother, Shout," a gospel-style swinger accompanied by the tremendous dancing trio Tip, Tap and Toe, each of whom delivers a routine of singular, jaw-dropping steps. This combination of musical and terpsichorean performance is not only unique to the Abbott and Costello films, it is one of the finest such scenes in the "golden age" of Hollywood film. The Ink Spots were underused in the cinema (1944 was a rough year for the group: Hoppy Jones died at the age of 42 and Charlie Fuqua was drafted into the Army), so *Pardon My Sarong* offers modern viewers a rare glimpse at their artistry, as well as the prodigious talents of Tip (Samuel Green), Tap (Ted Fraser) and Toe (Ray Winfield), who were popular in vaudeville and on Broadway, but only appeared in one other film, *All By Myself* (1943), also at Universal. (An enormous influence on future doo wop, pop and soul performers [especially the Platters], the Ink Spots were ultimately inducted into the Vocal Group and Rock and Roll Halls of Fame.)

Pardon My Sarong (1942). Wellington Phlug (Lou) and Algernon Shawhang (Bud) with Marco the "Magicken" (Sig Arno) in one of the team's most unusual and consistently funny films.

Apprehended by Kendall, the boys are ordered to drive the bus back to Chicago. When Wellington drives onto a small ferry, Algy tells him to "back up ... go ahead!" Kendall reiterates with "Go ahead and back up!"

"What kind of a bus do you think this is?" Wellington asks. "I'll satisfy the both of yous. I'll go sideways!"

"Back up!" shouts Algy. By the time Wellington takes action, the ferry has moved away from the pier and the bus ends up on the bottom of the Pacific Ocean! Costello puts some icing on the comic cake when Wellington turns on the windshield wiper before swimming to the surface. Kendall paddles off, and the boys end up on the anchor of Layton's yacht, *The Bounding Main*. "We're hitchhiking to Chicago!" announces Wellington.

Costello reportedly disliked being drenched while shooting the seafaring scenes in a huge tank on the Universal process stage. When Alex Gottlieb wanted him to do a retake of a scene, he refused but eventually relented when the producer actually resorted to begging.

Joan Marshall (Virginia Bruce), the sister of Tommy's seafaring rival, has been hiding out on the boat. Pulling a fast one, Layton sends her dinghy adrift and shanghais her for the voyage. Also aboard is a friendly seal named Sharkey who repeatedly nuzzles the bum of Algy, who has stuffed a can of sardines into his back pants pocket. Thinking that Wellington is goosing him, he slaps his pal across the face. Demonstrating his own nautical ignorance, he orders, "Keep your course northeast by southeast."

Boardman and Perrin's dialogue is particularly clever in the yacht scenes. "I think we can stand more canvas, boys," says Layton. "Ease the main, douse the jib, and break out the spinnaker."

Wellington heads for the gallery, prompting Algy to ask, "What are you going down there for?"

"Gonna eat," replies Wellington.

"Naw," says Algy. "Didn't you hear what the skipper said?"

"Yeah," Wellington answers. "He said, 'Peas and giblets and break out a can of spinach.'"

There are also some classic burlesque bits courtesy of John Grant. Observing Tommy and Joan together, Wellington comments, "They hate each other enough to get married."

"Wouldn't you marry a pretty girl like that?" Algy inquires.

"No," Wellington replies. "I'd marry a homely girl."

"Why?" asks Algy.

"Well," says Wellington, "if you marry a pretty girl like her, she's liable to run away."

"Well," adds Algy, "a homely girl is apt to run away, too."

"Yeah, but who cares?" Wellington concludes.

Pardon My Sarong (1942). Wellington (Lou) and "Algy" (Bud) aboard the yacht *Bounding Main* with Joan Marshall (Virginia Bruce) and Tommy Layton (Robert Paige) (original lobby card).

Joan deliberately throws the boat off course as a typhoon begins to rage. Wellington tries to shave, but the mirror keeps sliding away. Unable to see his reflection, he says to himself, "How do you like that? I cut my head off."

The doings become even more macabre when Algy steals Layton's gun. "I can't stand to see you starve to death," he tells Wellington, handing over the piece.

"Oh, I can't eat that," says Wellington.

"Who wants you to eat it?" Algy asks. "It's the only way out."

"You mean you want me to demolish myself?" Wellington realizes.

"It's the only honorable thing I could do," Algy admits.

Wellington offers a handkerchief to Sharkey, who blows his nose, then hides his eyes as the gun goes off. Fortunately, the bullet misses its mark just as Wellington spies land. While the boys keep a lookout for "cannibals" on the island, Costello slips in some brilliant bits of improvisation. Picking up a large native shield—or "protector" as Algy calls it—and a club, Wellington sings a few notes as he pretends to play a cello. A hilarious scene ensues as Algy blows a whistle and Wellington whacks a "cannibal" with the club. When they switch roles, Algy is placed in a precarious position because his pal can't blow the whistle.

The "natives"—particularly Universal contract player Samuel S. Hinds as the chief—are the most ludicrous element in the film. As Varnoff, the slimy leader of a gang of jewel thieves seeking "The Sacred Ruby of Mantua," Lionel Atwill, wearing a heavy double-breasted suit in the tropical climate, says, "The natives here speak a little English." (After all, they're all Caucasian contract players—and not all of them are wearing skin-darkening makeup!) The presence of Atwill is one of several Universal horror elements, which also include a "haunted temple" and some excerpts from the musical score of *The Ghost of Frankenstein*, composed by Hans J. Salter.

Wellington accidentally rings an enormous bell and is declared the "moola," or hero of the island, who will protect the natives from the evil spirit of the volcano. To solidify his new position, he is ordered to marry the beautiful Luana (Nan Wynn, a role originally suggested for Martha Raye!), daughter of the chief, a development that enrages the burly Whaba (Leif Erickson), who threatens to kill him if he accepts.

The native dress is taken up by Algy and Wellington, who holds up his sarong with a pair of suspenders. Accompanied by a chorus of seven decidedly *non*–Pacific beauties, his "fiancée" sings the Don Raye-Gene de Paul number "Lovely Luana," then takes him to the "Tree of Truth," where she reveals, "If you tell a lie under this tree, something will happen to you." (Nan Wynn consistently strikes poses to show off her exquisite dancer's legs.)

"Well, I've got nothing to worry about, because I never tell any lies," claims Wellington, who is immediately conked on the head by a falling coconut. He maintains a solid stream of fibbing—including several attempts to tell the old "traveling salesman and the farmer" story—and receives a coconut to the melon each time.

Worse than the tree's onslaught is the return of Whaba, who reminds him, "Remember, if you marry Luana, you be dead husband."

"Get your hand off me!" orders Wellington. "I am a hero. You are a *stinker*."

"What do you mean?" Whaba asks. "What you call 'Stinker'?"

"Well, you see," Algy explains, "a stinker is a great man."

"You bet your life me stinker," Whaba announces proudly. "My father was stinker. My brother stinker. My whole family stinkers!"

"Yeah," agrees Wellington, "but you're the biggest stinker of 'em all." When Whaba offers thanks, the "moola" emphasizes, "You're the biggest stinker on the whole island!"

Pardon My Sarong (1942). One of the most impressive character lineups ever to grace an Abbott and Costello picture: (left to right) unidentified, Ferna (Marie MacDonald), Dr. Varnoff (Lionel Atwill), Wellington Phlug (Lou), Whaba, the "Stinker" (Leif Erickson), Algernon Shawhang (Bud), Lovely Luana (Nan Wynn), Tommy Layton (Robert Paige), Joan Marshall (Virginia Bruce), Chief Kolua (Samuel S. Hinds), unidentified (original lobby card).

At the wedding feast, Costello and Leif Erickson enact the vintage "switching of the glasses" burlesque gag. Whaba has spiked Wellington's libation, and the two men distract each other so the drinks can be swapped. At one point, Lou looks directly into the camera and announces to the audience, "I'm gettin' a mickey," but the "Stinker" ends up passing out.

A lavish production number, featuring a group of muscular African-American dancers, follows. "Vingo Jingo," another Raye-de Paul song, begins as an island chant but kicks into a Big Band swinger as Nan Wynn and her supporting lovelies trip the light fantastic with some Katherine Dunham choreography. (Censor boards in Massachusetts, Pennsylvania and Ohio cut some of the more "suggestive" shenanigans.) When the jewel thieves deliberately set off the volcano, Wellington must prove himself as Luana's bridegroom by passing through the temple to the forbidden side of the mountain. Trying anything to prove that he is really a coward, he admits, "I'm a *bad* boy!"

Algy, however, refutes his cowardly claims: "This boy is an honorary member of the Campfire Girls."

As Wellington, wearing an absurd fish hat on his head and the sacred jewel around his neck, prepares for his hazardous journey, the thieves plan to purloin the gems and "hold the little fat guy hostage" until they can leave the island. Before his pal ascends the mountain, Algy hands over the "dollar" he owes him. "You pick out a fine time to pay me!" Wellington protests. "Where am I going to spend a dollar up there?"

"Go on up those stairs," Algy orders. "Be brave! Do you want these people out here to think I'm a coward?"

An epic chase ensues, during which the boys pose as an (ever-changing) statue, with Wellington knocking out each of the criminals with a club. Pursued by Tabor (Jack La Rue), the leader of the henchmen, Wellington halts at one point. "Wait a minute. I'm out of breath," he says. "I get this way every time I run up stairs. I'm a little too fat." He pauses for another moment, motions to Tabor and commands, "Okay, let's go!" and scampers out of the temple, gliding onto a tree branch below.

Layton grapples with Varnoff, but Joan accidentally K.O.s her boyfriend with a clay pot and is taken hostage. During a furious battle—the boys use coconuts for "ammunition"—Wellington lands on the back of a zebra. "Get me off this jail horse!" he shouts as the animal gallops through the jungle. Worse yet is his encounter with three male lions (another

Pardon My Sarong (1942). Dr. Varnoff (Lionel Atwill) menaces Wellington (Lou) as "Algy" (Bud) and Lovely Luana (Nan Wynn, next to Atwill) look on.

incongruity on the Pacific island). After attempting to swing on a vine, a la Tarzan, he swims after Varnoff's speed boat, receiving a helpful tow from Sharkey. Costello brawling with Lionel Atwill—at one point biting his leg—is a hilarious event unique in the great English actor's career. Wellington winds up riding the detached outboard motor, nearly broadsides the boat, and forces Varnoff and his pilot into the sea.

Now a true hero, Wellington is embraced by Luana. Afraid they'll "miss the boat," Algy scolds, "This is no time for that sort of thing!" As Wellington begins to sweat profusely, Luana lays on a passionate kiss, sending him diving into the lagoon. As a geyser of steam erupts, "The End" also rises from the water.

Again, an Abbott and Costello film was supposed to end differently. The original scripted scene depicted the principals back on Layton's yacht, where Wellington has allowed Luana to stow away, wrapped in a canvas. Attempting to kiss her, he instead plants one on Sharkey, then falls headfirst into the galley. The seal's applause was to conclude the film.

Pardon My Sarong premiered in Lou's hometown of Paterson, New Jersey, to raise money for St. Anthony's Catholic Church. Released nationwide on August 7, the film provided widespread comic relief for millions of Americans as the second biggest Hollywood box-office hit of the year. Only MGM's British home-front drama *Mrs. Miniver* (which went on to win the Best Picture Academy Award) raked in more money. Erle C. Kenton's effort was so

Pardon My Sarong (1942). This still photograph shows footage deleted from the final cut of the picture: "Algy" (Bud) and Wellington (Lou) have succeeded in trussing up Detective Kendall (William Demarest) and Marco (Sig Arno) in straitjackets!

impressive that he would be assigned to the next two Abbott and Costello pictures. After appearing in two more Universal releases, *Night Monster* and *Arabian Nights* (both 1942), Leif Erickson was twice wounded in action while serving overseas.

While working-class Americans were flooding into theaters to see Bud and Lou, British General Bernard Montgomery took command of the Eighth Army in North Africa, squaring off against "The Desert Fox," German Field Marshall Erwin Rommel. In Europe, the Nazis began deporting Polish Jews to concentration camps, including the recently opened Treblinka, a complex designed solely for extermination, located 60 miles northeast of Warsaw. Without Abbott and Costello, there wouldn't have been a hell of a lot to laugh about.

Erle Kenton was solidly in his element for *Who Done It?*, an atmospheric comic mystery with a sparkling script by Stanley Roberts and Edmund Joseph, a selection of choice gags from John Grant, the boys—particularly Costello—improvising brilliantly, and—most noticeably—no musical numbers to interrupt the flow of the narrative.

Shooting on this exciting project began at Universal on May 25, 1942. (During production, Bud, Lou and Kenton filmed the new ending for *Pardon My Sarong*.) Kenton and producer Alex Gottlieb assembled a top supporting cast including the romantic duo of Patric Knowles (who had recently costarred in *The Wolf Man* [1941] and *The Ghost of Frankenstein* at Universal and was very nervous about appearing with burlesque comics) and the gorgeous Louise Allbritton, plus William Bendix, William Gargan, Thomas Gomez, Jerome Cowan, Don Porter and Mary Wickes, the perfect physical and comic complement to Costello.

Lou intended to dedicate *Who Done It?* to Charles Chaplin, who recently had invited him to dine at his Beverly Hills home. After watching his idol do impressions of himself and his partner, Lou discussed a potential future project with the comic genius. He wanted to buy the rights to Chaplin's 1921 masterpiece *The Kid*, and the director suggested that Lou recreate the character he had played in the silent version. Costello later revealed that the project was shelved when Chaplin was deported due to his leftist political beliefs.

While the boys unleashed their shtick on a Hollywood soundstage, director John Ford shot a *real* movie on Midway Island, a tiny atoll in the North Pacific between Japan and Hawaii, during a victorious U.S. Navy rebuff of a major Japanese attack lasting three days. This decisive U.S. victory was the most important single engagement in the Pacific Theater of War.

In a much safer zone, *Who Done It?* transported audiences to the studios of GBS radio, where network head Colonel Andrews (Thomas Gomez) tangles with Marco Holler (Jerome Cowan), the writer of the popular show *Murder at Midnight*. Indirectly referring to another of Universal's current film series, Holler boasts, "Right now I could devise a murder that would baffle even Sherlock Holmes." Regardless of his expertise, Andrews has hired English professor Jim Turner (Patric Knowles) to pen future episodes.

When Turner realizes that his old flame, Jane Little (Louise Allbritton) is the show's producer, he walks out. Bud and Lou first appear at the network's lunch counter as Chick Larkin and Mervyn Milgrim, two aspiring radio writers who pay the bills by serving sandwiches and malted milk. (Stanley Roberts, who left Universal for MGM, originally had cast Bud and Lou as Radio City Music Hall groundskeepers who dream of becoming mystery writers. The Andrews Sisters and Phil Spitalny and His All-Girl Orchestra were also to appear.)

Mervyn's first order is for a Limburger cheese sandwich. Nearly rendered unconscious by the pungent aroma, he manages to cut a slice, then arrives at the counter wearing a gas mask! Though Chick tears it from his face, he has a clothespin on his nose as a backup. When Juliet (Mary Wickes), Andrews' secretary, sits down, Chick encourages his pal to show some

Who Done It? (1942). Donning deerstalker caps, would-be detectives Chick Larkin (Bud) and Mervyn Milgrim (Lou) call to mind another successful Universal series of the time: the Basil Rathbone and Nigel Bruce Sherlock Holmes adventures (original lobby card).

romantic interest to land writing jobs. Taking one look at the lanky, hawk-faced woman, he replies, "I've seen better heads on malted milks."

Using ice-cream scoops as makeshift microphones, Chick and Mervyn play detectives named "Muck" and "Meyer" as they perform a scene from their script, "The Midget Gets the Chair; or, Small Fry." Mervyn's teenage nemesis, an obnoxious elevator boy (Walter Tetley), arrives to bet that he can drink orange juice faster than it can be prepared. While Mervyn serves the glasses as fast as possible, the kid gulps down five, then concedes, tossing him a nickel for the lot. Later, the kid, calling Mervyn "Chubby," cons him out of his *Murder at Midnight* tickets, gets the best of him with the old "two dimes for a nickel" routine, and offers to "squeal" for half a buck. Taking the 50 cents, he walks off, making high-pitched dog noises.

Outside the radio studio, Chick spies Juliet. "There's the girl you've gotta make love to," he reminds Mervyn. In the film's one botched scene, her line, "Do you want me to be your Juliet?" obviously was dubbed in during post-production, and Mary Wickes' mouth movements do not match the dialogue as Juliet walks through a nearby door. Throughout their film career, Bud and Lou weren't concerned with watching the dailies or shooting retakes. Due to their frequent improvisations, dialogue sometimes had to be dubbed to provide a transition from one shot to the next.

Who Done It? (1942). Chick (Bud) encourages his pal Mervyn (Lou) to "make love" to Juliet Collins (Mary Wickes).

The boys manage to enter the studio for the *Murder at Midnight* broadcast. Admiring Miss Little, Mervyn asks Turner, "Is that your girl? Boy, is *she pretty*!" then slams his head into the wall. During a moody sequence beautifully lit by cinematographer Charles Van Enger, Kenton demonstrates his talent for the macabre as the organist plays, an actress screams, and the announcer, in sepulchral tones, begins his eerie narration: "Two men shall die this night. Two men shall die in this, "The Steel Chair Murder Case."

Colonel Andrews is about to speak when he suffers an apparent heart attack, as diagnosed by network physician Dr. Marek (Ludwig Stossel), but it is soon discovered that his steel chair has been wired with high voltage. "Murder?" Mervyn queries. "Murder!" Costello creates one of the film's funniest moments when he runs onto the pedals of the organ, raising quite a cacophony as Mervyn attempts to exit the room.

Outside the studio, Chick suggests that they pose as actual detectives and solve the case. "Let's go inside before rigor mortis sets in," he says.

"Rigor Mortis?" Mervyn puzzles. "Is he on this murder case, too?" Back in the studio, Costello has a field day improvising as Mervyn "interrogates" the suspects with such questions as "Where were you on the night of January 16?" He also insists that the dead man must "have an alibi." In a single take, Bud and Lou ad-libbed an entire bit not in the shooting script, as Chick attempts to explain "watts" and "volts" to his partner.

"What's volts?" Mervyn asks.

"That's right," replies Chick.

"Well, go ahead and tell me," Mervyn requests.

"Well, that's it!" Chick insists.

"What are volts?" Mervyn asks again.

"That's right," repeats Chick.

Fed up, Mervyn claims, "Next thing you know, you'll be telling me What's on second base!"

A rubber glove is found outside the control room door. "You know, if we find the hand that fits that glove, we've got the murderer," observes Chick.

"And it fits me perfect," says Mervyn, just before Inspector Moran (William Gargan) and his sidekick, Brannigan (William Bendix, in a perfectly clueless performance), arrive. The real detectives' interrogation is no more effective than that of "Muck" and "Meyer."

Mervyn and Chick's encounter with a water fountain is one of the funniest scenes in Abbott and Costello's 15-year career at Universal. Initially, Mervyn is blasted in the face, then is unable to get a drink because the water stream recedes every time he moves his mouth toward it. Costello's talent for pantomime is effortlessly demonstrated (particularly when Mervyn *crawls* up to the fixture in an attempt to "fool" it) before the shenanigans *really* break loose: When Chick goes for a drink, Mervyn steps on the pedal too hard, twice soaking his pal. "What are you sweatin' about?" he asks. The showdown culminates with Mervyn flogging the fountain with his hat.

Miss Little informs Moran that Colonel Andrews was involved in "some serious government business—and, only yesterday, he talked to the FBI in Washington over his private wire." Referring to "The Steel Chair Murder Case," she reveals, "It features exactly the same device by which the Colonel was murdered."

The coroner (the ever-creepy Milton Parsons) and two assistants arrive to discover Mervyn sitting, nearly trance-like, against a wall. "Well, we didn't have far to look," he says joyously, examining Mervyn's eyes. "Looks like he's been dead for weeks. Put him in the basket, boys."

"I'm not the guy! I'm not the guy!" he shouts. "I'm still alive. Look!" He runs in place, then speeds off to find Chick and Juliet—who, according to Mervyn, "is too nice a girl to commit a murder." Reaching into her purse, he pulls out a book titled *57 Convenient Ways to Murder a Man*. Shrieking, he immediately puts it back.

"What'd you find?" Chick asks.

"A cookbook," Mervyn replies.

"What do you mean?" says Chick.

Mervyn explains, "It tells fifty-seven ways to cook a guy's goose."

Referring to the boys, the dimwitted detectives vow to "get those murdering cutthroats, dead or alive." The remainder of the film includes an extended chase, as Chick and Mervyn elude the cops while trying to find the real killer. In another sidesplitting scene, Mervyn accidentally switches on a turntable that plays a recording of a crime show. "You have lived too long," it tells him. "You are about to die. It will be a beautiful death."

Three shots ring out. Mervyn begins to slide toward the floor. "Right in the back," he winces. "You dirty rat, for lettin' me have it in the back." Trying to stay on his feet, he leans on the record machine with his right arm, switching on another turntable.

"The bullet didn't kill ya," a wiseguy's voice says. "Maybe this knife will." Costello feigns being stabbed just as a "knife" sound effect is heard.

Gasping, Mervyn says, "First, you shoot me in the back, then you stab me in the heart. What a dirty culprit. Chick!" He switches on a third turntable.

"Do you have halitosis?" the record asks.

"What difference does it matter now?" Mervyn replies. "Chick!" A fourth and final turntable is switched on for good measure.

"Chief, you can't kill this guy," another wiseguy's voice commands. "I'll get him. I'll fix him," another voice replies. "Here comes the Midnight Express. Lay him across the tracks. As Mervyn continues to yell for Chick, the sound of a locomotive fills the room. Kneeling on the floor, the shot, stabbed and run over "victim" thinks his legs have been ground off.

"It's only a transcription," Chick explains. "What's wrong with you?" When Mervyn continues to monkey with the records, Chick implores, "Now stop this nonsense, please!"

After this fantasy experience, Mervyn is brought back to reality when he discovers the corpse of Dr. Marek hanging in a closet. Remarkably, Chick sees it, too; but, by the time the cops arrive, the body has disappeared, to be replaced by a cowering Juliet. In a shadowy sequence, Mervyn is throttled by the murderer, who is shown only in silhouette.

The scene was originally scripted to include Juliet smashing Mervyn over the head with a stack of records, initiating a dream sequence in which the "couple" was to appear as Romeo and Juliet. When Chick entered to duel with Romeo, Juliet was to drop a flower pot, accidentally braining Mervyn, who was then brought back to reality. (A variation on this premise was resurrected for *Buck Privates Come Home*, but again abandoned, five years later.)

In Andrews' office, Jim and Joan discover that, in 1917, the Colonel was an agent for the Cryptograph Bureau. Just before he was murdered, he was attempting to decipher the code of a "foreign power." This plot device is the first wartime element in Abbott and Costello's Universal films referring to the Axis, though no actual nation is mentioned.

As the chase continues, Mervyn runs onto a stage where a variety show is being broadcast. Falling in with an acrobatic act known as "The Flying Bordellos" (a name that went totally unnoticed by the Breen Office), he ultimately splinters a teeter totter and crashes through the floor.

Jumping onto a departing truck, the boys hear a radio announcement that Mervyn will win $10,000 on the *Wheel of Fortune* program if he contacts the station within the next five minutes. Racing to the phone booth in a nearby drugstore, he attempts to call "Alexander 2222," but the operator repeatedly insists that "the line is busy." His frustration is compounded by other callers who effortlessly reach Brazil, Alaska and Russia, while he can't even connect with the building across the street. Just in time, the boys reach the studio as the orchestra strikes up "You're a Lucky Fellow, Mr. Smith." Required to prove his identity, Mervyn Q. Milgrim announces, "I belong to the Campfire Girls, troop number thirty-four."

Sharing the winnings with his pal, he gives Chick the $10,000 check but keeps a brand new radio for himself. Switching it on, he tunes into a broadcast of "Who's on First." "Oh, no, no, no," the boys groan in unison. "That little fat guy ... no good," adds Mervyn. (The microphone in the scene was first used by Bud and Lou during their 1938 *Kate Smith* radio debut.)

Getting the best of the bulls, Mervyn handcuffs Brannigan's hands behind his back. While distracted, the swell-headed "little fat guy" doesn't notice Juliet unlocking the cuffs before he returns to taunt his "hostage." But the detectives' pursuit of the boys ends when Jim and Joan stage a recreation of the *Murder at Midnight* death of the Colonel. Andrews, the code breaker, and Dr. Marek, "a Czechoslovakian patriot" (now the audience knows it's the Nazis who are up to no good, as usual), died "because they knew too much."

Who Done It? (1942). Lieutenant Moran (**William Gargan**), Chick (**Bud**), Brannigan (**William Bendix**), Mervyn (**Lou**), Jimmy Turner (**Patric Knowles**) and Jane Little (**Louise Allbritton**) in the GBS Radio office.

During the broadcast, Mervyn plugs in his radio and shorts out the electricity, flushing out the real killer, Art Fraser (Don Porter), who escapes, running up to the roof of the skyscraper. Coincidentally, the boys also have lammed it to that location. Following several dangerous escapades—including dangling from a flagpole, teetering on a ledge and being shocked with thousands of volts while walking on some high-tension wires—Mervyn foils the rod-toting criminal by using the rubber glove as a slingshot to knock out several letters on a sign advertising, "VOTE FOR TOWNSHEND PHELPS." The revised sign reads, "SEND HELP."

The police arrive and take the crazed Fraser into custody. Mervyn, the intrepid "hero," picks up a light bulb, only to realize that he has been super-electrified by the high wires. He tosses the bulb at the sign, which now reads, "END." Pat Costello again doubled for his brother in the more dangerous shots. (The original ending included Mervyn falling into a huge air conditioner, where he becomes encased in a block of ice.)

After production wrapped, Bud and Lou went on their first personal tour for the Army Emergency Relief Fund. Initially intending to spend eight weeks raising $350,000 to purchase a bomber for the Air Corps, they were persuaded by Under Secretary of War Robert Patterson to aid the dependents of combat soldiers. Increasing their target amount to $500,000, the boys personally paid all expenses incurred during the tour.

During 34 days on the road, they visited 78 cities and 100 war production plants while selling a whopping $85-million stack of war bonds, quite a testament to their rising popu-

Who Done It? (1942). The intrepid Mervyn (Lou) apprehends the murderer, Art Fraser (Don Porter), as witnessed by Jimmy Turner (Patric Knowles), Jane Little (Louise Allbritton), Lieutenant Moran (William Gargan), Brannigan (William Bendix), Juliet Collins (Mary Wickes) and Chick (Bud).

larity. In each major city, supporters received a souvenir flyer titled "from U.S. to You" including the team's portrait and facsimile autographs. The Treasury Department spoke for the boys:

> Congratulations on your involvement in U.S. War Savings Bonds for Victory, and thanks for making our visit to [city] a happy occasion because of your enthusiasm at the war bond meeting this [date] 1942.
>
> The real thanks comes from Uncle Sam who needs all the savings everyone of us can invest in war bonds to buy ships, guns, tanks and planes to crush the Axis.
>
> Yours for Victory and Freedom,
>
> Bud Abbott
> Lou Costello

In Indiana, they auctioned off a cocker spaniel donated by Irene Dunne for $103,000 in war bonds. Governor Henry F. Schricker named Bud and Lou Number One and Number Two honorary members of his "White Hat Club," though as "badges" they received *gray* fedoras!

In Manhattan, they appeared in Central Park, where they raised $30,000 prior to the

Who Done It? (1942). The original ending, depicting Mervyn (Lou) encased in a huge block of ice, was deleted prior to the film's release.

arrival of Mayor Fiorello LaGuardia, who addressed the crowd of 17,000. The rally was organized by the New York State War Activities Committee of the Motion Picture Industry.

After a show in Omaha, Nebraska, on July 31, 1942, the boys improvised a second one in the backyard of Jerry Young, a 14-year-old boy who had approached them after climbing up six flights of stairs to their room at the Fontenelle Hotel, claiming that he and his pals would collect local funds to purchase war savings stamps. By the time the boys arrived with a police escort, the yard was packed with children and adults who had contributed several hundred dollars. Abbott told a reporter, "That kid will be a millionaire by the time he's 16."[2]

The superior *Who Done It?* was released nationwide on November 6. In North Africa, U.S. forces began "Operation Torch," joining General Montgomery in driving back the Panzer divisions of the Desert Fox. The Allies had broken through the Axis lines at El Alamein, and Rommel was forced to withdraw from El Agheila on December 13. Four days later, British Foreign Secretary Anthony Eden revealed to the House of Commons that Germany was executing Jews en masse. In Washington, FDR, surrounded by Yuletide cheer, vowed to avenge these crimes against humanity.

8

STALLIONS AND SKATERS

It Ain't Hay (1943) and *Hit the Ice* (1943)

It was impossible to be sad with Lou around. — Patsy O'Connor[1]

Universal moved Bud and Lou from a comic mystery sans music into a full-blown musical, *It Ain't Hay*, one of the most unusual films directed by Erle C. Kenton. In fact, all three of Kenton's Abbott and Costello films are quite different, making him one of the team's most versatile collaborators.

The screenplay by Allen Boretz—with the usual material contributed by John Grant—was based on the Damon Runyon story "Princess O'Hara," which Universal previously had filmed with Chester Morris in 1935. The original title of the project, "The Sky's the Limit," was changed to "Hold Your Horses," but ultimately was christened *It Ain't Hay* by Alex Gottlieb to acknowledge the success of Bud and Lou's recent fundraising tour for the war effort.

Kansas-born Damon Runyon (1884–1946) began his career as a journalist, but is famous for his fascinating short stories based on actual people he had known and observed on the streets of New York. Gamblers, con men, gangsters and all-around operators populate his works, which are written in an entertaining vernacular style. *It Ain't Hay* is crawling with crooked gamblers, touts and wiseguys, including Harry the Horse (Eddie Quillan), Chauncey the Eye (Dave Hacker) and Umbrella Sam (Shemp Howard), who is asked why he carries his namesake at all times—even when "it ain't rainin'." "How should I know?" he says. "I'm a Damon Runyon character."

Armed with a six-week schedule, Kenton began shooting the film on September 28, 1942. Unlike earlier Abbott and Costello projects, which include song performances placed strategically among the comedy routines and romantic subplots, *It Ain't Hay* is the only true musical the team made at Universal. Rather than working in singing acts like the Andrews Sisters or the Ink Spots, the film features several characters, including Private Joe Collins (bandleader Leighton Noble), Peggy, Princess O'Hara (Patsy O'Connor), and even Wilbur Hoolihan (Lou), participating vocally in lavish production numbers.

The opening credits feature the names of Bud Abbott and Lou Costello on the shoe soles of two bums passed out under a park bench. The initial scene opens with 12-year-old hack driver Princess O'Hara singing "Sunbeam Serenade" as she guides her horse, Finnegan, around Central Park (actually Griffith Park in Los Angeles). The carriage transports Army man Collins and his sweetheart, Kitty McGloin (Grace MacDonald), who lend their voices to the upbeat number. At their destination, Princess is harassed by Reilly (Wade Boteler), a beat cop (Irish, of course), who threatens to lock her up.

It Ain't Hay (1943). This once copyright-entangled, rarely seen musical inspired by the tales of Damon Runyon features a hilarious scene involving Grover Mockridge (Bud) and Wilbur Hooli-han (Lou) actually hitting the sack with the racehorse Teabiscuit! (original title lobby card).

"She's twelve years old," says Kitty, while Joe adds, "Her old man's laid up with arthri-tis."

Reilly continues to act the tough bull, but quickly caves in. "Hello, Princess!" he exclaims as he lifts the girl down from the rig. The boys then make their entrance as Wilbur nearly runs over several pedestrians as he careens down the street to park his taxi. He completely removes the front passenger-side door as the one in back falls onto the street, allowing his "fare"—actually his pal, Grover Mockridge (Bud)—to get out. On a four-day pass, Collins has been ordered by his captain to round up "every big star on Broadway" for a show at Camp Saratoga. Out of money for phone calls, the private is loaned a quarter by Grover, who grabs the coin from Wilbur's hand.

"Hello, Princess. How's my best girlfriend?" Wilbur asks the child. "How's my best boyfriend, Finnegan?" he adds.

"He's hungry," she replies.

"I love this horse," Wilbur says to himself as he feeds some peppermint candy to the animal, providing an opportunity for the boys to slip in a classic burlesque bit.

"You've spoiled the horse's appetite," Grover accuses. "Now he won't eat his fodder."

"Eat his Fodder?" Wilbur asks. "What do you think Finnegan is—a cannibal?"

"No. She's gonna hang his fodder on his nose," Grover explains.

"Ain't he gonna look funny with his Fodder on his nose?" suggests Wilbur.

"He eats his fodder every day," continues Grover.

Wilbur requires clarification. "Finnegan eats his fodder *every day*?"

"Well, *sure*," Grover replies.

"What's his Fodder eat?" asks Wilbur.

"He eats *his* fodder," Grover answers, matter-of-factly.

Wilbur continues, "And what's his Mudder eat?"

"Well, she eats *her* fodder," says Grover.

"It's gettin' worse all the time," Wilbur concludes. After the disgusted Grover walks away, the confused cabbie adds, "It must be Fodder's Day."

Princess offers a sandwich to Wilbur, but Grover grabs it away, holding it behind his back. Pretending to have something caught in her eye, she distracts Grover long enough for the starving Wilbur to take a bite of—his partner's hand! This gag, depicting Lou inflicting actual physical pain on Bud, is a rarity in the team's films.

Outside Grant's Cafeteria (an inside joke), Umbrella Sam invites Grover and Wilbur to have lunch with him and his fellow touts. Clumsiness and gambling results in Wilbur's acquisition of six checks, none of which he can pay. Gregory Warner (Eugene Pallette), a "new

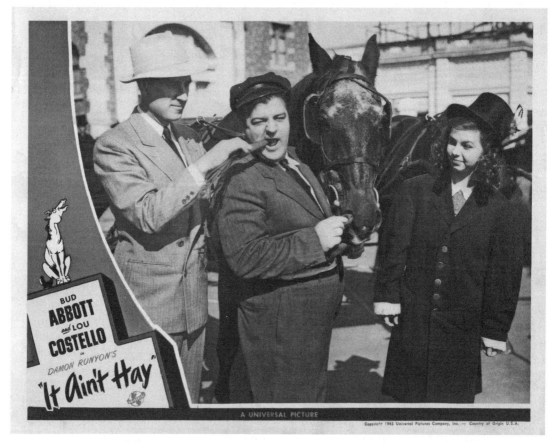

It Ain't Hay (1943). Grover (Bud), Wilbur (Lou), Teabiscuit and Peggy, Princess O'Hara (Patsy O'Connor) (original lobby card).

efficiency expert" is "plenty tough," according to Joe. "Anybody that can't pay his check winds up in the alley, all cut up and bleeding."

Grover hits the street to "dig up some money," leaving Wilbur at the mercy of three tough bouncers (Mike Mazurki, Sammy Stein, Matt Willis). As the frightened cabbie salts the checks and begins to eat them, Warner orders, "Pay your check and get out!" Told to stay until Grover returns, he instead prepares to eat a platter of spaghetti. Attempting to dine under the threat of violence, Wilbur ends up devouring a large portion of his necktie.

Outside, Princess tells "Uncle Grover" that Finnegan has fallen seriously ill. "I'm afraid it was that peppermint candy," she adds.

The three goons are about to toss Wilbur into the alley when Grover runs in, claiming that his pal is "a millionaire" who must go outside to sign "some legal papers." Princess remains in his stead, and Joe tells Reilly, "A poor, little, innocent Irish girl is being held in that cafeteria against her will."

"That big, fat guy in there said, 'I don't like the Irish!'" adds Wilbur.

Reilly storms in, protesting the "$4.55 worth of food" the girl is supposed to have eaten. Kitty is fired from the cafeteria by Warner, who, in turn, is sacked after only four hours on the job. Worse yet, the manager holds "his $100 bond" and charges him the $4.55!

The boys arrive at Finnegan's stable with veterinary medicine as Princess sings the ballad "Old Timer" to the horse. Wilbur tries to take its pulse, but Grover advises him to check the "forelegs." Knowing there are only "two front legs," he is assured that "the horse's forelegs are in front."

"What's those things in the back—crutches?" Wilbur asks. Using a rubber hose, he attempts to blow a large pill into the horse's mouth. Gagging, wheezing and unable to talk, he uses pantomime to show Grover "what happened": "The horse blew first!"

Finnegan rises from the hay, inspiring Princess to rouse her father and all the neighbors, who are led in the number "Glory Be" by Kitty and Joe. The Vagabonds, a vocal trio in hardhats, emerge from a manhole, followed by an accordionist and two guitarists. Skaters then roll in from a nearby beverage stand, and the Step Brothers, an African-American tap-dancing quartet, carry out a furious routine on the loading dock of the Monarch Department Store. Wilbur joins the marching throng, only to transform the Vagabonds into a quartet after falling into the manhole.

This optimistic home-front ramble depicting an entire Manhattan community coming together is quickly countered during the next scene, in which Wilbur is shunned by everyone on the street. He then sees that an "SPCA Humane Ambulance" has pulled up to the stable. Costello is given a chance to demonstrate his talent for pathos when Wilbur looks into the empty stall, quietly mentions "Finnegan" twice, then slowly walks back outside. He masterfully uses only the backside of his body to communicate the genuine sadness the character is feeling, placing his hands into his pants pockets and taking short, infant-like steps (a technique he would later repeat for his tour-de-force performance in *Little Giant* [1946]). "You're a murderer!" a small boy (Alex Gottlieb's son, Stephen), standing rigid with hands on hips, accuses him as he reaches the sidewalk. "You killed that horse," the kid adds.

"Honest, kid, I didn't mean to do it," Wilbur explains.

"Oh, yes, you did!" insists the boy. "I don't want to talk to you, and nobody else wants to talk to *you*!" he claims, then walks off.

Subtly expressing guilt with his eyes and mouth, Costello slowly turns around and leans his forehead against a brick wall. Though he loved being a comic, this was the type of scene he longed to play. Throughout the team's career, Bud was appreciated by audiences for his peerless talent as a straight man, but his characters were consistently bossy and downright cruel to those of his partner. Without lapsing into undue sentimentality, Lou was able to combine an uncanny talent for inciting riotous laughter with an understated ability to be genuinely lovable.

The boys visit the Sportsman's Club, a racketeering front, to raise money for a new carriage horse. "Stinky Fields sent us up here," Grover claims.

"Yeah," adds Wilbur. "He's a good friend of Shorty McAllister's." (Fields and McAllister were a burlesque team well known to Bud and Lou. During the team's 1952–54 television series, the characters "Stinky" and "Mr. Fields" were played by Joe Besser and Sidney Fields, respectively.) After borrowing $100 on a fishing rod, Wilbur bets on a series of bogus horse races, at one point putting dough down on the nose, tail and "rest of the horse ... in case [it] comes in sideways."

Fooling the mugs that the cops are raiding the joint, Grover grabs the announcer's microphone and they split with the winnings. As soon as they hit the street, Wilbur gives the roll to a con man who "sells" him a police horse. (It was inevitable that the boys, being compulsive gamblers, would include such a scene in one of their films. Costello loved going to the track, and eventually began raising his own race horses. One of the horses mentioned in the scene is called "Lolly C," the nickname of Lou's mother and the name of one of his future racers.)

A companion to the earlier "Fodder" routine, "Mudder" involves Grover telling Wilbur that "sometimes a he makes a better mudder than a she."

"How can you tell if a horse is a Mudder?" Wilbur asks.

"By looking at his feet," Grover replies.

"Ain't we livin' in a wonderful age?" exclaims Wilbur. "Mudder or Fodder, I gotta have a horse."

Umbrella Sam and his cohorts suggest a visit to Colonel Brainerd, the owner of "the world's fastest race horse," Tea Biscuit, whose companion, Boimel, will be given away "to the first person who calls." Just as the boys reach the stables at the Empire track, the Colonel puts Warner on his payroll, telling the "efficiency man" that "this track is situated in country Washington Irving wrote about. Remember 'Sleepy Hollow'? Some night you're liable to see the Headless Horseman around here."

Wilbur runs into the stable wall, gets a pitchfork stuck in his rear end, and ends up with a bucket over his head, but the boys manage to gallop away with the horse from Boimel's stall. Warner sees only Wilbur with the bucket, thinking it's the Headless Horseman. (As usual, Lou was doubled by his brother, Pat, in this scene.) When the morning paper hits the streets, the headline reads, "TEA BISCUIT KIDNAPPED." "It's propaganda!" Wilbur exclaims.

The wartime references in *It Ain't Hay* are sporadic and indirect. A gag involving a flower pot dropping from a window onto Wilbur's head is followed by his comment, "Made in Japan. That's the closest hit they'll ever make around here." When Grover asks him what he's wearing on his head, he replies, "Oh, I just planted a Victory Garden."

Princess' father, King O'Hara (Cecil Kellaway) has driven Tea Biscuit to Saratoga, to take a drunk there for "the cure." The boys locate the hack and horse, who is asked by Wilbur, "Don't tip off the cop, will ya?"

"I'm no stool pigeon," replies Tea Biscuit! (This incident is a forerunner to the "Francis the Talking Mule" series produced at Universal from 1950 to 1956. The boys' former collaborator, Arthur Lubin, directed six of the seven films, then went on to repeat the speaking equine premise for the *Mister Ed* television pilot in 1958.)

The boys hide the horse in their hotel room. One sequence, "borrowed" from the Marx Brothers' superlative *Duck Soup* (1932), shows Grover, Wilbur *and* Tea Biscuit in bed together, with their respective shoes lined up on the floor below. The three touts aren't far behind, and the hotel manager now hires Warner to be his efficiency expert! The Colonel has offered a reward of $10,000 for the animal's safe return, and Wilbur's ordering of "a bail of hay and a bag of oats" has put them on the scent. But Wilbur has provided a "disguise"—a huge pair of sunglasses—for the horse, whose hooves have been "quieted" with pillows from the bed.

A carriage chase ensues, and the King's hack, driven by Wilbur, is cut in half by a speeding train. Grover and Princess are abandoned in the rear half, while Wilbur speeds off on Tea Biscuit to the Saratoga Handicap. Though the horse is not actually in the race, the Colonel enters him "for sentimental reasons."

To lend the film some racing realism, Universal dispatched a newsreel crew to shoot the opening of the summer season at Saratoga. Though shots of the town and track were included in the final cut, the actual racing footage was filmed at the Los Angeles County Fairgrounds in Pomona.

A prime contender, Rhubarb, waits at the ready. Before the jockey (Rod Rogers) can mount the horse, Wilbur is tossed onto its back by Tea Biscuit, who is then mistaken for the other animal. Grover weasels $100 from Warner (as a down payment on the "nag" Wilbur

It Ain't Hay (1943). While hiding Teabiscuit, the "incognito" Wilbur (Lou) and Grover (Bud) fool inept "efficiency expert" Gregory Warner (Eugene Pallette) (original lobby card).

is riding) and bets it on Tea Biscuit—at 100 to one odds. During the race (another scene "suggested" by a Marx Brothers film, *A Day at the Races* [1937]), Wilbur/Rhubarb stays neck and neck with the jockey/Tea Biscuit mistaken for Rhubarb, but rides back for his cap after it blows off his head. Rhubarb is declared the winner, but after the horse's teeth are examined, the judges realize that the horse is actually Tea Biscuit. In the meantime, Grover has made good on his deal to sell the horse ridden by Wilbur to Warner for $500, but the Colonel bought it back for $10,000 before being told the animal's true identity!

A knock is heard in the boys' hotel room. "Go answer the door," Grover commands. "It might be Warner."

"It won't do no good," Wilbur points out. "We're signed up with Universal."

The Colonel has arrived to pay Grover his $10,000 winnings from the race, but he has thrown the tickets out the window. After Wilbur discovers them under the windowsill, the boys joyously buy a new horse and carriage for King O'Hara.

A lavish production number follows, with Joe and his band, dressed in their Army uniforms, performing "Hang Your Troubles on a Rainbow." Warner is ordered to return the money to Colonel Brainerd and chases the boys onto the nightclub stage, where Wilbur falls in with the Step Brothers. Costello's inept choreography amid the four formidable tap dancers is a comic high point. Disguised as a Revolutionary fife and drum trio, Wilbur, Grover and Princess toss Warner from the stage.

"How do you think he landed?" Wilbur asks. "Heads or tails?"

"Who cares?" replies Grover.

Glancing down, Wilbur discovers that Warner's bankroll has fallen out of his pocket. "Am I Lucky!" he exclaims, pulling a band off the money. "Rubber! Good rubber!" He throws away the dough and then rejoins the patriotic march with his pals. This gag and the Army uniforms are the film's final brief, indirect references to the wartime situation.

This acknowledgment of rationing originally was to be followed by much more blatant propaganda delivered in song by Bud and Lou—

GROVER:

Come on, let's all sing a toast
To the ones we hate the most

WILBUR:

Let Heinie and Fritz'll
Choke to death on Weiner Schnitzel

—followed by a chorus (rejected by the Breen Office):

Hats off to Old Glory
To Hell with the Heil!
Hang your troubles on a rainbow
And rally 'round a smile!

Erle Kenton wrapped *It Ain't Hay*, his final, unusual Abbott and Costello film, on November 11, 1942. Pat Costello, having shouldered the overly strenuous scenes for his brother, was pleased to have his head back on his body; but more pressing family business was on Lou's mind. Five days before the wrap (the same day *Who Done It?* was released), Anne Costello had given birth to a son, Louis Francis Cristillo, Jr., whom the proud papa referred to as "Butch." *It Ain't Hay* was delivered to mixed reviews on March 10, 1943.

True Boardman's original story for the next Abbott and Costello opus, tentatively titled

"Oh, Doctor," was to feature Lou as a hypochondriac. By the time Robert Lees and Frederic Rinaldo finished their script, none of the original remained. Retitled *Hit the Ice*, the screenplay now focused on two aspiring newspaper photographers who get mixed up with a trio of gangsters who hide out in a hospital while pulling off a bank heist.

Though Kenton had planned to direct "Oh, Doctor," he was removed from the project before production began. Bud and Lou joined new director Charles Lamont at Universal on November 23, 1942, to begin shooting the film. Like Kenton, the Russian-born Lamont began his career with Mack Sennett in 1919, and directed scores of two-reel comedies before graduating to features. He is credited with discovering Shirley Temple at a dance studio during the casting of one of his shorts. During the 1950s, he would direct eight Abbott and Costello films for Universal.

Lamont filmed the majority of *Hit the Ice* on Universal soundstages. The Sun Valley resort in central Idaho, located near the city of Ketchum, had been reserved for location shooting, but Universal turned over the area to the U.S. Army when its Ski Troops required the specialized space for important maneuvers. In January 1943 some location work was done at Soda Springs, California, and at Sonja Henie's ice-skating rink in Westwood.

The winter sports setting is immediately established in the film's opening credits, which include snowmen resembling Bud and Lou, here playing "Flash" Fulton and "Tubby" McCoy.

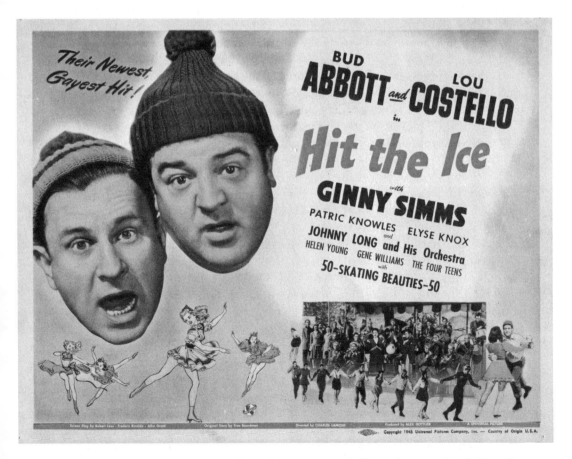

Hit the Ice (1943). Bud and Lou in another of their most unfailingly funny and satisfying films (original title lobby card).

The opening scene set at the hospital outlines the major gangster plot, as Silky Fellowsby (Sheldon Leonard) and his two henchmen, Buster (Joseph Sawyer) and Phil (Marc Lawrence), plan to rob a bank across the street. Referring to two heavy hitters who are scheduled to arrive soon, Fellowsby explains, "We don't move out of here until the boys from Detroit arrive.... I've never seen these boys from Detroit, but they tell me they handle a gun like it was a blonde."

On a nearby street, photographer Flash Fulton meets his old University of Wisconsin chum Dr. Bill Burns (Patric Knowles, sporting his usual English accent). Ascending from under the sidewalk on a garbage lift, Fulton's partner, Tubby McCoy, peeks out of his "dark room" trash can. Both neophytes have been promised a newspaper job if they can provide a scoop. Hopping into an ambulance with the doc, they race to a high-rise fire. Falling out the back door, they ride a stretcher to the scene, where they skid to a halt on the street. A frantic "triple gag" follows, with Costello being slammed in the head with the ambulance door three times.

Attempting to snap a photo, Tubby stands on an extension ladder that raises him all the way up to a smoke-billowing window. He grabs the sill, dangling high above the street as flames repeatedly roast his rear end. He falls onto a trampoline-like firefighter's net, bounces onto the roof of a car and hits a stretcher. Rushed to the hospital, he is mistaken for a woman who has just delivered a baby! Seeking a hiding place, the boys run into the gangsters' room, where Tubby admits they've been working by "shooting people—perfect day for it." Flash adds, "I was shooting a cop down on the corner." Of course, Fellowsby mistakes them for the "boys from Detroit."

Rather than providing armed protection for the wiseguys, Flash and Tubby set up their cameras outside the bank. Making some adjustments, Tubby focuses on a passing woman's shapely derriere. "You're not getting paid to do that!" scolds Flash.

"I thought I'd pick up a little on the side," Tubby admits.

Discovering that a robbery has been committed, Flash observes, "The bank's stuck up!"

"What's this bank got to be stuck up about?" Tubby asks. "It's no better than any other bank." Lees and Rinaldo's dialogue—combined with John Grant's contributions—is uniformly witty throughout the film. But the boys' performances, as usual, rise above the scripted material. At the door of the vault, Costello grabs the turning device, pretending it's the wheel of a ship. Barking out imaginary orders to his "crew," he sounds like W. C. Fields, one of his comic heroes. After ineptly setting off the alarm, Tubby manages to slip by the police: He has placed his shoes at the ends of two long poles. Covering the poles with a sheet, the boys walk out to the sidewalk, creating the effect that Flash is single-handedly carrying the injured Tubby on a stretcher. "I was shot. Some guy stabbed me," Tubby tells a cop. Of course, another officer steps on the sheet, and their ruse is uncovered. As they flee, Tubby stops to take the policeman's picture.

The following morning, a sketch artist's rendering of the boys hits the front page of the newspaper—impetus for Abbott to launch into the classic routine "Pack/Unpack," during which Flash, debating the pros and cons of either staying in town or taking it on the lam, repeatedly orders Tubby to "pack that grip!" or "unpack that grip!" This provides a tour de force scene for Costello, who first packs and unpacks their clothes very carefully, then gets frantically sloppy, shoving one of the bed pillows in with the garments, and finally whistling to send everything automatically flying into the suitcase. The sequence ends with Tubby being slammed through the wall by the Murphy bed, then emerging from under the covers, between the couple sleeping in the adjacent room!

Tubby did snap a photo of the three crooks as they emerged from the bank, although only their backs are visible. A full frontal view of Flash *can* be seen, however. Nonetheless, the boys plan to use the image to blackmail the gang. Dr. Burns agrees to continue as Fellowsby's physician, joining Flash and Tubby in tailing the mob to Sun Valley. Nurse Peggy Osborne (Elyse Knox) also accompanies them. At the train station, Tubby runs into an African-American porter (Mantan Moreland, in a brief cameo) carrying some snowshoes. Tubby thinks they're "tennis rackets," prompting the porter's response, "Don't you recognize a flyswatter when you see one?"

Tubby's confusion is overwhelmed by love at first sight when he spots the beautiful Marcia Manning (Ginny Simms), the singer in Johnny Long's orchestra. He immediately runs over to the young woman, offering to carry her bag. She declines and walks off, leaving Tubby in a daze. Flash tries to snap him out of it and nearly receives a kiss for his trouble. "Not me!" he insists.

As the musicians from the band file past the steward, they call out the name of their instruments. Following two bass players, Flash calls out "third base" and Tubby shouts, "short stop!" but they manage to climb aboard.

The first Harry Revel-Paul Francis Webster song staged by Sammy Lee is "I'm Like a Fish Out of Water" featuring Ginny Simms and Johnny Long's orchestra in their own private car. One of the finest Big Band singers, the subtle yet sultry Simms (who is billed third, just after Bud and Lou) was also an attractive actress in 11 films, including several with popular bandleader Kay Kyser, with whom she performed from 1938 to 1941, when she left the band to headline her own radio show. *Hit the Ice* provided one of her best roles, after which she signed with MGM (where he quit after one too many amorous overtures from Louis B. Mayer), perhaps topped only by a major role in Warner Bros.' *Night and Day* (1946), starring Cary Grant as (a fictionalized) Cole Porter.

The Four Teens vocal quartet supports Simms during the number, during which Lamont inserts reaction shots of Tubby being captivated by Marcia's crooning. At the end of the song, he runs over to hug her, but she instead embraces Johnny Long, who also happens to be one of the boys' old college chums.

In a passenger car, a conductor asks the boys for their tickets. Pretending to be handcuffed to his partner, Flash states, "FBI, Washington."

"C.O.D., Alcatraz," adds Tubby. The train speeds through a tunnel, and mayhem rages in the darkness. When light is restored, a candy butcher (Bobby Barber), with his toupee covering his eyes, shouts, "I can't see. I can't see!" (A pal of Bud and Lou's, Barber, who appeared in several of their films and TV shows, would be the brunt of many baldness jokes over the years.)

Fellowsby, who gave Marcia "her first break," conscripts her into the gang as bait. "She comes in so the Detroit boys can go out," he tells his henchmen. At Sun Valley, the elegantly attired canary sings "I'd Like to Set You to Music" as Tubby again watches in rapture. As swimsuit-clad beauties walk by, he merely scoffs. Intending to impress "his girl," he pretends to play classical masterpieces on a piano while Flash spins records on a hidden player. "We're going to *flim flam* her," he tells Flash, then shouts "All right!" each time he wants the music to begin or end. The plan hits a snag when she says, "All right" and is foiled after Flash falls asleep behind the piano.

"You ought to be ashamed of yourself," Marcia scolds the would-be virtuoso. "I thought you were a nice little fellow."

He backs toward the swimming pool and then looks into the camera. "You thought I

Hit the Ice (1943). Beautiful songbird Marcia Manning (Ginny Simms) works her wiles on the smitten but innocent Tubby McCoy (Lou) (original lobby card).

was going to fall in, didn't you?" he asks the audience. Another supremely built beauty walks past, and he plunges into the water.

Hired as waiters, the boys deliver room service to Fellowsby, whom they offer the photographic negative in return for the "25 Gs" he owes them for the bank job. He accepts, telling them to meet him at his mountain cabin, but then orders Marcia to work her wiles on Tubby. Wearing another ensemble that accents her considerable charms, she feeds the little man and then inquires about the negative. "May I see it?" she asks. Tubby's refusal prompts a kiss. "Now many I see it?" she repeats, receiving another "No." She lays on an even more passionate smooch, causing him to slap the wall several times. She attempts, "Now may I see it?" one more time.

Tubby tries to respond, scans the room, looks out the window, motions for her to wait, walks over and locks the door, and returns to the window seat to sit beside her. In words of one syllable, his answer is still "*No.*"

"I give up!" she responds. "I've had enough!"

"You've had enough?" asks Tubby. "Not me!" He plants a *long* one on her as sweat beads on his face and smoke rises from his rear end. "I've never had a kiss affect me like this before." Marcia screams as he discovers that the seat of his pants has been burned away by a heating vent!

Simms sings in a major production number, "Slap Happy Polka," as skaters enjoy the ice at the Sun Valley rink. Dr. Burns and Nurse Osborne cut an impressive routine (Knowles and Knox are doubled by professional skaters in the long shots) during the extravaganza staged by Harry Losee. Following his effort, the doc is informed of the bank robbery by Flash. "Where's Tubby?" Burns asks.

Tubby "skates" into the shot and falls flat on his back. (Pat Costello again doubled for Lou.) "There he is," Flash replies. Crawling back out into the middle of the rink, Tubby falls down several times and then uses a little girl to get back on his feet. A remarkably accomplished skater, the wee lass puckers up to *blow* him back to the ice. Grabbed up by a long chain of skaters, he then is flung into the fence, tears down the awnings, and finally crashes over the barrier into a snow bank.

The gang nabs Nurse Osborne, and Burns follows them to the cabin. The doc has ordered the boys to join him there; but, before embarking via dog sled, Tubby straps a small keg of booze around a St. Bernard's neck. "In case we meet W.C. Fields," he explains to Flash. (This bit is the second Fields-related moment in the film.) By the time they reach the cabin, the dogs are *riding* the sled, which is being pulled by Tubby!

The crooks knock Burns cold, but Tubby runs in brandishing a "gun" in his pocket. "Drop that gun or I'll drill ya," he commands Buster. "I got a gun that shoots bullets for twelve miles and throws rocks the rest of the way." Tubby and Marcia exchange winks.

Hit the Ice (1943). Tubby takes to the frozen rink with a lineup of skating beauties (original lobby card).

Buster drops his rod but grabs Tubby by the collar. "You ain't so tough, you little pig!" he says.

Tubby grabs Buster's collar. "Who are you calling a pig?"

"You!" insists Buster.

"Well, with the price of pork nowadays, is that an insult?" Tubby asks. (This line is the film's only indirect reference to the wartime home front.) The little man then assumes a "wiseguy" attitude, handing Buster's gat to Flash, whom he calls "Killer." "Take this gun," he orders, pointing to the doc and nurse. "Take them outside. Use them bullets on 'em. If you come back with any, I'll use 'em on you."

"Okay, boss," Flash replies. (Here, Costello glances into the camera and registers a brief "what am I doing?" expression.) Outside, the couple rides off in the sled and "The Killer" blasts two shots into the air to fool the gang.

Buster discovers the negative, and Fellowsby realizes that their faces are not visible in the photo. Tubby knocks out the two mugs with a clay pot, and Marcia smacks the leader on the melon with the money bag. "Mush!" Tubby yells as she speeds off on the dog sled, leaving them—and the cash—behind in the snow. The usual grand chase follows, with the

Hit the Ice (1943). Tubby mistakenly believes he is to be married to singer Marsha Manning (Ginny Simms), who has already been wed to bandleader Johnny Long (far left), as observed by Dr. Bill Burns (Patric Knowles), Peggy Osborne (Elyse Knox) and his pal Flash Fulton (Bud) (original lobby card).

boys skiing down the mountain. Tubby and the crooks play "catch" with the money bag before he slams into a tree, rides piggyback on the skiing Buster, swings on a telescope, and crashes through a mine and a cabin. At one point, a bear hitchhikes on the back of his skis. "You've got a bear behind!" Flash points out. The mayhem culminates with the brawling Tubby and Fellowsby becoming encased in a giant snowball as they roll down the mountainside. The police arrive to take the mugs into custody, but Tubby chases everyone off when he pulls a skunk out of the snowball.

At the train station, the boys are dressed to the nines in tuxedos and top hats. Tubby thinks he's going to marry Marcia, who arrives, but already wed to Johnny Long. Before reaching the station, however, she sings one more number, "Happiness Bound," while riding in a sleigh with Long and a gang of musicians and vocalists.

Costello again conveys sadness with the back of his body as he does his slow walk toward the train. After seeing Marcia and Johnny kiss through the car window, he spots Flash doing the same with a gorgeous blonde. "If I ever fall in love with another girl, I hope they hang me," he says, just as a sweet young thing winks at him from another car. He begins to wave at her, but is hung up by the mail arm at the end of the train. As he is carried away, his pants are torn off, and "The End" is superimposed over the seat of the garment. (This is the third Abbott and Costello film to use Lou's rear end as a way to conclude the shenanigans.)

9

SICKNESS AND SLAPSTICK

Lost in a Harem (1944)

I asked Anne to keep that baby up tonight to see if he would be able to recognize my voice, and wherever God has taken my little boy, I want him to hear it. — Lou Costello, to his sister, Marie[1]

Hit the Ice wrapped on December 31, 1942. During the boys' radio show that evening, producer Walter Wanger, President of AMPAS, presented them with a special scroll from the Motion Picture Herald announcing their status as the number one box-office attraction in the United States. While working at Universal, a "minor" studio, they had managed to nudge out former top dogs Clark Gable, who currently was a lieutenant in the Army Air Force, and Mickey Rooney, two of MGM's most bankable stars.

On the heels of this tribute came an even more prestigious honor: Bud and Lou received a request from President Roosevelt to embark on another major nationwide tour to promote war bonds. Hitting 85 cities in 38 days, they were flown from one performance to the next in an Army bomber and then sped to the stage by local state troopers. Lou's brother, Pat, who was on active duty, received permission to join the team during the tour. Bud and Lou opened each show at opposite sides of the stage, trying to outdo each other in selling bonds before launching into classic routines, including "Who's on First?"

From January 14–24, 1943, Roosevelt joined Winston Churchill at an Allied conference in Casablanca, French Morocco, to plan war strategy for the European Theatre. Soviet premier Josef Stalin also had been invited, but refused to attend. When General Charles de Gaulle also declined, Churchill threatened to recognize another general, Henri Giraud, as leader of the Free French. The conference resulted in the "Casablanca Declaration," which called for the unconditional surrender of the Axis Powers, Allied aid to the U.S.S.R., the invasion of Sicily and Italy, and the joint Free French leadership of de Gaulle and Giraud. Back in Washington, FDR explained the plan to the American people during his radio address on February 12.

In the Pacific, the Japanese had begun evacuating Guadalcanal after five long months of bloody fighting, and ceased all resistance by February 9. From March 2–4, during the Battle of the Bismarck Sea, U.S. and Australian air forces successfully attacked a Japanese convoy relocating troops from China and Japan to New Guinea.

On March 3, the exhausted Lou began fighting his own personal war after collapsing suddenly. Having survived rheumatic fever as a child, he now was diagnosed with rheumatic heart disease. Unable to work, he was aided by several guest stars who paired with Bud for their weekly radio show. But the airwaves were dominated by official war reports, including news of Allied gains in North Africa and the Pacific.

Lou's health remained poor, and he was confined to a wheelchair. His doctor delivered the discouraging news that he might never work again. When Bud decided to forgo future performances until his partner could recover, Lou became determined to make a comeback, an attitude bolstered by visits from many friends, including the Andrews Sisters, David Rose, Joe and Dorothy DiMaggio, Martha Raye and her husband, Nick Condos, Clark Gable, and his hero, Charles Chaplin. A special bed was built for him, and it could be wheeled into the home theater, where Lou enjoyed screening films. The prolonged illness, which laid him up for close to a year, brought the Abbott and Costello families closer together. Lou also was able to spend time with his daughters and little son, whom he watched grow before his eyes as he convalesced.

While laid up, Lou read stacks of letters sent to him by others suffering from rheumatic fever. He was particularly moved by the get-well wishes from children who asked if he could finance a cure for the disease. He thoughtfully answered these missives, advising the youngsters to get plenty of bed rest. Supported by Bud, he intended to establish the Abbott and Costello Rheumatic Fever Foundation to provide treatment for those who couldn't afford health care. They agreed to split the $500,000 cost of building a hospital and research facility in Palm Springs, then finance its operation with profits from personal appearance tours.

Lou, accompanied by his butler, Mitch, finally returned to work on November 4, 1943, to rehearse with Bud for their NBC radio show, which would reunite them for a national audience that evening. During the rehearsal, Eddie Sherman took a phone call from Lou's sister, Marie, one of several family members who had been preparing for the first birthday celebration of Lou, Jr., scheduled for two days later. Marie asked Eddie to take Lou home; and, instinctively, Sherman knew that something had happened to "Butch."

When Lou walked into his house, he immediately went to the den, where the family doctor sadly informed him that little Lou, Jr., was dead. In the confusion created by preparations for the party and the baby's nurse having the day off, the baby accidentally had been left in his playpen, alone, in the backyard near the swimming pool. Apparently, he had worked some hooks loose and crawled out and into the water, where he eventually was discovered by Anne. Two firefighters had worked on Butch for an hour and 40 minutes, to no avail.

Lou secluded himself in his office, but was joined by his father, Eddie Sherman, and Bud's brother, Harry Abbott. Word of the tragedy spread fast, and though Lou received several offers from major stars to fill his spot on the radio show, he ordered his sister to phone NBC and tell them he'd be there as scheduled. For the first time in a year, Lou joined his partner to make the nation laugh, as if nothing out of the ordinary had happened. But when the shtick ended, Abbott, summoning almost as much grit as his devastated associate, got serious while addressing the audience over the airwaves:

> Ladies and gentlemen, now that our program is over and we have done our best to entertain you, I would like to take a moment to pay tribute to my best friend and to a man who has more courage than I have ever seen displayed in the theater. Tonight, the old expression "The show must go on" was brought home to all of us on this program more clearly than ever before. Just a short time before our broadcast started, Lou Costello was told that his baby son—who would have been one year old in a couple of days— had died.
>
> In the face of the greatest tragedy which can come to any man, Lou Costello went on tonight.... I know you all join me in expressing our deepest sympathy to a great trouper.

Instead of celebrating the first birthday of the Costello heir, Lou, walking with a cane, struggled through his funeral, on November 6. Thinking that his wife might have been negligent with his son (an opinion shared by other members of his family), he was permanently scarred by the event, and his home life was never the same. Though he rarely spoke about it, one day, shortly after the funeral, he opened up to comic Bobby Barber, telling his friend that his dream of becoming a movie star, complete with a big swimming pool, had taken his only son's life.

Right on the heels of his prolonged illness and death of his beloved son, Lou was summoned to appear before the Paterson Draft Board. On November 19, he received permission to be inducted in Hollywood, should he pass the tests and physical examination; but, of course, a 37-year-old father who suffered from heart disease couldn't have been drafted even if he wasn't a movie star.

From November 28 to December 1, Roosevelt met with Churchill and Stalin at the Tehran Conference, the first summit attended by all the leaders of the "Big Three" Allies. Their discussions focused on opening a second front in Western Europe, recognition of the independence of Iran, and planning a final strategy for the defeat of Nazi Germany.

Following his rejection by the draft board, Lou and his partner soldiered on with their 1943–44 radio season, distinguished by an impressive lineup of guest stars, including Humphrey Bogart, George Brent, John Garfield, Cary Grant, Charles Laughton, George Raft and Lana Turner. Sid Fields and Mel Blanc continued as regulars, but the show became aggravating for Lou, who—being a supremely *visual* comic—was limited by the audio format. Confined to delivering lines from a script, he had to rein in his improvisational talent.

After a hiatus of 15 months, Bud and Lou finally returned to a Hollywood soundstage on March 22, 1944. But their home base of Universal would have to wait. MGM originally had announced that the team's second film for the studio would be "The People's Choice," from a screenplay by Lou and Gene Schrott. Set in Chaos City, the plot pitted Abbott's corrupt mayor against Costello's innocent street cleaner, who accidentally becomes a hero when he tidies up the town. Bearing no resemblance to this ambitious premise, the film that *was* made—*Lost in a Harem,* shot on leftover sets from *Kismet*—is a completely fantastical hodgepodge set in "the teaming mythical city" of Port Inferno, with only a single brief reference to "America" and no topical wartime material whatsoever.

In fact, on April 16, *New York Times* Hollywood correspondent Fred Stanley reported:

> Studio executives have estimated that the major companies will take a loss of at least $2,000,000 on war story properties that were acquired during the last two years and since have been shelved because of the fast-changing status of the conflict and the decreasing theatre-goer interest in war plots.[2]

A complete inability of the studios to churn out topical films fast enough to keep up with daily headlines had created an "apathy to this kind of material." Stanley added, "Besides, who in Hollywood can outguess the real war developments coming up, such as the Allied invasion of Europe?"[3]

Before the shooting of *Lost in a Harem* began, Eddie Sherman met with Louis B. Mayer to renegotiate the boys' salary. They were guaranteed $80,000, yet could have grabbed a quarter million had they made the film at Universal, where they enjoyed a piece of the back end. Mayer agreed to double their pay, but when Sherman pushed to make the deal retroactive to *Rio Rita,* the mogul was furious. Wartime salary stabilization measures wouldn't permit such extravagance, he argued. Sherman claimed he could work around the red tape with the help of two attorneys at Universal, who wanted no problems with Bud and Lou. This impressed Mayer, who agreed to pay the team a total of $450,000.

The uneven *Lost in a Harem* script by Harry Ruskin and Harry Crane was improved somewhat by John Grant's usual re-workings of tried-and-true material, and the boys benefited from the comic expertise of Charles Reisner, who served as assistant director on 10 Chaplin classics—including *A Dog's Life* (1918), *Shoulder Arms* (1918), *The Kid* (1921) and *The Gold Rush* (1925)—and directed Buster Keaton in *Steamboat Bill, Jr.* (1928) and the Marx Brothers in *The Big Store* (1941). For additional box-office appeal, producer George Haight cast sumptuous blonde Marilyn Maxwell and the top-flight Jimmy Dorsey Orchestra, who are certainly a curious but solidly swinging presence throughout the film.

During production, Lou lightened his spirits by indulging in one of his favorite pastimes: "removing" major props from sets and adding them to his own household furnishings! At Universal, he often had lifted items from sets before scenes were completed—resulting either in extensive and *expensive* retakes or the studio promising him the props if he returned them temporarily—but he at least *thought* he had waited until scenes were completed at MGM before running off with the goods. Following the completion of a harem sequence, he grabbed all the large, stuffed pillows from the set and took them home in a delivery truck.

Lost in a Harem (1944). In this "Arabian Nights" spoof, Bud and Lou share the screen with eye candy (Marilyn Maxwell) and a swingin' Big Band (Jimmy Dorsey and His Orchestra) (original title lobby card).

The next day, workers in the prop department were searching for the pillows to use in another scene. Finally a studio suit approached Lou, pitching him the old Universal offer.

Working on *Lost in a Harem* by day, Lou then moonlit as a producer at Monogram, sitting in on story conferences and supplying gags for *A Wave, a Wac and a Marine* (1944). Having been impressed with Elyse Knox's performance in *Hit the Ice*, Lou gave her top billing in this Poverty Row potboiler. He had intended to direct this picture and another Monogram project, *Blockbusters* starring the East Side Kids, under the pseudonym "Lucas Tello," but Universal shot him down.

Lost in a Harem opens in typical MGM style with an anachronistic production number at the Café of All Nations. On the bill are Hazel Moon (Marilyn Maxwell), Alioop and His Captivating Cobras, The Three Fezzes and Mother (!), and—at rock bottom on the sandwich board—Garvey and Johnson, a stranded vaudeville duo. Hazel takes the stage first—at one point singing the lyric, "I can even get to second base with Frank Sinatra" (in actuality, Maxwell was one of Sinatra's extramarital dalliances at the time)—followed by Harvey Garvey (Lou) and Peter Johnson (Bud), whose inept act outrages the club's proprietor, Mr. Ormulu (Ralph Sanford, whose face is buried beneath an outrageous prosthetic nose and mustache). A full-scale riot erupts among the disgusted patrons, and Harvey and Peter are tossed into a jail cell with a mentally unhinged "Derelict" (Murray Leonard). (Ubiquitous freelance bit player Harry Cording plays the Police Chief.)

For this lengthy scene, John Grant re-wrote the old burlesque standard "Slowly I Turned," here featuring the Derelict recounting his unfortunate relationship with an unfaithful wife who left him for a man on "the banks of the Pokomoko." "Every time I hear the word 'Pokomoko,' I just want to *kill*!" he warns Harvey. Of course, the prisoners mention the name repeatedly, resulting in Harvey being throttled and pummeled each time.

Ramo (John Carroll), the deposed Prince of Barabeeha, helps the boys escape by bringing them a large loaf of bread containing a saw. The "beloved" leader, accompanied by his new pals and Hazel, is reunited with his desert troops, the "Sons of the Desert" (a reference to the 1933 Laurel and Hardy masterpiece) who perform a ludicrous production number on horseback before bedding down for the night. Harvey is awakened several times by the flowing beard of Chief Ghamu (Adia Kuznetzoff, the nemesis of Laurel and Hardy in *Swiss Miss* [1938]), who also unintentionally stabs him in the bum with a scimitar, before an ornery goat rams the aforementioned posterior, tearing down the entire tent.

In classic MGM style, the exterior desert scenes were filmed on a huge interior soundstage. Instead of transporting the cast and crew to the Arizona desert, the studio maintained its "ars gratia artis" image by trucking in 10,000 square feet of sand, 25 date palms, Arabian horses and camels—a move that perfectly complements the 100-plus faux "Arabs" who populate the scenes. The script originally included a scene requiring Costello (in a variation on his hammock mayhem in *In the Navy*) to fail five times to mount a camel, but his recent illness nixed the idea.

A clever gag, masterfully directed by the silent film veteran Reisner, is achieved without dialogue: Observing a beautiful woman (Katherine Booth), Harvey subtly indicates his interest by facial expression only; after slapping him, she walks into a building marked "Mind Reader."

At the Barabeeha palace of Ramo's "evil uncle" Nimativ (Douglas Dumbrille, in another "ethnic" role), the boys encounter Bobo (J. Lockard "Lock" Martin, later to play Gort, the robot, in *The Day the Earth Stood Still* [1951]), who becomes convinced that they are Hollywood scouts looking for star material. Attempting to steal the "hypnotic" rings worn by

Lost in a Harem (1944). In the dungeon of Port Inferno, Peter Johnson (Bud) and Harvey Garvey (Lou) are nearly done away with by The Derelict (Murray Leonard) and the seven-foot Bobo (J. Lockhard Martin) (original lobby card).

Nimativ, Harvey and Peter are mesmerized into believing they are termites. They respond by eating the elaborately carved wooden palace furniture.

Exactly at midpoint, Jimmy Dorsey, playing some "Middle Eastern blues" on his clarinet, kicks off a tremendous Big Band swinger. Lester White's chiaroscuro cinematography and George Hively's editing complement the pulsing rhythm of the instrumental number; and, though Bud and Lou don't appear in the sequence, it is one of the film's highlights. Playing himself, Dorsey is the one "realistic" element in the film's fantasy milieu.

The sole direct reference to the contemporary United States is Nimativ's racially charged mention of the "beautiful, blue-eyed blonde" who will become "wife number 38." The only way he can manage this feat, however, is by hypnotizing her with his rings. Meanwhile, Ramo awakens the "termites" with a pin, and they immediately flee into Nimativ's harem, where "men are forbidden." Some less-than-subtle humor involves the boys hiding under a sofa, upon which the evil despot then sits, announcing, "If I get my hands on them, I'll bash their heads in." Plopping down his posterior a second time, he adds, "I'll put a heavy price on their heads."

A brief chase is followed by another lengthy jail scene—the best in the film—during which the boys are reunited with the Derelict, who "leads" them into the imaginary home of "Mike," his "crazy" brother. Using Chaplin-esque long takes and compositions showing all three characters, Reisner allows Costello to create one of his most brilliant pantomimes, as Harvey "plays" an invisible piano and smashes a nonexistent punch bowl before the Derelict "guns down" his own crazed sibling. After Peter and the Derelict walk out of the frame, Harvey is menaced by the still-living Mike, whom he attacks with a knife, which is accompanied by the sound of a gunshot. "I shot him with a knife!" he exclaims. (During the first season [1952–53] of their TV show, Costello reprised his superb performance, again with Abbott and Murray Leonard.)

In another tour de force, Lou appears in drag (his first on film) as Harvey impersonates Nimativ's plump wife, Teema (Lottie Harrison), in yet another attempt to swipe the rings. He throws a tantrum on the sofa, then *flips* Nimativ onto his back (Costello actually performs the stunt in a single shot, with Reisner using no editing). Borrowing another bit from the Marx Brothers, Abbott, dressed as Nimativ, contributes his own pantomimic magic as Peter pretends to be the despot's mirror image.

Bobo, Teema and all the harem girls, set on going to Hollywood with the two "scouts," join the resistance against Nimativ. Just as Harvey is about to be beheaded, they all dance into the chamber and "strangle" the despot's men, just as the Sons of the Desert arrive in the nick of time. Nimativ is hypnotized into thinking he's a dog, and Garvey and Johnson ride off in a desert taxi, driven by none other than the Derelict, who hears "Pokomoko" and chases them into the final fadeout.

Lost in a Harem (1944). Peter (Bud) and Harvey (Lou) are supported by the beautiful Hazel Moon (Marilyn Maxwell) during their harrowing Arabian adventure (original lobby card).

The film's only connection to the home front arrives in lieu of end credits. As "Overseas Program No. 820" sponsored by the War Activities Committee of the Motion Picture Industry, *Lost in a Harem* concludes with the following note: "Pictures exhibited in this theatre are given to the armed forces for showing in combat areas around the world."

Regardless of the film's "mythical" setting and cartoon-like representations of "Arabs" (solid conventions of the popular 1940s Arabian Nights sub-genre), some real-life Muslims were not amused. Along with the usual objections to revealing costumes and "suggestive movements," the Breen Office had warned against any dialogue referring to Islam that could be misinterpreted. Producer George Haight wisely suggested blending together elements from various Middle Eastern cultures to create the ambiguous locale. This move was primarily successful, with only Syria (where several edits were made) and Morocco (where it was banned outright) finding offense. *Lost in a Harem* was released in the United States on August 18, 1944.

While the film was in post-production, the Allies marched into Rome on June 5 and hit the murderous beaches of Normandy the following day. "Full victory, nothing else," General Dwight D. Eisenhower had told the paratroopers before they set out on a mission whose odds were certain death in a hail of bullets from German machine guns on a blood-soaked beach in France.

10

CLIQUE AND CAMPUS

In Society (1944) and Here Come the Co-Eds (1945)

Probably no other comedy team in pictures has been so sincerely and enthusiastically supported by screen observers and critics generally. Whatever criticisms have been leveled, they have been pointed, not at the comedians, but at their vehicles. This almost universal loyalty from the press springs from the personal warmth of the comedians themselves plus a deep faith, on the parts of most critics, in the real comedy potentialities of the two men.—Paul P. Kennedy, *New York Times*, August 20, 1944[1]

Lou was back at full throttle, making films, performing on the radio with his partner, and dedicating many of his off-hours to the war effort. When he and Anne weren't welcoming servicemen into their home, he was seeing to their comfort when he was out on the town. At the Brown Derby one evening, he witnessed the maître d' turning away a sailor who hadn't phoned in a reservation. After inviting him to the table for dinner, he took the young man home, where he stayed for the weekend.

The filming of *Lost in a Harem* wrapped at MGM on June 3, 1944. Nine days later, Bud and Lou finally returned to Universal to work with director Jean Yarbrough on *In Society*, using a variety of burlesque gags and improvised mayhem to poke fun at the ways of the idle rich.

Alex Gottlieb, wanting to move beyond producing formula pictures for a comedy team, had left Universal for Warner Bros., where he applied his talents to a variety of genres. As his replacement, Milton Feld hired screenwriter Edmund L. Hartmann, who worked on the next three Abbott and Costello pictures for the studio.

Jean Yarbrough had been working in film comedy since 1921, when he began his career as Hal Roach's chauffeur, then as a prop man at the studio that created Our Gang and teamed Laurel and Hardy. After directing several Leon Errol shorts at RKO during the 1930s, he graduated to features. *In Society* was the first of five major projects with Abbott and Costello, with whom he collaborated extensively during their television run from 1951 to 1953.

Anxious to rush Bud and Lou's "comeback" into theaters, Universal brought in Erle C. Kenton to direct two production numbers, Bobby Worth and Stanley Cowan's "Rehearsin,'" a poolside romp featuring Anne Gillis, the Three Sisters, and a bevy of bathing beauties, and Kim Gannon and Walter Kent's "What a Change in the Weather," a romantic canoeing duet between Marion Hutton and Kirby Grant clearly patterned after the "duck boat" scene in *Keep 'Em Flying* (although Bud and Lou are completely excluded from the sequence this time around). The musical numbers (featuring none of the dynamism of the Andrews Sisters or the Ink Spots) proved the most lackluster in the Abbott and Costello films to date; and, though Yarbrough's directorial style is visually more pedestrian than those of Arthur Lubin and Erle Kenton, his handling of new variations on old chestnuts like "Fleugel Street" (Lou's personal addition to the film) and "Go Ahead and Sing" feature a deft combination of ace Abbott and Costello timing and spare editing. Much of the "society" footage was shot on location at the Jewett Estate in Pasadena.

Burlesque veteran Sid Fields was hired by the boys to add his comic touches to the script by Edmund L. Hartmann, Hal Fimberg and John Grant, and he thereafter remained in Hollywood, where he later wrote many of the Abbott and Costello TV shows, on which he also played their ever-exasperated landlord and other characters. Yarbrough also directed Fields in "The Language Scene," in which he played an elocutionist who attempted to teach Lou's Albert Mansfield proper grammar, but the sequence was cut from the finished film.

Marion Hutton, previously a vocalist with the Glenn Miller Orchestra (1938–1942) and elder sister of Betty Hutton, is appealingly innocent as the girl Albert is nuts about, but there is no tangible chemistry between her Elsie Hammerdingle, "Lady Cab Driver," and Kirby Grant's wealthy bachelor, Peter Evans. When Albert and his plumbing partner, Eddie Harrington, arrive at the posh Van Cleave mansion to "repair" a leaky bathroom faucet, Elsie dances with Peter and then takes the stage to perform the nonsensical Mann Curtis-Vic Mizzy song "No Bout Adout It" with the Will Osborne Orchestra.

In Society (1944). Impossible plumbers Eddie Harrington (Bud) and Albert Mansfield (Lou) (original lobby card).

Hired by Parker (William B. Davidson), the Van Cleave butler, Albert and Eddie (who operate as two plumbing companies: Ajax, at $6 per hour; and Atlas, at $4) wreak havoc on the master bath and flood the bedroom of the sleeping patriarch (Thurston Hall). One of the great Abbott and Costello set pieces, the scene (which took two days to shoot) is the high point of the film. Classic dialogue such as "Walk this way"—prompting Albert to mimic Parker's pompous gait—and Van Cleave's suggestion that the noisy plumber "stop fooling around and come to bed"—inspiring Costello to do a take directly into the camera—peppers the scene.

Following the flood, which culminates with the boys floating through the bedroom in the bathtub, Mrs. Van Cleave (Nella Walker) writes a note, threatening to have them "assaulted physically by our servants" should they ever show their faces again. Parker, however, mistakenly replaces the missive with an invitation to a weekend soiree at the Winthrop estate before mailing the envelope. Prior to *walking* to the mansion, Albert and Eddie are visited by Drexel (Thomas Gomez), whom they owe $1,000. Of course, the low-rent gangster views the event as an opportunity to use the boys as stooges. An ironic bit of dialogue has the portly Gomez referring to Lou as "a little fat guy."

Originally performed on burlesque stages in 1918, the classic "Fleugel Street" routine was transformed into Bagel Street for the film. Asked to deliver a container of $15 straw boaters to the Susquehanna Hat Company, poor Albert is accosted by an assortment of irate,

In Society (1944). An attempted delivery of Susquehanna Hats on Bagel Street gets the best of poor little Albert (Lou).

violent and insane pedestrians (one man claims he was killed by a falling safe!) who quickly destroy the merchandise. The performances and straightforward visual style guided by Yarbrough create a scene that is a direct forerunner to his work on the Abbott and Costello television show.

At the estate, Albert and Eddie are accompanied to their room by Pipps the Butler (Arthur Treacher, providing the perfect pompous counterpoint to the "unsophisticated" boys). "Well, sir, if I may start undressing you now," he tells Albert.

"The last person that ever undressed me was my mother, and that was a *year* ago," he admits. Soon, he and his pal are attired in finery misappropriated from two VIP guests, Baron Sergei (George Dolenz) and Count Alexis (Steven Geray), but Albert is saddened upon discovering that "his" girl is actually smitten with Peter, whom she joins after singing Curtis and Mizzy's "My Dreams Are Getting Better All the Time."

Albert is amazed that he must shell out $5 to view "The Plunger," which Mrs. Winthrop claims is worth 150 grand. Soon, Drexel arrives to heist the painting, joining forces with the family chauffeur. In a sequence that eerily reflects Costello's tragic loss of his son, Albert jumps into the swimming pool to save a drowning man (Don Barclay). Abbott launches into a variation on the "Mustard" routine, bawling out his buddy for "putting lifeguards out of work"

In Society (1944). Much to the dismay of Pipps the Butler (Arthur Treacher) and Professor Mellonhead (Sidney Fields, whose footage was deleted from the final cut), Albert (Lou) and Peter (Bud) crash the high-class Winthrop gathering at Briarwood (original lobby card).

by inconsiderately rescuing someone. To end the squabble, the inebriated man jumps back in, and the boys immediately forget about him as they spot Drexel coming their way. Albert survives an onslaught of knives thrown at him by the chauffeur (whose final blade *does* drop the victim's drawers), then takes part in a rousing fox hunt. Following a wild ride on a bull, he ends up with the fox in his lap.

In Society features three major chase sequences: a runaway sofa that carries Albert and Eddie from the back of a moving van into a pond; the fox hunt; and a climactic, frenzied ride on a fire engine, the result of their attempt to retrieve the purloined "Plunger" from the crooks. This final pursuit includes several long shots lifted from Universal's W. C. Fields feature *Never Give a Sucker an Even Break* (1941). Interestingly, the Winthrops are so rich that their estate has its own fire department!

"You may be plumbers," Mrs. Winthrop reminds them, "but you're *wonderful* plumbers. Thank goodness my 'Plunger' is safe." But they again take it on the lam when Sergei and Alexis reappear to accuse them of the clothing theft, prompting Albert to damage the painting irreparably. The film concludes in Three Stooges–style as the boys are knocked out by rocks tossed at them by the two dishonored guests.

Released on August 18, 1944 (13 days *before* the debut of *Lost in a Harem*), *In Society*

In Society (1944). Albert (Lou) and Peter (Bud, center) are about to destroy the famous painting *The Plunger* in the film's closing scene (original lobby card).

(which wrapped on July 21 at a cost of $659,000) proved the team's most expensive film to date, but was a big hit at the box office. As promoted in the trailer, Bud and Lou were "back with a bang." Following their 18-month absence from the screen, Universal chose to focus solely on comedy; though providing a light satire of the upper class, the film — like *Lost in a Harem*—includes no topical references to the home front.

On August 25, the Allies liberated Paris. During the first week of September, the troops followed suit in several cities throughout France and Belgium. Soviet troops continued to make progress from the East, and the Germans continued to be trapped between two encroaching fronts. On October 21, the Allies forced a massive surrender at Aachen, the westernmost city in Germany, bordering Belgium and the Netherlands.

Back home, the boys weren't experiencing a "bang" off screen. They often made sarcastic remarks about each other, and matters were made worse by Eddie Sherman's attempts to exclude Pat Costello from team discussions. Sherman also angered Lou by asking for more money, suggesting that he become their manager *and* agent, which would land him 25 percent of their take. The turmoil reached an apex when Lou proposed that Sherman make a *separate* deal with Abbott, but leave him completely out of any such agreement.

This wrangling led to a near split-up after Bud hired a household servant who had been fired by his partner. Lou angrily phoned Sherman, insisting that Bud dismiss the maid if he ever wanted to work as a team again. Eddie informed his client that such a demand could result in a multi-million dollar lawsuit that he definitely could not afford. Lou backed down, but swore not to talk to Bud except while performing.

Back on a Universal soundstage, the tension between the boys took a backseat to their professionalism. *Here Come the Co-Eds*, their entry in the "campus comedy" sub-genre, eschewed wartime concerns for solid laughs. Despite several unconnected musical interludes that break the flow of the comedy, the film—one of their funniest—offered them the widest array of settings since *Pardon My Sarong*. John Grant (who, with Arthur T. Horman, reworked an earlier script by Edmund Hartmann, Edmund Joseph and Hal Fimberg) was promoted to producer this time around. Jean Yarbrough, armed with a budget of $702,000, directed his second Abbott and Costello assignment from October 24 to December 6, 1944, shooting many of the Bixby College scenes on location at North Hollywood Park. A 43-day shooting schedule was a luxury on a Bud and Lou opus, but Yarbrough still managed to spend an additional $15,000. The boys raked in $102,000 plus a percentage of the take.

The film opens at the Miramar Ball Room, where Slats McCarthy (Bud) and Oliver Quackenbush (Lou) are paid to escort ladies onto the dance floor. While conversing with attractive patrons, Oliver is accosted by a nearsighted husband (Richard Lane) who twice tosses him into a large potted plant. "May I apologize on the floor?" the now bespectacled man asks one of the lovely dames.

"Why don't you apologize to me?" Oliver replies. "*I'm* on the floor!"

After Slats lands in one of the plants, Oliver accidentally punches out their boss, and they flee out the front door, where they heist a conveniently waiting car. Speeding down the street, they hear an announcement on the radio:

> Calling cars 11, 12, 14 and 15. Calling cars 11, 12, 14 and 15. Be on the lookout for car 13.
> It has just been stolen. Here is a description of the men who stole the police car. Number One: medium height, slender, blue eyes. Number Two: short, fat and stupid.

Oliver is careless with a match, blows up the car, and he and his pal accept jobs as assistant caretakers at Bixby College, where Slats' sister, Molly (Martha O'Driscoll), has accepted

Here Come the Co-Eds (1945). Oliver Quackenbush (Lou) with Slats McCarthy (Bud) and his sister, "Miramar" Molly (Martha O'Driscoll).

a scholarship. Pondering the opportunity to be "caretakers for two- or three-hundred girls," Oliver does the famous Costello wolf whistle. When Benson (Donald Cook), Dean of the College, knocks at their apartment door, Oliver, assuming the cops have arrived, decides to "hide on the fire escape," not realizing that there isn't one!

"Miramar Molly" immediately finds trouble with Jonathan Kirkland (Charles Dingle), the conservative Head of the Board of Regents, while the boys become the assistants of Johnson (Lon Chaney, Jr., fresh from playing the Wolf Man in Universal's *House of Frankenstein* and Kharis in *The Mummy's Curse* [both 1944]). Two attractive co-eds drop their handkerchiefs as Oliver innocently walks by, and Johnson threatens to fire him; when he tosses his own, a third beauty is beat to the pick up by Patty (Peggy Ryan), a super perky, garrulous young lady, who calls him "Butterball." "She's *cute*," replies Oliver (as Lou looks directly into the camera.)

"This is the caretaker's quarters," Johnson announces as he leads the boys into a room that resembles a landfill.

"Then you should get a caretaker to take care of it," Oliver adds.

Ordered to "get busy and clean up," he and his pal execute one of the funniest slapstick scenes in the Abbott and Costello films. When Slats tells him to "go in the kitchen there and wash the dishes," he suggests, "Why don't I just take the dishes and throw 'em in the spare room?"

Costello single-handedly creates another comic tour de force as Oliver turns a grease spot into the portrait of a pig, puts "fresh water" into the drip tray under the ice box, and climbs onto the kitchen counter, where he stumbles into a large pan of dough. Rejoined by his buddy, he initiates a hilarious exchange of sticky tin containers that become cemented to their hands and clothing.

While Oliver and Slats do all the work, Johnson does nothing but "shoot dice." Oliver swipes the dice, then hides them in his mouth when Patty approaches. Of course, the girl kisses him, and the dice slide down the hatch. "I paid two bucks for those dice!" rages Johnson, who vows, "I'm gonna get 'em out of you if I have to choke 'em out!"

Placed behind an x-ray machine, Oliver becomes a tumbler as Slats and Johnson each bet $5, then shake him up, let it ride, and spin him around on an operating table. Coughing up the dice, he produces two sixes—boxcars—and Johnson grabs the loot.

Though the first musical interruption is prefaced by Patty's explanation that Benson has given the college a cultural "facelift" with music and athletics, the second performance comes out of nowhere. The sequence opens with a sign indicating "Music Appreciation Class with Evelyn and Her Magic Violin." Bowing melodies heavily reminiscent of the Hungarian Dances of Johannes Brahms, she is accompanied by Phil Spitalny and His Hour of Charm All Girl Orchestra. The film credits Edgar Fairchild and Jack Brooks for the music and songs, but excerpts from Hans J. Salter's score for *House of Frankenstein* can be heard throughout the performance.

John Grant adapted the "Jonah and the Whale" tale first used in *One Night in the Tropics* for Oliver to entertain a classroom of co-eds. This familiar bit is followed by a charming duet sung by Costello and Peggy Ryan, whose Patty is kissed by Oliver three times before launching into "Let's Play House." Lou's first singing and *dancing* since *Buck Privates* concludes with Oliver admitting, "I feel just like Donald O'Connor." A multi-talented performer, Ryan made her film debut at age five in Warner Bros'. *The Wedding of Jack and Jill* (1930), memorably played a hungry girl in John Ford's *The Grapes of Wrath* (1940), and co-starred with O'Connor in eight Universal musicals before becoming Costello's girl in *Co-Eds* at age 20.

Lou and Peggy share another energetic scene, in which Oliver attempts to prevent Johnson from lying down on a bed under which Patty is hiding. Grabbing the lumbering caretaker, he pretends to dance with him and then moves him from one rack to another, as the girl likewise rolls under them before finally exiting the room. The sight of Costello wrestling Chaney to the mattress, pulling his jacket over his head, which is then thrust between the metal bars at the foot of the bed, is a comic highlight.

A Stan Laurel–like scene is also a winning bit of comedy: While raking leaves, Oliver opens a pocket knife, slices a piece of sod away from the sidewalk, and shoves the leaves underneath. Meanwhile, Kirkland (a Capra-esque creep if ever there was one) demands the expulsion of Molly (Martha O'Driscoll appears rather fetching in her brief shower scene, a racy inclusion in a 1945 film) and the resignation of Dean Benson. And if the delinquent mortgage payments aren't met, he threatens, the school will be closed.

Odds are 20 to 1 against Bixby in the big basketball game against Carlton, so the co-eds need only raise $1,000. A benefit recital is held, providing an excuse for another intrusive appearance by Phil Spitalny's gang of girls, here billed as the "Bixby Orchestra and Glee Club directed by Prof. Spitalny." "This ought to bring in enough money to bet on the basketball

Here Come the Co-Eds (1945). Oliver and Slats attempt to buffalo Johnson (Lon Chaney, Jr.), the hot-headed caretaker of Bixby College (original lobby card).

game," a sign-painting co-ed proclaims. The number, "I Don't Care if I Never Dream Again," is the film's nadir—absolute filler—again featuring Evelyn and her Magic Violin and a decidedly masculine vocalist with a husky voice.

Costello lifts the film back to its comic senses with some fine nonverbal improvisation during the classic "Oyster Stew" routine. "I think there's a wild oyster in there," Oliver tells Slats. He feeds it soda crackers, stabs at it with a fork and knife, splashes broth on himself and his pal, and then attempts to catch it by sticking a pin in the end of his necktie. He whistles for the oyster, which grabs the pin, pulling his face into the stew. Of course, Slats never sees the broth-spewing seafood. Originated by silent comic Billy Bevan during his early tenure with Mack Sennett, this gag previously had been revived by Jerome "Curly" Howard in the Three Stooges short *Dutiful But Dumb* (1942).

The girls need another $500, so Slats approaches his pal Tiger McGurk (Sammy Stein), who wrestles as The Masked Marvel. Slats offers to split the $1,000 purse with him if he agrees to let Oliver win an upcoming match. Before the bout, McGurk becomes sick on banana fudge sundaes, so "Strangler" Johnson takes his place. Shown in two-shots and close-ups only, Costello and Chaney were doubled in the scene by two professional wrestlers whom Yarborough hired at an arena on Hollywood Boulevard.

The announcer introduces "The Bixby Bulldog, Oliver Quackenbush." Witnessing "The

Masked Marvel" effortlessly hop into the ring, he attempts to follow suit, tripping over the ropes and falling to the mat with a towel covering his face. Yarborough filmed the stunt in a long take sans editing, with Costello very deftly swinging the towel onto its mark with head and body movements only; his hands never touch it.

During the bout, the referee warns Oliver, "I'll disqualify you if you don't keep your head out of the ropes." After pulling up the mask to reveal Johnson, Oliver manages to knock him out with a left upper cut to the jaw.

Costello had a field day filming the basketball game on Universal's Stage 28, where the Lon Chaney, Sr., classic *The Phantom of the Opera* (1925) had been filmed 20 years earlier. Lou made a stunning series of difficult shots himself, blending his talent for comic improvisation with considerable athletic skill. Broadcasting from Carlton College, sportscaster Bill Stern introduces "the unknown, unheralded basketball team from Bixby, as they attempt to upset the undefeated conference champions from Carlton."

At halftime, Bixby leads Carlton 20 to 16. Delayed by a flat tire, the Amazons, a professional team hired by Johnson to don Carlton uniforms, hitch a ride with Kirkland as the "between the halves entertainment" takes over. Patty sings "Jumpin' on Saturday Night," a

Here Come the Co-Eds (1945). To raise $500 for the college mortgage payment, Slats (Bud) "encourages" Oliver, "The Bixby Bulldog," to wrestle "The Masked Marvel," who turns out to be none other than the dreaded Johnson!

breath of fresh Big Band air in a film filled with inappropriate, stilted orchestral perform-ances. Peggy Ryan finally is able to strut her terpsichorean stuff, now making *Co-Eds* seem like a true Abbott and Costello wartime release.

"Look at those big *Amazings*," Oliver says as the new "Carlton" players take to the court. "Amazons," corrects Patty.

The big bruisers immediately knock Molly to the floor, then trip up two additional play-ers. When the official threatens to "forfeit the game to Bixby," two Amazons tackle him. "Now the referee is knocked out cold," announces Stern, as Carlton leads 22 to 20. The Breen Office objected to the violence, warning Universal not to show the professional players delib-erately sabotaging the college girls. Though the studio complied with the edict "to avoid ... any suggestion that the Bixby girls are injured badly or suffering intensely from their injuries," the Amazons remained deliberate villains on the court.

Slats takes over the officiating duties, and Oliver, disguised as "Daisy Dimple, the World's Greatest Girl Basketball Player," becomes the substitute center. After several terrible mis-takes result in eight additional points for Carlton, Oliver is hit on the head by the rebound-ing ball, a blow that makes him think he truly is the legendary Daisy. In the second drag appearance of his film career, Costello becomes "a one-girl tornado." Daisy scores 10 unan-

Here Come the Co-Eds (1945). Lou, an avid home-movie enthusiast, captures one of the "lady bas-ketball players" with his 16mm camera during a break on the set.

swered points (each basket is actually made by Costello in a single long shot, sans editing), but again receives a blow during a pile up on the floor. Patty whacks him on the head with a water dipper and—voila!—he's Daisy again. But a Carlton player slams the ball into his head and, as Oliver, he tosses the ball toward the Bixby backboard. It bounces off and (in a trick shot) flies all the way across the court to swish through the Carlton net. The champions win 32 to 30, and Oliver is abandoned by the entire crowd. The scene ends with Costello doing his trademark "walk of sadness" framed in long shot; the camera, placed behind the Carlton backboard, shows the empty gymnasium as he slowly leaves.

Now Oliver is snubbed by all the girls, including Patty, and Slats, who slaps him hard in the face, knocking off his hat. Luckily, the despondent "little guy" overhears Johnson receiving the game's payoff from Honest Dan (Lou's brother-in-law, Joe Kirk), sneaks into the locker room, grabs the dough, and he and Slats run into the film's climactic chase scene. Jumping into a sailboat towed by a passing car, they raise the canvas in an attempt to elude the crooked gamblers and Amazons. Costello receives another pain in the posterior when Oliver accidentally "picks up" a pick axe from a road crew, and the scene culminates in a railroad tunnel. This mad chase took six days to shoot, including locations at the UCLA campus, Mulholland Drive, and the corner of Ventura and Sepulveda Boulevards.

Oliver, riding a *tricycle* (one of the most bizarre Costello images *ever*), pushes the boat back to Bixby, where Kirkland and some girls send Johnson and Honest Dan packing. Oliver is truly toasted at a celebratory bonfire when Kirkland announces, "Well done, Oliver! Well done!"

"It certainly is," the "hero" agrees, as Patty roasts his rear end with a flaming torch. Again, an Abbott and Costello film ends with a focus on Lou's bum.

11

WHO'S IN UNCLE TOM'S CABIN?

The Naughty Nineties (1945)

The brightest spot in the film is a repeat of the famous Abbott and Costello "Who's on First"
routine; this sequence, in which Costello tries to find out the names of a baseball team, is
always good for as many laughs as any one can spare.

—*New York Herald-Tribune*[1]

November 1944: The Japanese began to use suicide flyers known as *Kamikaze* against
the U.S. Navy in the Leyte Gulf. U.S. forces, continuing to make progress in the Pacific,
bombed Iwo Jima, a volcanic island located 650 nautical miles south of Tokyo. Intent on
capturing the strategic airfields on the island, American troops engaged the intrepid Japanese in a fiery Hell during February and March 1945.

Here Come the Co-Eds was released on February 2, while Bud and Lou were knee deep
in their next Universal project, *The Naughty Nineties*, which Jean Yarbrough had begun on
January 14. Totally removed from the contemporary wartime milieu, this period piece is
heavy on timeworn routines, and the 1890s riverboat plot devised by Edmund L. Hartmann,
Edmund Joseph and Hal Fimberg was "burlesqued" by two gag men this time: John Grant
(who co-produced with Hartmann) and Felix Adler, whose "additional comedy sequences"
are nothing more than hoary old bits previously flogged by the Three Stooges.

Perhaps the filmmakers assumed they could trot out the same tired material in a new
costume atmosphere, taking them back in time to an era that was witnessing Abbott and
Costello for the first time. But the comedy material is not the only element re-used by Universal in *The Naughty Nineties*: the *River Queen* piloted by Captain Sam Jackson (Henry Travers) is none other than the *Cotton Blossom* first seen in Universal's *Show Boat* (1936), directed
by James Whale and starring Bud and Lou's old pal Allan Jones, Irene Dunne, Paul Robe-
son and Hattie McDaniel. A second connection to this classic musical is the presence of Hattie's brother, Sam McDaniel, who plays a cook (listed as "Matt" is the credits, but called
"Sam" by the boys in the film).

During production, Lou's daughters, Patricia Ann ("Paddy") and Carole Lou visited the
set. Paddy remembered:

> I loved going to Universal. Dad would take us there on weekends when he was shoot-
> ing. We, at that time, had pretty much free reign of the place. We would run around
> and do whatever we wanted. We knew when we had to be quiet, where we could go or
> where we couldn't go.[2]

Yarbrough wrapped *The Naughty Nineties* on March 1, 1945. Bud and Lou returned to
Universal on May 13—during production of *Abbott and Costello in Hollywood* at MGM—to
shoot some re-takes.

The Naughty Nineties (1945). In their first period costume picture, Bud and Lou are members of a drama troupe traveling aboard the 1890s showboat *River Queen* (original title lobby card).

The musical sequences of *The Naughty Nineties*, staged by John Boyle with songs by Edgar Fairchild and Jack Brooks, are necessary to the period setting and not merely so much "filler" this time around. Bud plays "the greatest actor on the river," Dexter Broadhurst, introduced to a crowd gathered on the Ironville docks by Captain Sam, as Sebastian Din-widdie (a stuntman filling in for Lou), strapped to an enormous bass drum, literally *rolls* into the film. Sebastian attempts to join a marching band, but the drum's size completely blocks his view. Separated from his fellow musicians, he ends up marching into a trench in the dirt street.

Aboard the riverboat, Dexter and Captain Sam's daughter, Miss Caroline Jackson (Lois Collier), are performing in "Bill Bassler's Revenge." During this hammy Victorian melo-drama, Sebastian is backstage, performing all the sound effects: a train is achieved with a large wooden whistle, wheezing shrieks, and some frantic footwork; "the footbeats of [a] trusty steed" are merely two coconuts banged on a table; and the horse's whinny is really Sebastian's own. At one point, the clueless stagehand wanders on to the stage, and then pro-ceeds to knock over the set and dump artificial snow on the actors. When two babies begin to cry in the audience, he attempts to quiet them by pouring milk into a rubber glove and piercing two of the fingers with a pin from one of the mother's hats. Unsuccessful, he begins to bawl himself.

Three crooked card sharps, Crawford (Alan Curtis, Bud and Lou's costar in *Buck Privates*, here made up to resemble Clark Gable), Bonita (Rita Johnson) and Bailey (Joe Sawyer), board the boat, where they watch a (mercifully brief) minstrel show featuring three dancers in blackface. At the Gilded Cage saloon in St. Louis, Dexter and Sebastian, arriving in top hats and tails, try to prevent Captain Sam from betting the *River Queen* in a poker game. Lou revives his "I think I'm gettin' a mickey" shtick from *Pardon My Sarong* in a reworking of the "switching of the glasses" routine, this time involving champagne with the shifty Bonita. After discovering the act "Crestello's Boxing Bears" (a Costello in-joke), Dexter tries to scare off the other patrons by dressing in a bear suit, but Sebastian ends up being accosted by a *real* bear whom he thinks is his pal.

Back on board, Sebastian auditions for a show by singing "My Bonnie Lies Over the Ocean" as Dexter barks directions to some stagehands. Commands such as "try it to the left," "try it to the right," "get low enough to touch the floor," "higher," "lift up the right leg," "lift up the left leg," "lift up both legs" and "bring it forward" result in Sebastian's toppling into the orchestra pit!

This Costello feat is followed by several others, including Sebastian's "shooting" of several birds with six-guns as a warning to the interlopers to stay off the boat, and his acciden-

The Naughty Nineties (1945). Sebastian Dinwiddie (Lou) and Dexter Broadhurst (Bud) trap Bailey (Joseph Sawyer), a hulking henchman of the gang who commandeers the ***River Queen*** (original lobby card).

tal inclusion of a pot holder in a cake that he *attempts* to frost. Interestingly, in this scene, Sebastian is given orders by Matt/Sam, who says, "Ever since them gamblers took over this *River Queen*, we ain't been doin' nothin' but servin' 'em drinks, and then servin' 'em coffee—to sober 'em up. Mr. Sebastian, you better hurry up with that cake, 'cause they'll be callin' for it any time now."

This rare instance of a Caucasian character deferring to an African American one is followed by Sebastian carrying the cake into the gambling room, where he tells Bailey, "I baked it myself, with my own little, white hands."

The film's most famous sequence is a complete, six-minute version of "Who's on First?" originally intended to appear earlier in the film. When Costello begins by telling Abbott, "When we get to St. Louis," the *River Queen* is already docked there. To preserve Bud and Lou's crackerjack timing, Jean Yarbrough filmed the entire routine in real time, using two cameras, one framing a two-shot of the team, and the other set up farther back to capture Costello at the beginning of the bit, retrieving his hat after knocking it off his own head with a baseball bat. Even though the camera crew can be heard laughing on the soundtrack, the director chose to keep the superlative take in the final cut of the film. After all, Dexter and Sebastian are performing their shtick in front of a live audience, though the 40 extras in the

The Naughty Nineties (1945). Lou with his daughters, eight-year-old Paddy and six-year-old Carole Lou, on Father's Day, just prior to the film's release.

crowd were ordered *not* to laugh and drown out the dialogue. However, they were allowed to slap their knees and *pretend* to laugh. Yarbrough planned to dub in strategically placed giggles during post-production.

The scene opens with the pit orchestra playing "Take Me Out to the Ball Game," and Lou adds a new line just after Bud mentions the "very peculiar names" of current baseball players. "Funny names?" he asks. "Not as funny as *my* name, Sebastian Dinwiddie." (This name, like the "Who's on First?" routine, is one of the most memorable elements in *The Naughty Nineties*, and one of Costello's all-time funniest monikers.)

Back in the galley, Matt/Sam is still issuing orders, telling his coworker, Effie (Lillian Yarbo), "Move out the way, Sister!" When some stray kittens run in, he threatens to chop them into "cat burger," then discusses "cats" (actually catfish) with her. The atmosphere is far more macabre than funny as Costello registers terrified facial expressions while chopping, and feline groaning and wailing sounds are heard in the background. Dexter enjoys his chopped meat (obviously hamburger), while Sebastian pours milk over his two patties, which seem to be "meowing" (two cats are hiding under the table). When the meat "drinks" the milk and Sebastian *barks* at the plate, the routine becomes genuinely funny.

A fishing scene involving plastic props and concluding with Sebastian being pulled into the river is followed by a ludicrous, unconvincing version of the Marx Bros.' "mirror scene" so recently mimicked in *Lost in a Harem*. Bailey's ignorance knows no bounds as he thinks Sebastian's undisguised face is his own reflection, and he finally realizes the ruse when the little pudgy guy's rear end (yet another Costello bum incident) is hauled up in front of the window by Dexter.

Caroline sings the (pure 1940s) love ballad "I Can't Get You Out of My Mind" and is briefly romanced by Crawford, who then pulls a fast one on his partners, who lose the *River Queen* after Captain Sam agrees to play Bonita in "one hand of open poker, winner take all." Bailey pulls a piece, and the climactic chase is on. Following some savage head bashing by Sebastian, who wields a mean wooden plank like a baseball bat, the Captain regains control and the show goes on. Appearing in *Uncle Tom's Cabin*, Sebastian plays an angel who crashes through the stage. "I think I went in the wrong direction," he observes.

Costello originally had a much different plan for the Gilded Cage scene. An admirer of Harold Lloyd, Lou wanted to re-create, shot for shot, the silent comic's classic "Magic Coat" routine, in which he accidentally dons a magician's jacket at a party, and then must deal with a rabbit and other unexpected interruptions while on the dance floor. In Costello's version, Dexter orders Sebastian to dress in a policeman's uniform so they can save Captain Sam from the villains. Of course, the little guy has no idea that "Officer 666" is a magician who wears a cop's garb. Inundated by a pigeon, an egg and a rabbit, he then squirts Bonita in the face with water from his carnation. As Bailey tries to drag him out, he drops a box of white mice, and the entire joint clears out instantly.

The sequence was shot but cut from the film after someone at Lloyd's company threatened to sue Universal. Lou had intended, not to steal, but pay tribute to one of his heroes. In an effort to bury the evidence, the studio destroyed the scripted scene and locked the footage in a safe-deposit box, but still photographs of Lou in the fake policeman's uniform have survived.

Opposite, top: The Naughty Nineties (1945). This still photograph depicts Lou and Bud in a portion of the Harold Lloyd-inspired "Magic Coat" routine that was cut from the film. *Bottom: The Naughty Nineties* (1945). Lou and Rita Johnson in more excised "Magic Coat" footage.

A fast-moving 76-minute musical comedy, *The Naughty Nineties* was released on July 6, 1945, to mixed reviews. Some critics praised the first complete visual version of "Who's on First?" which had taken more than five years to reach the screen, but others without an eye to posterity complained that the boys were merely relying on their "oldest chestnut."

12

LUCY AND LOU

Abbott and Costello in Hollywood (1945)

I think when they could play around and fool around and have other people join in—and they had a lot of their old buddies with them on- and off-camera—that made them comfortable.

—Jean Porter[1]

Though the boys made most of their films at Universal (who had just announced their next two pictures, "She Meant No Harm" and "The Phantom Pirates," neither of which was made), MGM was responsible for first putting their names in an actual title, *Bud Abbott and Lou Costello in Hollywood*, which director S. Sylvan Simon shot from April 10 through June 1, 1945. During this loan-out, Bud and Lou returned to Universal to shoot retakes for *The Naughty Nineties* on May 13. *Abbott and Costello in Hollywood* (the film is also known under this shorter title) also required some additional takes, completed at MGM in July.

On April 12, as Bud and Lou were preparing to welcome the Andrews Sisters to their radio show, they were given some devastating news. At 3:35 P.M. that afternoon, President Roosevelt, just beginning his fourth term, had died of a massive cerebral hemorrhage while posing for a painting by artist Elizabeth Shoumatoff at his retreat in Warm Springs, Georgia. Harry Truman, who had been Vice President for only 82 days, had just been sworn in as the 33rd President of the United States.

Less than a month after FDR's untimely death, the war in Europe ended on May 7 and 8, when unconditional surrender documents were signed by members of the German high command and witnessed by Allied representatives from the United States, the USSR, Great Britain and France. "V-E Day" was celebrated in the U.S. on May 8, when President Truman—who was also celebrating his 61st birthday—dedicated the event to FDR, who had been unable to witness the ultimate victory for which he had worked since December 1941.

John Grant didn't join the boys on the loan-out this time around. The screenplay by Nat Perrin and Lou Breslow, based on an original story by Perrin and Martin A. Gosch, featured several new routines for Abbott and Costello, although the team did manage to work in a few burlesque bits here and there. Perrin, who thought actors should follow the scripted material, disliked the improvisational style favored by Bud and Lou, whose modus operandi, he thought, was to try anything to complete a scene on the first take.

Simon was assisted by Charles Walters, who directed the dance sequences, and the songs by Ralph Blane and Hugh Martin, performed by Robert Stanton, solidly anchored the film in a contemporary MGM Frank Sinatra–like style (Walters would later direct two Sinatra classics, *The Tender Trap* [1955] and *High Society* [1956], at the studio.) Stanton, making his film debut, was the brother of Dick Haymes, whom Sinatra had replaced in the Tommy

Dorsey band in 1940. Prior to being cast in the film, Stanton had performed under his real name, Bob Haymes. Leaving much to be desired as an actor, he later found success as a song-writer.

Making another switch from Universal to MGM didn't abate Lou's on-set larceny. After a huge black telephone used in the film's final scene made its appearance on camera, it promptly disappeared, only to turn up in a Costello 16mm color home movie, shot—like so many of Lou's other amateur productions—by the family swimming pool.

In the brief home-movie clip, Lou, dressed in a yellow cloth shirt, white shorts, and a sailor's cap, sits on the diving board, beside the phone. Picking up the receiver, he asks, "Hello, Gene Lester?" as his friend, a cameraman who shot many of his home movies, quietly walks up behind him.

"Hello, Lou," says Gene.

"Hello, Gene," Lou answers, launching into the familiar burlesque telephone routine. "How are you?"

After the familiar banter subsides, Lou hangs up the receiver, turns to his pal, points to the phone, and explains, "*Gene Lester.*" Registering a classic double take and his trademark wheezing sounds, he retrieves the receiver to examine it as Lester laughs.

Abbott and Costello in Hollywood opens at the Hollywood Shop, "Barber to the Stars," where young Ruthie (Jean Porter) takes a phone appointment from MGM's own Clark Gable. Ace tonsorial artist Buzz Kurtis (Bud) is conducting "barber college" in the store room, where Abercrombie (Lou), who is smitten with Ruthie, is undergoing his third year of study, which involves practicing shaving techniques on a lathered-up balloon with drawn-on face. Ruthie complains to Buzz about his "racket," so he agrees to let his pupil shave the next cus-tomer.

Abercrombie's very first victim proves to be comic "Rags" Ragland, who, still dressed in a costume for a "back woods" film, undergoes quite a tortuous session. (Bud and Lou's *Buck Privates* nemesis, Nat Pendleton, was originally cast in the part.) The would-be barber first lathers up his moccasins, one of which is used to smear the soap on his face. Before using the dull side of a straight razor to *not* shave off any whiskers, Abercrombie applies a steam-ing cloth. "What's the idea of dropping that hot towel on my face?" Ragland shouts.

"It was burnin' my hands," replies Abercrombie, who uses an MGM publicity photo of the actor as a "mirror" to show him that the job has shorn "about ten years" off his appear-ance!

On their way to an "emergency call—a very important shoe shine" with agent Norman Royce (Warner Anderson), they meet Claire Warren (Frances Rafferty), a former manicurist now cast in a major Hollywood musical, "Romance for Two." Gregory LeMaise (Carleton G. Young), the famous womanizing crooner, pulls alongside in his convertible to ask her to lunch, but Abercrombie replies that she already has a date.

"Well, break it," suggests the "wolf."

"Oh, no, she's not going to break it," insists Abercrombie. "She has a date with my girl-friend; and, someday, *I* hope to have a date with my girlfriend." (Frances Rafferty can be seen stifling a laugh as she sits in Claire's convertible.)

LeMaise won't take Abercrombie's "no" for an answer. "We'll take a run down to my beach house."

"Oh, no, you don't!" continues the protective proxy. "You're not going to take her down to *your* beach house and get her all *sun burned.*"

LeMaise points out that, as her costar in the musical, he needs "to get better acquainted with [his] leading lady," but Abercrombie orders him to "hit the road." The fading crooner's predatory behavior ends with his threat to pull out and sink the picture.

While delivering a shipwreck of a shoe shine, the boys are impressed by the vocalizing of young, Sinatra-like crooner Jeff Parker (Robert Stanton), who has ridden the bus out from Des Moines, which also happens to be Royce's home town. The rejected LeMaise arrives to drop out of "Romance for Two"; but, when Royce gives the part to "Jeffy Boy," "Greg Boy" complains about "fresh young punks" and the non-exclusive representation of his agent.

LeMaise is assured that the kid will be sent back on the bus, and star and agent leave for lunch, as Royce exits with black shoe polish smeared all over the legs of his trousers. "That's a dirty trick they're gonna play on that kid—especially a neighbor of mine," says Abercrombie.

"A neighbor of yours?" puzzles Buzz.

"Yeah," replies Abercrombie. "Didn't you hear him say he was ripe from Des Moines, Iowa? Ain't that right near Paterson, New Jersey?"

"Des Moines, Iowa, is two thousand miles from Paterson, New Jersey," Buzz points out.

"Can I help it if I have a big back yard?" Abercrombie asks.

At Mammoth Studios, the boys are denied entrance to see director Dennis Kavanaugh (Donald MacBride), so they sneak in with a group of extras. While Buzz dons a cop's cos-

The boys give a movie executive a shave and a shine... with extras!

Abbott and Costello in Hollywood (1945). Ace tonsorial artist Buzz Kurtis (Bud) watches as his partner, Abercrombie (Lou), expertly administers "an important shoeshine" to Tinsel Town agent Norman Royce (Warner Anderson) (original lobby card).

tume, Abercrombie, wearing his usual street clothes, is considered "perfect" by an assistant director who is casting bums for a picture. A studio guard chases them around the lot, and Abercrombie ducks onto several sets: First attempting to tell the story of "Red Riding Hood" to MGM child stars Jackie "Butch" Jenkins and Sharon McManus, he then interrupts Lucille Ball (who accidentally sits on his lap) and Preston Foster—who are shooting with director Robert Z. Leonard (who also plays himself), and finally becomes a "prop dummy" in a Klondike adventure film. Twice dragged up a flight of stairs and tossed off a balcony, he then replaces a "real actor" (future John Ford stalwart Hank Worden) for a third take, this time jumping off to land on a roulette wheel.

The boys celebrate Jeff's good fortune with champagne at Ciro's, where Abercrombie and Ruthie "trip the light *fanatic*," "the dancing champion of East Des Moines High" croons "I Hope the Band Keeps Playing" to Claire, and Greg LeMaise meets with Kavanaugh to get the kid dropped from "Romance for Two" a second time.

Later that night, Abercrombie fights insomnia as Buzz refuses to let his pal resort to drugs. "They're sleeping tablets!" he warns. "That's dope! Do you want to be a dope fiend?" Instead, Buzz plays a sleep-inducing record that makes endless noise when reaching its end, then offers to turn off the phonograph after Abercrombie dozes off. Buzz quickly goes comatose instead, so Abercrombie devises an even brighter idea: tie one end of a string to the power switch and the other to his toe; but when he rolls over to sleep, he yanks the switch past "off" to "radio," with predictable results.

To get LeMaise fired from "Romance for Two," the boys decide to frame the arrogant actor with an incriminating photograph. They stow away on his yacht, and then Buzz attempts to snap a photo when LeMaise punches Abercrombie. Unfortunately, the little fat guy is knocked into the ocean, where he disappears without a trace. At a waterfront tavern, Buzz laments the loss of his partner—"Why, that Abercrombie was the sweetest guy that ever lived"—just as the "drowned" man quietly walks up behind him, his jacket stuffed with small fish. Buzz continues:

> Oh, the rightest, royalist pal that ever drew breath, and me always playin' him for a sucker. Why, with just one little barber college racket alone, I clipped him for every cent that he had in the world. Oh, if he could only come back to life just long enough for me to tell him how sorry I am—tell him how miserable I feel—tell him how much I miss him. (Buzz begins to cry, as Abercrombie, still behind him, follows suit.) Oh, I miss that poor kid. It's all my fault. I've always treated him like—like a sucker.

"Here you are, Buzz," says Abercrombie, handing a soaked handkerchief to his buddy, who says, "Thanks," then backhands him across the face. Fish fall out of his hat and onto the floor. Outside, Buzz tells him, "Now, listen. This is even better than you getting socked. You're dead."

"Dead?" asks Abercrombie. "Then why am I so hungry?"

Buzz intends to claim that LeMaise killed his pal. With the crooner on the lam, Jeff will again land the "Romance for Two" role. Declared a fugitive in the newspapers, LeMaise dons a beard and gets drunk on brandy flips. Disguised as an Indian, with turban and beard, Abercrombie idiotically reveals his identity to the inebriated actor.

Kavanaugh is shooting the elaborate conclusion of his musical on an amusement park midway set. An indicator is calibrated, and when the pointer reaches the number "4," an explosive charge will detonate the entire set. Unknown to each other, Abercrombie and LeMaise are costumed as "Pekinese Twins."

Abbott and Costello in Hollywood (1945). Stumbling onto a set at Mammoth Pictures, Abercrombie (Lou) meets up with director Robert Z. Leonard and stars Lucille Ball and Preston Foster.

Refusing to remove his fake nose and mustache, LeMaise admits, "I don't want to be seen around here."

"You don't want to be seen around here?" echoes Abercrombie. "You don't have to worry. If anybody recognizes you, I'll tell 'em it's me," he adds, just before identifying his nemesis in a funhouse mirror. The obligatory Abbott and Costello chase begins, culminating in LeMaise and Abercrombie's wrestling match on a speeding roller coaster inter–cut with "Midway," a production number featuring Stanton, Rafferty, and a gang of hoofers in familiar MGM sailor suits (*Anchors Aweigh*, costarring Frank Sinatra and Gene Kelly, was released by the studio on July 14, 1945).

LeMaise knocks Abercrombie onto the detonator, and billowing smoke dissolves to the boys, seated behind their own agents' desk (in the barbershop), reading *Variety* and *The Hollywood Reporter*. Ruthie brings a $100 bill, requesting change for a customer. Abercrombie dials an oversized telephone, out pops a wad of cash, and he picks up the huge receiver.

MGM released *Abbott and Costello in Hollywood* on August 22, 1945, with little fanfare from the publicity department. Louis B. Mayer didn't lament this self-engineered box-office disappointment, and the team's loan-out agreement wasn't renewed.

Such a personal setback hardly seemed significant in the wake of Japan's acceptance of unconditional surrender on August 14. One week earlier, the U.S. had dropped atomic bombs on Hiroshima and Nagasaki, prompting Emperor Hirohito and Prime Minister Suzuki to seek an immediate peace agreement. While Japanese troops in the Philippines, Korea, Burma,

Abbott and Costello in Hollywood (1945). Fellow insomniacs Buzz (Bud) and Abercrombie (Lou).

They're Hollywood big-shots now... with a phone to match!

MGMerriment
Bud ABBOTT and Lou COSTELLO IN HOLLYWOOD
A Metro-Goldwyn-Mayer Picture

Abbott and Costello in Hollywood (1945). In the film's closing scene, Abercrombie (Lou) and Buzz (Bud) operate their own talent agency at the Hollywood Shop, "Barber to the Stars." (The oversize telephone was actually heisted by Costello for gag use on his home patio!) (original lobby card).

and on Wake Island held out until mid–September, the formal surrender ceremony was held on board the battleship USS *Missouri* in Tokyo Bay on September 2, designated by President Truman as "V-J Day" (although the American people already had considered August 15— the date of Hirohito's acceptance of the Potsdam Declaration, the surrender terms issued by Truman, Churchill and Chiang Kai-shek—as such).

During the summer, Bud and Lou, on hiatus from their radio show, played the Roxy Theater in New York for three weeks, earning a tidy $45,000, then went on tour, performing in Atlantic City, Baltimore and Philadelphia. These personal appearances, combined with propaganda issued by their publicity machine, did much to refute rumors of the "break-up" that had been circulating for two months. Off stage, they only communicated with each other through their attorneys. The ice finally thawed as they prepared to return to the West Coast, where plans for a youth foundation named after Lou's beloved "Butch" were under way. "Everything's fine now," Bud told a reporter. "Lou's a great guy—and we're going to have a swell reunion when we get back to Hollywood."[2]

13

POSTWAR EXPERIMENTS

Little Giant (1946) and *The Time of Their Lives* (1946)

In romantic scenes my father would become very excited and take on the demeanor of a nine-year-old boy. You got the feeling he was so innocent, he didn't know why he was so excited. People loved that.

—Chris Costello[1]

World War II had ended on August 14, 1945, with the celebration of "V-J Day" in the United States, sparked when news of the Japanese surrender broke in U.S. time zones. However, President Truman officially declared V-J Day on September 2, after the Japanese signed the surrender on board the battleship U.S.S. *Missouri* in Tokyo Bay. Abbott and Costello had made their last cinematic references to the war in *It Ain't Hay*, released more than two years earlier, but their films had continued to provide laughs on the home front and at U.S. military installations.

The year 1946 was one of experimentation for the boys at Universal. Because of tensions between the team during the previous year—and the studio's intention to bolster flagging box-office receipts—they released what became the two most original, ambitious and *underrated* films of their career. Leaving the burlesque repertoire behind, the boys abandoned their familiar team personae to play actual characters blending drama with—contrary to some past critical assessments—plenty of belly laughs.

With the end of World War II, the Abbott and Costello films finally abandoned the popular pop song interruptions for more developed story lines. But Universal had planned to experiment with the formula before the end of the war. In late 1944 and early 1945, various writers had prepared treatments titled "Once in a Lifetime" and "Hired Husband," both intended to feature Bud and Lou as individual characters.

In particular, Lou Costello was given the opportunity to mine his masterful talent for characterization, coming as close as he ever would to achieving his dream of becoming a dramatic actor. (Today, reviewers might toss around comments about an Academy Award.) His ability to engage audience interest and identification is at its peak in *Little Giant* and *The Time of Their Lives*, which also feature fine performances by Bud Abbott, who pulls off two characterizations (each sporting a noticeably different, highly lubricated toupee) in both films.

For *Little Giant*, producer Joseph Gershenson, at Costello's request, hired Sennett-trained comedy specialist William A. Seiter, who directed scores of silent shorts (1915–1919), several Wheeler and Woolsey features (1931–1933), the Laurel and Hardy masterpiece *Sons of the Desert* (1933), and *Room Service* (1938) with the Marx Brothers. His expertise earned him a fee of $100,000 (13 percent of the film's $775,000 budget), but also—ironically—the

enmity of Costello, whose on-set relationship with the director during the November 1–
December 17, 1945, shoot was problematic at best. The main bone of contention was Seiter's
literal adherence to the script, which often stifled Lou's improvisational tendencies.

Little Giant opens in Cucamonga, California, at the gas station store owned by "Mom"
Miller (Mary Gordon), the Scottish-accented mother of devoted son Benny Miller (Lou),
who is listening to his latest lesson from the Record Correspondence School. "Boy, am I
dumb," he says at one point, looking into the camera.

Costello is teamed with Abbott in only a few subsequent scenes, but he enjoys other
opportunities to display his crackerjack timing, including engaging in some humorous shtick
with the instructor on the phonograph records and a hilarious scene with Sid Fields (the
replacement for Eddie Waller, who appeared in an earlier take) as a motorist who pulls in
for nothing but free air. No matter what Benny says, the driver reacts with ridiculous argu-
ments about produce, vitamins, his wife and his children.

When the over-anxious salesman mentions that "even the worst cook" could make a
good meal from their Leghorn eggs, the unreasonable man replies, "Oh, the worst cook?
Now you're draggin' my wife into the argument! ... Why don't you just come right out and
say it? My wife is a miserable old hag. Just the thought of kissing my wife makes a person
sick and disgusted!"

"Wait a minute, Mister. I wouldn't say that," Benny counters. "I think kissing your wife
is a pleasure." As the man grabs his bib overalls, he pleads, "Look, Mister, please. I don't
mean any harm. Please leave me alone. I'm only trying to be a good salesman, and a good
salesman should never take 'No' for an answer. What do you say?"

"No!" the man shouts, releasing his grip.

Thinking he's made a sale, Benny answers, "Good! That's all I wanted to know," grabs
a crate of goods and shoves it into the back of the man's car as it speeds away. Anxious to
tell his mother, he runs frantically toward the house. Framing the action in a single medium
shot, Seiter tracks the camera backwards as Costello does a spectacular acrobatic pratfall:
Benny flips over the bottom of a split door, landing flat on his back inside. (Lou does protect himself by grabbing the door with his left hand as he flips.)

Back outside, Benny is interrupted by a loudly honking car horn. "Aw, keep your shirt
on!" he yells before realizing that the "customer" is Martha Hill (Elena Verdugo), his girlfriend, who arrives in a U.S. Mail vehicle to deliver his final lesson from the Record Correspondence School. Also included is his official diploma awarding him the degree of
"B.S.—Bachelor of Salesmanship."

Encouraged to seek a sales position in the big city, Benny prepares to hitchhike, but kisses
Martha for the first time, becoming "engaged," before he goes. (The well-developed *Little
Giant* gives Costello an actual girlfriend at the beginning of the story—another "first" for the
film.) In Los Angeles, he drops in at the Hercules Vacuum Cleaner Company, where his
Uncle Clarence (George Cleveland), the longtime bookkeeper, is secretly forced by the slick
general manager, E. L. Morrison (Bud), to keep "two sets of books." Morrison and the advertising manager, Hazel Temple (Jacqueline De Wit)—who is also his "secret bride"—are "inter-
viewing" candidates for a model to pose as Hercules. (E. L. and Hazel were originally scripted
as unmarried lovers, but the Breen Office quickly had them hitched.)

In Morrison's office, Benny is ordered to take off his clothes. Understandably puzzled,
the possessor of "the biggest muscles in Cucamonga" drops his drawers. "You certainly don't
look like Hercules to me," observes Morrison.

"Who wants to look like a vacuum cleaner?" Benny asks.

Little Giant (1946). Record Correspondence School graduate Benny Miller (Lou) receives his mail-order diploma from his mother (Mary Gordon) as his girlfriend, Martha Hill (Elena Verdugo), admires her beau's great achievement (original lobby card).

"Who's talking about a vacuum cleaner?" Morrison replies. "I'm talking about Hercules—a *man*. Surely you've heard of Hercules?"

"What's his last name?" asks Benny.

"What?" queries Morrison.

"His *last* name—like Hercules Brown, Hercules Ginsberg. Everybody has a last name," Benny explains.

"No last name, just *Hercules*, an old Greek hero," Morrison insists.

"Oh—*him*. What's he do?" Benny asks.

"He cleaned out some stables," replies Morrison.

"Cleaned out stables? That's nothin,'" claims Benny. "I clean out stables every week up in Cucamonga."

"Yes, but these stables were *different*," explains Morrison.

Benny leans in slightly. "Did they have horses in 'em?"

"Certainly they had horses in 'em!" Morrison declares.

Benny steps back slightly and then leans in again. "Then, if there was horses in 'em, it's *no different*."

Stripped down to his underwear, Benny quickly puts on his hat after Hazel enters the room. He glances down at his boxer shorts, crawls under the desk and places his hand over his eyes. "Hercules," suggests Morrison.

Benny slowly surveys the statuesque woman. "It ain't my fault. He *made* me do it."

Hazel shows him to a restroom, where he may "re-pants" himself. "He's cute, isn't he?" she remarks. "Why didn't you introduce me?"

When the real Hercules candidate walks in, he is hired instantly. Hazel suggests that the man getting dressed might be Cupid, but Morrison is more concerned about the company president: "If Van Loon hears about this, I'll be the laughing stock of this office."

"I can hear them now," adds Hazel. "They'll be calling you 'Take 'Em Off' Morrison."

Benny suggests that Morrison make up for the mistake by giving him a job, then launches into a Record Correspondence School spiel. Recognized as a "salesman with housekeeper appeal," he is told to report for work the following morning, when he hits the street with a vacuum cleaner. This sequence involving Benny's door-to-door efforts is reminiscent of *Big Business* (1929), one of Laurel and Hardy's most memorable silent shorts, in which Stan and Ollie try their hand at selling Christmas trees to uninterested homeowners. Marx Brothers veteran Margaret Dumont (personally cast by Seiter) also appears in the scene, as Mrs. Henderson, who files a $2,000 lawsuit after Benny stains her carpet and blows soot all over her living room while demonstrating the functions of the machine, which is subsequently stolen. (An incident that was cut from the film involved Benny littering the floor of a woman who ultimately admits that the farmhouse has no electricity. The sketch was later revived for the Abbott and Costello TV show.)

Back at the office, Morrison fires Benny and threatens to sack whoever "sent that apple-knocker in." Uncle Clarence exercises damage control by sending him to Stockton, where his friend, Tom Chandler (Bud), Morrison's cousin, is branch manager. In a scene lifted from the Laurel and Hardy short *Berth Marks* (1929), Benny attempts to sleep on a train while traveling to the new job. When a Pullman conductor (the versatile Donald MacBride) asks, "What's your berth?" he replies, "March 6, 19 ..." (Costello's actual birthdate).

While the conductor leaves to fetch a ladder, Benny steps on a sleeping man in the lower berth while trying to climb into the upper one. After falling out into the corridor, he attempts to undress while lying in the berth, becoming childishly frustrated as he slams his hands into the compartment wall and wraps a clothing net around his head. (In the 1929 precursor, the scene lasts much longer, with both Stan and Ollie creating a tour de force of comic chaos.)

In Stockton, Benny mistakes Chandler for Morrison. "I bet he took the shirt right off your back," Chandler remarks.

"And my *pants*, too!" Benny admits.

"He's a dirty, slave-driving, double-crossing skunk!" Chandler claims. "He's a crook" who devised the "no-relative rule" to get his cousin out of town. Here, Bud and Lou (in a last-minute addition) worked in the film's one major burlesque routine, when Benny proves that the seven salesmen at the office will need to sell 13 vacuums each to reach the weekly quota of 28. Following a short-wave radio broadcast by Van Loon and Morrison, who announce a "special cash prize to the best salesman of the year," Chandler offers to double the commission on every vacuum sold by his men.

Two weeks pass, and Benny fails to sell a single machine. Chandler orders his secretary, Ruby Burke (Brenda Joyce), to type up a dismissal notice, and Benny accompanies her to Joe's bar, where the other salesmen are having a drink. In the pre–PC world of postwar America, one of the men calls Ruby "Cute and Cuddly" and "Baby" as they all sit down to play the "old Egyptian pastime" of mind reading, a "rib" that leaves Benny thinking that he's

Little Giant (1946). Tom Chandler (Bud), Stockton branch manager of the Hercules Vacuum Cleaner Company, shows the portrait of his lovely grandmother (also Bud) to Benny Miller (Lou).

clairvoyant. While walking Ruby home, he refuses to believe the game was a fake; and when she tries to give him the memo, he assumes she has become infatuated with him.

The next day, Benny—confident that he can read minds—lands his first customer, then proceeds to sell machines to every member of the woman's sewing club. Back at the office, only two coworkers have made minor sales, but Benny breezes in to rack up *nine* stars on the board, breaking the "all-time sales record for one day." He is immediately sent back to Los Angeles, where Van Loon is casually playing golf in Morrison's office. During the ride from Union Station, Benny arrogantly boasts of his success to Uncle Clarence. "I penetrate people's brains—and leave my mind blank," he explains.

Clarence prevents Benny's imminent dismissal by telling him about the stock price juggling, the two sets of books, and the "G.M.E."—General Manager's Emergency Fund—account, which now is fed by skimming four percent from the company's receipts. During a meeting with Morrison, Hazel and Van Loon, Benny "reads" E. L.'s mind, mentioning, "me taking off my clothes in the office, getting fired, and the G.M.E. thing."

"I'm sorry," Van Loon interrupts. "What is 'the G.M.E. thing'?"

Benny attempts to stammer a reply, but Hazel interjects, "Benny tuned in on the wrong wavelength, that's all. G.M.E. are the initials of my favorite uncle, Gregory M. Elliott. That's what I was concentrating on."

In his office, Morrison asks Hazel, "Who told him about that G.M.E. account? And what

Little Giant (1946). The Hercules staff proves to Benny (Lou) that he's a "mindreader" (original lobby card).

else does he know about my business? Is he a company spy, a blackmailer, or can he really read minds? Well, that's your job, this afternoon—pumping Benny dry."

Martha arrives in Los Angeles to visit Benny, while Hazel treats him to a day at the Venice Amusement Pier and a drink (which he spits out) at her apartment. Slipping into something more comfortable, she elicits a "Hubba, hubba" from the naïve bumpkin, then is told, "Lips that touch liquor will never touch mine."

"You know, you're a frightfully interesting character," she cons him. "I imagine most women find you *fascinating*." Jacqueline De Wit became the first in a long line of femmes fatales who attempt to "seduce" Costello into providing information (or something *more*— like his brain!—in *Abbott and Costello Meet Frankenstein*), and she is one of the most appealing and least heavy-handed of them all. Hazel is essentially a harmless character manipulated by her crass embezzler of a husband, a creep who uses his "secret" wife to further his own business ends. Merely blowing in Benny's ear is enough to spark his quick retreat from the sofa. "I gotta get out of here before you lose control of yourself," he tells her.

When alcohol and seduction fail, Hazel resorts to tobacco, persuading the non-smoker to try a cigar. Furious puffing immediately leads to serious sickness, and Benny ends up, fully clothed (including his hat and shoes), in the bathtub, with the shower running. "I'm *so sick*," he groans as he struggles his way into the bedroom. Wearing Morrison's bath robe, he whines,

"I want my momma" as Hazel tucks him into one of the twin beds and hands him a sleeping pill. He can't stand the taste, however, and drops it into her drink on the nightstand.

Silent comic Chester Conklin makes a cameo appearance as a tailor who arrives to take Benny's clothes. Checking on her sleeping guest, Hazel sips her drink and passes out in the other bed. Morrison soon arrives to find both of them sleeping soundly, declares he is about to go "completely insane," and threatens to toss her "boyfriend down the elevator shaft." Martha then drops in to witness the sordid spectacle, and Morrison, on his way to the door to collect the clothes from the tailor, orders her to "wake him up, so I can kill him when I get back!"

Martha wakes Benny, who softly says, "Hello, Martha. How are you?" before snuggling back onto his pillow. Slowly opening his eyes, which gradually widen, he then starts up, stammering, "Mmmmm*martha*!" pulling the covers over his head. (This might be the most elongated double take in Costello's entire screen career. He originally was going to say, "I'm a *baaaad* boy!" but the Breen Office also nixed that.)

Morrison threatens to brutalize Benny, but Martha offers to take him back to the farm at Cucamonga. Emerging from the bedroom, Benny sees Morrison holding his clothes. "Well, how do you like that?" he says. "Trying to steal my pants again!"

Little Giant (1946). Hercules general manager E. L. Morrison (Bud) discovers his "secret bride," Hazel (Jacqueline De Wit), sacked out in the bedroom with Benny Miller (Lou) (original lobby card).

Morrison holds a meeting with Van Loon and the home office staff, who learn the truth about the mind-reading gag from Ruby. Benny arrives, seeking his cash prize, but Martha sees Ruby and, thinking she's another "girlfriend," runs out. Costello again communicates dejection and sadness with the *back* of his body as Benny follows her to the door, which is slammed in his face. Eavesdropping on Ruby's revelation, he then turns and walks slowly out of the office and—as the scene dissolves to a locale one mile from Cucamonga—down a lonely country road.

Carrying his suitcase and a birdcage housing a canary for his mother, Benny meets up with Mr. Perkins (William "Red" Donahue), a farmer having trouble with his stubborn mule, Ashtabula, who refuses to budge, then furiously kicks the front of his egg wagon. "I got him by the head," the farmer reassures Benny, who replies, "Never mind!" pointing to the animal's rear. "*This* is the end that worries me, not the head."

The mule kicks itself free and chases Perkins down the road, leaving the canary cage smashed on the road. Benny sadly shuffles home, where Martha joyously runs out to greet him. A welcome from Mom is followed by cheers from Chandler, Uncle Clarence, Ruby and Van Loon, who appoints him sales manager of the new Cucamonga branch. Morrison has been replaced by Chandler, who presents him with his double commission, which is followed by a second check from Van Loon: the "special cash prize" of $10,000, the exact amount he had promised to bring home to his mother.

The happy couple retreat to the citrus grove, and Benny swiftly runs back to the house. "Momma! Momma! Martha just said, 'Yes!,'" he shouts, again flipping over the bottom half of the split door. This time, Costello outdoes his previous pratfall; rather than bracing himself by grabbing the top ridge, he overshoots it, instead palming the middle of the door on the inside, just before he hits the floor with his bum. "We're gonna be married," Benny giddily announces and the film fades to black.

Little Giant was released on February 22, 1946. The film is first-rate in every department, including Seiter's faithful direction of the excellent screenplay by Walter DeLeon, Paul Jarrico and Richard Collins, the uniformly superb performances, and the sweeping musical score by Edgar Fairchild. During the shoot, Elena Verdugo, then just 20 years old (and fresh from her role as Ilonka, the gypsy girl, in Universal's *House of Frankenstein* [1944]), married B-film screenwriter Charles R. Marion (who specialized in potboilers like the 1941 Bela Lugosi–East Side Kids "classic" *Spooks Run Wild*, but also contributed to the Abbott and Costello radio show).

Bud and Lou were back at Universal on March 6, 1946, again playing separate character roles while working with a new director, Charles T. Barton (who would helm their next eight films), for "The Ghost Steps Out," a historical comic fantasy that took two months to shoot, at a final cost of $830,625 (their highest to date). The original draft of the screenplay was written by Val Burton, who paired Lou's character, Gwinette De Rome, with an African-American valet, Cedric Brown. The final shooting script, however, which changed Lou's partner to a fetching female, was a collaboration between Burton, Walter DeLeon and Bradford Ropes—with additional dialogue by John Grant—and re-titled *The Time of Their Lives* by the time the shoot ended on May 15, 1946.

Barton had instant connections with the boys. He began his career as an actor in vaudeville and films, eventually graduating to assistant director under James Cruze, but comedy proved his forte. In 1933, he won an Academy Award for Best Assistant Director. (At that time, the Academy actually awarded an Oscar for this category, with a nomination for each studio. This particular award was a tie between *seven* assistant directors, from 18 nominees!)

Lou again was up to no good on the set, but this time his thievery resulted in a potentially disastrous situation. To achieve the illusion of ghosts wandering about, the camera crew first photographed a fully dressed set without the actors, and then draped the entire space with black velvet to use as a background for the performances. By superimposing the two shots, the effect was achieved. (This technique was the forerunner to the later blue and green screen processes.) Following a full day's work on one of the ghost scenes, a specific order was issued forbidding anyone to *touch* any props on the set, much less abscond with them. That evening, Lou—at least as mischievous as his character in the film—crept back onto the set and ran off with a fine selection of items. Though the same offer was made to him for their temporary return, the crewmen were unable to place them back on the set exactly where they had been before the heist. Universal had to allocate additional funds to retake all the shots, but the expense was far less than if an infuriated Costello had walked off the lot.

A few weeks into production, Lou did threaten to walk out after spending a few days at home. Thinking the studio didn't call him in so more scenes featuring Bud could be shot, he placed an angry phone call to Val Burton, demanding that his and Bud's roles be switched. Having shot considerable footage, Universal wouldn't consider such nonsense, realizing that Lou, who hadn't read the script, would return after cooling off.

Cinematographer Charles Van Enger was retained from the *Little Giant* shoot to aid Barton in creating a wonderfully atmospheric visual style, particularly in the early scenes set in 1780 at the King's Point, New York, estate of Thomas Danbury (Jess Barker), a secret comrade of Benedict Arnold. Barton and Van Enger open the film with fluid tracking shots that bring the audience right into the political intrigue. Horatio Prim (Lou), a patriotic tinker, lies asleep on his faithful steed, Lancelot, as the animal ambles toward the barn. Meanwhile, his sweetheart, Nora (Anne Gillis), a bond servant, overhears Danbury plotting to join Arnold in betraying George Washington and the colonists.

Danbury's butler, Cuthbert Greenway (Bud), is infatuated with Nora, and will stoop to anything to get Horatio out of the picture. "You're still in love with that little, fat, stupid tinker!" he accuses her. In their only scene together as a team, Bud and Lou tangle with a large trunk, which Cuthbert closes on the unsuspecting Horatio. For eloping with a bond servant, the butler informs him, "You'll get five years at hard labor, you penniless*stinker*!"

Horatio has entrusted Nora with an important letter of commendation personally signed by Washington, but she is kidnapped by the traitors led by Danbury, who hides the missive in the secret drawer of a clock in his library. Danbury's fiancée, Melody Allen (Marjorie Reynolds), also learns of the plot and, after freeing Horatio from the trunk, plans to warn the Continental Army. Unfortunately, the advancing patriots mistake Melody and Horatio for two of the traitors, shooting them dead as they attempt to ride away. Major Putnam (Robert Barrat) orders the bodies thrown "into the well—that's the only burial they deserve."

A truly chilling image of the murdered patriots (who appear to be holding hands in the dank water at the bottom of the well) is accompanied by Putnam's condemnation: "Hear me, ye faithless souls. May you lie there in everlasting torment with but one name to identify your rotting bones—traitors! And, unless some evidence proves us wrong, I curse your miserable spirits to be bound to Danbury Acres 'til Crack of Doom!" A soldier prepares a wooden plaque, which is nailed up by the Major, reading, "Here were buried two traitors, September 23, 1780."

After the revolutionaries depart, smoke immediately emanates from the well, and two spirits materialize. They laugh about thinking they're ghosts; then Horatio, attempting to slap Melody on the back, whips his arm completely *through* her form. Grabbing a dipper from the well, he drinks some water, which spurts out his chest and back. "That's funny. I'm still thirsty," he reports. Observing the plaque and the bodies in the well, they deduce the truth, then watch Danbury Manor being looted and torched by the American soldiers.

Horatio sees Cuthbert riding off on Lancelot, but is prevented from leaving the front gate by an unseen force. Recalling Putnam's curse, they vow to find Washington's letter to use as "evidence," but are disheartened by the remains of the manor burning to the ground. A series of lap dissolves leading to dates carved into trees include snow falling in 1830, buds blooming in 1873, and a rainstorm in 1910. Finally, 1946 arrives; and, after the two ghosts have been sitting up in a tree "for 165 years," Melody finally puts her arm around Horatio.

Danbury Manor has been rebuilt by Sheldon Gage (John Shelton), who also sought out the original furnishings looted by the Continental Army. He arrives, accompanied by his fiancée, June Prescott (Lynne Baggett), her Aunt Millie (Binnie Barnes), and Ralph Greenway (Bud), "one of the best psychiatrists in New York" and the great-great-great grandson of Cuthbert. "From butler to psychiatrist in six generations," he announces. "Now, that's democracy for you."

Emily (Gale Sondergaard), the strange housekeeper, is also on hand—inspiring a wisecrack (Binnie Barnes' specialty) from Millie, who asks, "Pardon me, but didn't I see you in *Rebecca*?" (Later, the "psychic" Emily follows up this nod to the 1940 Alfred Hitchcock hit by

The Time of Their Lives (1946). Revolutionary War ghosts Horatio Prim (Lou) and Melody Allen (Marjorie Reynolds) under the tree in which they sit "for 165 years."

making her own reference to a top-drawer cinematic mystery, Howard Hawks' *To Have and Have Not* [1944], when she tells Dr. Greenway, "If you want me, all you gotta do is whistle.")

The spirits decide to keep further visitors away by haunting the place. Horatio wants to begin immediately, but Melody counters, "You know no self-respecting ghosts do any haunting until midnight."

"Oh," he replies. "All right, I'll wait. But tonight, I *haunt*."

Melody easily floats through walls, but Horatio can't seem to achieve the proper rhythm, materializing inside a window seat or simply slamming into a door. At one point, he "wiggles" himself into invisibility, yet his shadow remains visible on the wall until he whistles at it to follow him. (None of this "dematerializing" makes any sense, because the living people can't see them in any state. The comic effect is substantial, however.)

The ghosts are frightened by the electric lights. "What an *astonishing* idea," says Melody. "They probably got it from Ben Franklin. He's always inventing things." They search the house, making a shambles of the library as they try to locate Washington's letter. While examining the furniture, they switch on a radio, and (in a reworking of the record-player gag from *Who Done It?*) are told to "stick up your hands ... or we'll fill you full of hot lead."

Dr. Greenway tells Sheldon (and himself) to "be calm, be reasonable," but is informed of an "invisible force" and "a gust of icy wind." Millie thinks Sheldon is crazy, but Emily knows he isn't. "It's them, all right," she says. "The ghosts from the well. They're up to their old mischief, throwing things around. Oh, there's a curse on this house, all right."

Lou was able to exact some "revenge" on Bud during the making of this film, particularly when Horatio begins to drive the neurotic, chain-smoking, self-psychoanalyzing Greenway (who he thinks is really an ageless Cuthbert) to near-madness. The chubby ghost plays the harpsichord, kicks him in the bum, and "toots" in his stethoscope. Paraphrasing one of the classic Abbott and Costello catchphrases, Melody tells Horatio, "You're a *bad* boy!"

Millie refuses to believe any of her companions' supernatural experiences, choosing to take "her spirits"—a decanter of brandy—to bed with her. On the way up the staircase, however, she sees an *evening gown* (Melody couldn't resist trying it on) walking past her, bids it "Hello," then screams and faints.

"Stop it! Stop it, all of you!" orders June. "I can't explain about the dress or anything else, but I do know there's nothing supernatural about it—and if you all don't stop acting like a bunch of crazy neurotics, I'm going to start acting like one myself!"

The lights begin to flash off and on, the result of Horatio's tinkering with the electricity in the basement. Melody rushes in, removes his hand from a switch, and suggests they return to the safety of the tree. Staggering around from the effects of the electrocution, he sits on a generator, takes another jolt (working in an obligatory Costello rear-end gag), throws wrenches at the device, and grabs a thin fluorescent light bulb, which glows in his hand. He attempts to *blow* it out, shakes it like a baton, causing an orchestral fanfare to emanate from thin air, then becomes invisible. The illuminated baton travels through the house, frightening the four "neurotics" and a Cairn terrier as he heads for the tree.

Emily gathers everyone for a séance. Sheldon reads about the curse in a record written by Major Putnam, but June still insists it's all "sheer medieval superstition." Greenway agrees with "Shelly" about the "two poor devils [who] can't get off this property," adding, "If we all intend to keep our sanity, we've got to get to the bottom of this."

"And *that* from a man who wrote a dozen articles exposing all séances as *fakes*," Millie points out. (Interestingly, the women are the skeptics, while the men—including a prominent psychiatrist—are quick to believe in the supernatural.)

The Time of Their Lives (1946). Specters Horatio (Lou) and Melody (Marjorie Reynolds) generate some mischief for Dr. Greenway (Bud), Shelton Gage (John Shelton), June Prescott (Lynne Baggett) and Aunt Millie Prescott (Binnie Bernes) at the reconstructed Danbury mansion (original lobby card).

"Let's do as Emily suggests," Sheldon appeals. "If this séance doesn't work, I swear I'll give up the whole thing and go back to New York with you in the morning."

"We've all got to make our minds *perfectly blank*," says Greenway.

Millie can't resist interjecting another wisecrack: "Well, that should be easy for you."

"It is," replies the doc. (Bud—his timing as razor sharp as ever—does a wonderfully startled double-take.)

Barton constructed an impressive, straightforward séance sequence (a forerunner to his "horror" approach pitting Bud and Lou against Dracula [Bela Lugosi], the Wolf Man [Lon Chaney, Jr.] and the Monster [Glenn Strange] in his masterpiece, *Abbott and Costello Meet Frankenstein*, released two years later). Emily's chanting immediately pulls the ghosts from their perch in the tree and back into the house. "Won't you please let us go back to the well?" Horatio asks. "I promise we will never bother you again." Emily replies with a repeat of her mediumistic gibberish, and he adds, "Oh, thank you—thank you, ever so much," walks over to Melody, and asks, "Did you hear what the nice lady said? *What* did she say?"

Sheldon tells the spirits they know of the curse and wish to help, but Horatio doesn't

The Time of Their Lives (1946). Ghosts Horatio (Lou) and Melody (Marjorie Reynolds) put a scare into Dr. Greenway (Bud) as Shelton Gage (John Shelton) and Aunt Millie (Binnie Barnes) question their own sanity (original lobby card).

trust them. "If you wish to cooperate with us," he continues, "rap on this table—once for no, twice for yes."

"Are you the spirits of the two traitors?" Greenway queries, receiving a hard rap on the foot that sends him toppling over in his chair. "Why do they always pick on *me*?" he asks Millie.

The group, aided in part by Tom Danbury's memoirs, learns the true identity of the ghosts and the existence of the letter from George Washington. Emily continues her trance; and, as the table rises from the floor, she begins to channel the spirit of Danbury, who speaks to Melody. "Oh, fine," Millie complains, "a ghost-to-ghost broadcast," as Horatio explains that Tom can't appear because "he's got his wings, while we're still grounded."

Tom's spirit gives these instructions—"Start at twelve, turn twice to three. At ten past one, 'twill open be"—then leaves Emily's body. As the group sets out to search all the clocks in the house, Horatio and Melody intend to tell them about the library, but (in a humorous special effect) accidentally run *through each other*, magically exchanging their clothes. They repeat the act to reverse the result, and Horatio commands, "Melody, don't ever do that again. I'm a *boy*!"

Sheldon explains that the library clock is a fine reproduction, whereas the original is on exhibit in a New York museum, from which he has been barred. Greenway offers to retrieve it, in an attempt to "atone for the sins of [his] forefathers," and is pursued back to the Danbury estate by Lieutenant Mason (the ever-entertaining Donald MacBride) and Sergeant Makepeace (Rex Lease) of the state police. Horatio—who tries to stop Greenway's car by swinging a cannonball on a chain he finds in the garden (Lou, in a single long take, masterfully wraps it around his head, causing the ball to hit him in the face and knock him down)—is heartbroken when the doc is nabbed before he can complete the combination on the clock.

Horatio initiates the mandatory Abbott-and-Costello climactic chase. Hopping into the police car, he yanks the Lieutenant's hat down over his eyes; aided by Melody, he prevents them from passing through the gate, and then takes the wheel after they get out to investigate. The invisible driver careens the car all over the lawn, pursues the police, who run to close the gate, and crashes into the well. "You know, a fellow could get killed doing this?" the already-dead Horatio observes.

Greenway is draped over a log, where the clock is found with its drawer open. Sheldon shows the letter to Mason, and Emily happily announces, "Now the curse is ended. This proves they weren't traitors, and their spirits are no longer bound to these acres. They're free—*free*."

The spirits cautiously walk through the gate, but Horatio is impeded one last time—by the tail of his coat, stuck on the fence! Melody is beckoned to Heaven by the voice of Tom. "Goodbye, Horatio. I'm going to miss you," she admits to her companion of 165 years.

Costello puts the finishing touches on what is arguably his finest screen performance as Horatio touchingly replies, "Goodbye, Melody. I'm gonna miss you, too. But don't you worry. Just as soon as Nora and I get settled, we'll have you and Tom over for dinner. I'll have Nora bake a big, nice angel cake." She gives him a farewell kiss on the cheek; and, in long shot, he gently waves, wipes his eyes with his coattail, and waves again. Following Nora's voice to the pearly gates, he kisses her through the bars, but she can't let him in. As the camera pans to the right, Horatio sees a neon sign, ironically reading, "Closed for Washington's Birthday," then looks into the camera, sighing, "Odds, bodkins" (his favorite phrase).

One major scene involving Horatio and Melody was cut due to typical objections from the Breen Office. Imagining what his life would have been like had he not been shot down, Horatio rattles off the names of fantasy descendants, including George Washington Prim and John Hancock Prim, as their images—exactly resembling Horatio—emerge from the ether. When Horatio Prim, Jr., is mentioned, the image that appears is dressed like Horatio but looks like Cuthbert. Horatio's "suggestive" response, "And they call me a traitor!" was instantly eradicated by Breen.

Released on August 16, 1946, *The Time of Their Lives*—the team's most unusual film, blending elements from numerous genres (this time going *Hold That Ghost* one better by including "real" spirits)—received mixed reviews and did less box-office business than expected. Audiences simply weren't used to seeing the team split up, playing characters who aren't "themselves." While Bud effectively created two related roles (one primarily "bad," and the other "good," though slightly annoying), Lou effortlessly merged his little funny man persona with a character who—like Benny Miller in *Little Giant*—patiently, sincerely triumphs against the odds. And being murdered this time around allowed him to gain even more audience sympathy! He and Marjorie Reynolds exhibit a subtle, moving chemistry as the platonic couple who stick by each another to weather more than one and one-half centuries while sitting in a tree! (Perhaps the space-time continuum doesn't exist for ghosts!)

Bud and Lou don't share many scenes together, but their "relationship" drives the story,

The Time of Their Lives (1946). Lou and Marjorie Reynolds take a break with director Charles Barton on the set.

A & C on Tour (1946). The official program for Bud and Lou's personal appearance campaign to raise money for the Lou Costello Jr. Youth Foundation.

with one Abbott making up for the tragic actions of an earlier one, ultimately providing redemption with respect to Costello. (Lou actually kisses Bud at one point, causing Greenway to smooch Millie, who slaps him across the face!) The boys anchor a fine cast, highlighted by Binnie Barnes, Donald MacBride, and the always memorable Gale Sondergaard, who specialized in mysterious, "dark" women and heavies (after winning the first-ever Best Supporting Actress Academy Award, for *Anthony Adverse* [1936], she co-starred in several Universal thrillers, including *The Black Cat* (1941) and *Spider Woman* (1944), both with Basil Rathbone, and *The Climax* [1944], with Boris Karloff; married to "Hollywood Ten" producer-director Herbert J. Biberman, she was unfortunately blacklisted in 1948 and didn't work again for 20 years).

After the shoot ended, Lou had headed for home on a mission to choose a suitable location for the Lou Costello Jr. Youth Foundation. To raise enough funds to open the center, he and Bud set out on a personal-appearance tour. Though their 20-page program included photo collages from their three previous films and a mention of *The Time of Their Lives*, the Foundation Directors made it clear that "the boys have expressly forbidden any gesture, in conjunction with this tour, that might be construed as a publicity tie-up for their current screen attractions."[2]

The program's introduction also explained:

> The marvelous thing about the Abbott and Costello Foundation [sic] is that it has been established to create playgrounds and club houses on the wrong side of town. Their first play center is in Los Angeles and is open to underprivileged kids—both boys and girls.
>
> If you are interested in this worthy cause, your encouragement will be welcomed and valued.[3]

Fans who came out to see the pair in person were informed that, "despite recent rumors that the noted comedy team would split, Bud and Lou will tell you today that they are more firmly united than ever."[4] The audience was also clued in to the constant friendly rivalry between the two comics:

> Abbott bought a home; Costello got a larger one. Abbott built a swimming pool; Costello built one one foot longer and one foot wider. Abbott bought a restaurant which specialized in Italian food. Costello bought a night club which not only served choice spaghetti, but served up a floor show and dancing as well. Each tries to top the other, when they talk about their business ventures. The only time the competition fell off was when Costello backed a bunch of other film stars in making the picture "A Wac, A Wave, and A Marine" under the corporate name of Biltmore Productions. This film also made money.[5]

Universal also included a brief tribute to the boys on the program's back cover: "Our best wishes to Bud Abbott and Lou Costello in appreciation of the fine constructive work they are doing in connection with the Youth Foundation." [6]

Lou carried his 16mm home-movie enterprise over into making a documentary about the Foundation. He shot black-and-white and color footage, both at home and on the work sites, which later was incorporated into short films promoting the funding of the center.

14

BACK FROM THE FRONT

Buck Privates Come Home (1947)

The world went wild when Bud and Lou went whacky in khaki ... now 10 million ex–G.I.s are ready to declare roar again! The laughs come marching home ... with those veteran funsters back in civvies!

—Universal publicity department[1]

Christmas was Lou's favorite time of year, and he went to extremes to out-do all his neighbors in decorating his home. Los Angelinos drove for miles just to see his display. Lou also was a home-movie maven, and he hired his pal, cameraman Gene Lester, to shoot family gatherings on Kodacolor 16mm stock. The Yuletide of 1946 was captured extensively, and—at Lou's insistence—Paddy and Carole were forced to sing in front of the Christmas tree. Along with the dolls and cameras, Lou made sure to buy his girls something he could enjoy—a pool table!

In his home movie, during a shot under the tree, Lou informs his daughters about "Santy Claus ... Thunder and Blitzen, and the three Andrews Sisters," then says, "Whaddaya say we set up the pool table?" and the gambling begins.

Preoccupied with plans for the Foundation, he stands up, then tells his daughters:

> This is going to be a very nice Christmas for all the children in Los Angeles—all the children down in the neighborhood where Daddy built the Foundation, for 4,300 little boys and girls.
>
> And next Christmas, they'll be able to use it. In fact, we're gonna open up the Foundation around January the 18th, and then it'll be open for all those poor kids down there....[2]

Buck Privates is the only Abbott and Costello film to have an actual sequel, and *Buck Privates Come Home* is a Hollywood rarity: a follow-up film that, in some ways, is an improvement on the original. World War II had been over for 15 months when Charles Barton began shooting at Universal on November 18, 1946, including location work at the U.S. Army base at Fort MacArthur in San Pedro and Gilmore Stadium in Los Angeles.

The studio, now called Universal-International, was under the management of Leo Spitz, an attorney, and William Goetz, the son-in-law of Louis B. Mayer. Neither boss cared much for the "low" comedy of Abbott and Costello, and they were much more concerned with creating "prestige product" that could rival the output of the Hollywood majors. Goetz, however, had a filmmaking background and realized that Bud and Lou could bring in profits to finance series dramatic projects. Lou, thinking that Goetz had been planted by the dreaded Mayer, didn't care for the new regime, but was back in top form for the new film.

Buck Privates Come Home (1947). This postwar Abbott and Costello service picture is a Hollywood rarity: a follow-up film that, in some ways, is an improvement on its predecessor (original
title lobby card).

Arthur T. Horman, who had written *Buck Privates*, penned the first draft of the new
screenplay, titled "The Return of the Buck Privates," based on a story by Richard Macauley
(who had contributed to such hard-hitting Warner Bros. classics as *The Roaring Twenties*
[1939] and *They Drive by Night* [1940]) and Bradford Ropes, but it was abandoned in favor
of a second script by John Grant, Frederic I. Rinaldo and Robert Lees.

Lou had been responsible for Universal's signing of beautiful young actress Joan Shawlee.
While performing in New York in 1945, the team had "discovered" her working as a dancer
at the Copacabana. Just 18 years old and still living at home with her mother, she was more
than surprised when a waiter walked backstage to give her Lou Costello's business card. Bud
and Lou then told her about the possibility of getting her a studio contract, but the one condition of her acceptance was their also providing accommodations for her mother, which
they accepted. After they all arrived in Hollywood, the gossip machine naturally painted her
as Lou's "girlfriend," but she countered that Costello was like her "big brother."[3]

Shawlee said, "For a couple of weeks after arriving in Hollywood, I thought I was having nutty dreams, but then they really put my nose to the grindstone, and I found out that
acting wasn't all luck."[4] Prior to her major role as Lieutenant Sylvia Hunter in *Buck Privates
Come Home*, she appeared in 13 films for Universal, who insisted she be billed as "Joan

Buck Privates Come Home (1947). In this University publicity photo, Bud feigns disapproval over Lou's apparent infatuation with his new "discovery," actress Joan Shawlee (a.k.a. Fulton, as billed in the film).

Fulton." (Later, she played several supporting roles on the Abbott and Costello television series.)

A former U.S. Army captain, Tom Brown, was cast as Shawlee's love interest, Bill Gregory, a G.I. who turns to car racing after returning Stateside. Prior to serving overseas during 1942–46, Brown had begun his New York stage career at age nine, then hit Tinsel Town for good in 1932, racking up nearly 60 film roles, including one as "Tom Brown" in Universal's *Tom Brown of Culver* (1932), directed by William Wyler.

Eight-year-old Beverly Simmons, cast as Yvonne ("Evey") Lebrec, a young French girl smuggled back to the States by Lou's Herbie Brown, came down with chicken pox shortly after the shoot began. Aside from Donald McBride, who recalled having the disease as a child, the other actors, particularly Bud and Lou, feared coming down with it. After a week passed, Simmons returned to work, and all was well.

Robert Arthur wanted to beef up the subplot involving midget-car racing, particularly the race-and-chase sequence that concludes the film. Four contenders from the 1946 Indianapolis 500—Ronnie Householder, Duke Nalon, Henry Banks and Louis Tomei—were joined on the track by five Pacific Coast drivers (Cal Niday, Al Sherman, Bob Pankratz, Chuck Barbo, Lyle Dickey), Australian champion George Davis, former motorcycle racer Mark Hilling, and Midwestern circuit driver Duane Carter.

Interestingly, U.S. military technology was used in a film about returning WWII soldiers. The publicity department reported:

> Army Air Forces photographic equipment was utilized at Universal-International to record a sequence which otherwise could not have been photographed. The script ... called for a midget racing car to streak along a highway with police in full pursuit. Trouble reared its ugly head in the problem of how to get a police-car's-view of the midget racer stepping along at more than 100 miles per hour, inasmuch as no camera truck could go that fast.
>
> The sequence was about to be junked when Producer Robert Arthur, who was recently discharged from an Air Corps photographic unit, went out to the Air Technical Service Command at Muroc Dry Lake and borrowed an automatic 16mm camera such as was used by pursuit planes in combat. Arthur had the unit bolted on another midget racer which took the place of the police car and photographed the speeding race car much like a fighter craft would record other planes in combat.
>
> Because the camera held enough film for only one minute's exposure, the scenes had to be re-shot 16 times before enough film was obtained for the cross-country race sequence in the movie.[5]

Universal also claimed that Lou had to crash through a wall "16 times" while shooting the climax of the race sequence, then unsuccessfully struggled for 10 minutes to get out of the midget car:

> Rescuers with hack saws finally were called from the metal shop and were put to work cutting out the side of the car to free the chubby star. The incident caused Lou to announce he will lose 20 pounds. Cost of the car was approximately $16,000, the damage, about $200.[6]

Bud and Lou had always competed, both as compulsive gamblers (Costello alone had lost approximately $1 million just playing cards over the years) and, to some degree, in the extravagance of their personal belongings. Since their early days at Universal, they had tried to outdo each other in the size of their trailers; but, after the war ended, Abbott was able to go all out. During the shooting of *Buck Privates Come Home*, Lou retaliated by buying "the biggest trailer ever seen in Hollywood," a 30-by-14 monster that he attempted to have towed onto the soundstage. As reported in *Movie Show* magazine, "Lou gleefully ordered the stage's doors opened so the truck could pull the trailer in, but suddenly the truck stopped. The doors were twelve feet wide. Abbott howled as Lou's pride and joy was hauled off the lot, probably to be sold as a house."[7]

Barton shot for over two months, wrapping on January 23, 1947, and racked up the largest tally ever lavished on an Abbott and Costello project: $1,202,000. Following the shoot, Tom Brown experienced a situation similar to that of the returning veterans in the film. Unable to find an apartment, he gathered together several of his pals to purchase an acre of land in the San Fernando Valley, where they subsequently built a cooperative eight-bunga-low housing project. Universal's publicity department emphasized that the sequel was intended as a comedy of "vet problems," adding a serious postwar home-front element to the solid shenanigans maintained by the boys throughout the film.

Documentary footage of the Allied Victory March through Paris briefly cuts to a shot staged on the Universal back lot, accompanied by "When Johnny Comes Marching Home" and an optimistic voiceover:

> The Victory March through Paris. The Buck Privates have fought their war and won, and they march in glory. Their reward: they're going home. It's one of the miracles of our time that this—the greatest fighting force the world has ever known—came into being one autumn day in 1940. On this day, Congress passed the Draft Act, calling the nation's youth to arms—and the young manhood of America answered the call. They came, millions strong, from all walks of life, farmers and schoolboys, and others of less creditable occupations....

Of course, *Buck Privates Come Home* is a comedy paying tribute to the U.S. fighting force, so this rosy picture doesn't include any mention of the 407,300 military personnel who *didn't* come home (and these U.S. casualties accounted for only *two* percent of the Allied total; the USSR lost 10,700,000, three million more than the combined Axis casualties of Germany and Japan). Since *Buck Privates* was produced and released before the U.S. entered the war, the sequel provided the first (brief) glimpse of the troops in "Europe." By the time Barton began shooting, Universal believed enough time had passed since the conclusion of the conflict to allow for another comic depiction of the nation's men in uniform.

Shots of the U.S. capitol are followed by two scenes from *Buck Privates* showing Slicker Smith and Herbie Brown selling ties in Times Square, then training at boot camp. The entire "drill routine"—concluding with Lou tripping over his belt—is included, providing a tall order for the new material, which begins more than six minutes into the film. "Even now," the narrator continues, "with the victory long since won, it's hard to believe that these pre-cision-like columns marching homeward were the awkward, raw recruits of short years ago." Somewhere in the back-lot approximation of Europe, Herbie again trips over his belt.

The returning servicemen are singing "We're Going Home" on the deck of their New York–bound troop transport. Nat Pendleton (in his final film role) is back as Sergeant Collins, still barking marching orders to Herbie, who, carrying a mop, turns and slaps a diminutive, Mickey Rooney–type mug upside the head. The little man nearly goes mad, babbling a stream of angry gibberish at his attacker. "Wait a minute!" Herbie shouts. "What are you talkin' about?"

"*I* don't know," the man shrugs, then walks away. Herbie continues his march, slapping Collins this time, before being slammed in the head with a hatch as the Captain (Don Porter) emerges. The men rush below, and Herbie tries to hide the contraband he's brought on board. The first item—a German booby trap disguised as a camera—eventually goes out a porthole, and the ensuing explosion sends a swell toward the ship. Initiating an exchange of hoary dialogue, the Captain asks, "What was that?"

"Thunder," replies Herbie.

Looking out the porthole, the Captain speculates, "Maybe we'll get rain," and receives a good soaking.

"Now we'll get *hail*," Private Herbie tells Slicker, who now wears a corporal's insignia.

Herbie's second item of contraband is not so easy to conceal in his duffel bag: Yvonne Lebrec, a six-year-old French orphan the boys call "Evey." The girl has grown attached to her self-appointed guardian, whom she calls "Uncle Herbie." Though Slicker doesn't approve of his pal's non-regulation actions, the rest of the men support Herbie's sentiments.

The inclusion of a European refugee is one of the film's semi-serious postwar elements. "Sergeant," Herbie tells Collins, "I know I don't know my right foot from my left, but I do know right from wrong, and if you send Evey back, that's *wrong*."

"Herbie, let the sergeant do his duty," Slicker interrupts. "After all, back in the States, we're just a couple of.... Look, let's face facts," he continues, "even if we get the kid through, we're not used to any responsibility. Where do we go from there?" (These remarks—suggesting they were better off overseas, in the military—is one of the film's several references to the difficulties experienced by returning veterans.)

The Captain returns, and Evey claims that Collins brought her on board. Until the child may be turned over to immigration authorities, she is temporarily placed in the care of Lieutenant Sylvia Hunter. Of course, Herbie is despondent over the entire affair, and twice asks Slicker to slap him in the face. After the initially reluctant corporal finally delivers the blow, Herbie remarks, "And I had to *coax* him for it."

In the Captain's cabin, Evey places Collins in even hotter water when she repeats one of his remarks: "If we lived up to all the regulations handed down by the brass tacks, we'd have lost the war." The sergeant receives further abuse when he is assigned to a mess detail preparing a party for the men. Of course, his two aides are Slicker and Herbie, whom he has difficulty locating as they shuffle in and out the two doors leading to the galley. "Where is that imbecile!" he shouts, just before both men exit, sandwiching him between the doors. Briefly incorporating material from *Hold That Ghost*, the scene is one of the funniest in the film.

The boys construct a makeshift table with a rectangular sheet of wood and *one* sawhorse, or "seahorse," as Herbie calls it. Intended to support snacks and eating utensils, it becomes as unbalanced as its engineers when Herbie drops a heavy fruit bowl, sending a large frosted cake hurtling through the air and onto the sergeant's head! (Nat Pendleton was forced to suffer through four takes—and *cakes*, requiring a shower to wash off the sticky frosting each time.) This fiasco is followed by their arrival Stateside, where the homecoming proves bittersweet for "Uncle Herbie."

At the Fort Dix Separation Center (San Pedro doubles for Burlington County, New Jersey), Barton and Charles Van Enger smoothly track their camera past the men anxious to be discharged from the service. "Say, what comes after the medical exam?" one soldier asks, as another answers, "You're a civilian."

"What's a civilian?" asks Whitey (future *Mickey Mouse Club* regular Jimmie Dodd).

"That's a guy who tells you about the grand times he had when he was in the Army," jokes Slicker.

"Yeah," Herbie agrees, "when they get you in the Army, they rush you to get up. They rush you here. They rush you *everywhere*. And when it's time for you to get out, *everybody* takes their time!"

Off-camera, Collins orders, "Stop griping."

Herbie grabs the sergeant's shirt. "Stop griping?" he asks. "Sergeant Collins, you and me got a score to settle. When you were a cop, if I hit ya, it was resisting an officer—and if I hit ya when you're a sergeant, it's insubordination—but when you and I go out that front gate, we're civilians."

"Then what?" Collins wants to know.

"I'll forget about the whole thing," Herbie admits. Observing a much shorter line on the opposite side of the compound, he tells Slicker, "I think I got a way of beatin' all this red tape." Standing behind the line of new recruits, he removes his shirt with the rest of them, then runs toward the sergeant, who asks, "What's your hurry, Bud? Keep your shirt on."

"You just told me to take my shirt off," Herbie reminds him.

"I told you to keep your shirt on taking your shirt off," the sergeant insists.

"How can I keep my shirt on and take my shirt off?" puzzles the veteran private. "Pardon me, is your name *Abbott*?"

"Abbott?" the sergeant asks.

Buck Privates Come Home (1947). At the Fort Dix Separation Center, Herbie Brown (Lou) "gets tough" with Sergeant Collins (Nat Pendleton) as his pal Slicker Smith (Bud) also puts on a front. (The actor playing the soldier behind Abbott's left shoulder is Jimmie Dodd, later of *Mickey Mouse Club* fame.)

"*Abbott*," repeats Herbie.

"Inside, rookie!" the sergeant shouts, slapping him toward the door.

Running back, Herbie taunts, "Rookie? Silly boy!" His final moments in the Army are painful ones as he receives the recruit's series of shots—including one in the bum with an enormous needle ("this is the end," the sergeant tells him)—before Slicker runs in to "comfort" him.

While Evey is waiting at the immigration office, some children accidentally send their baseball crashing through a window. (Though Beverly Simmons doesn't use a French accent, she does speak one line of dialogue in Evey's "native tongue" in this scene.) Fortunately for the girl, the duty shift changes while she is in a back room, and the officer, mistaking her for one of the street kids, scolds her for "smashing up government property," escorts her out the door, and commands, "Don't let me catch you around here again."

The boys are back in Times Square, "selling 15-dollar ties for 35 cents." As Slicker hypnotizes his "subject" into "a state of coma," the crowd laughs at their antics. (Bud and Lou's performance here, for an on-screen "audience," is pure burlesque shtick.) Discovering their con game, a disgruntled buyer runs to a nearby barber shop, where Collins—working "the first day back on [his] old beat"—is getting a shave. Forcing his way into the throng, he finds his two old platoon "pals." "Somebody hit you in the face with a cake again?" asks Herbie, who then notices that he's back on the police force.

"You leave my Uncle Herbie alone!" shouts Evey as she runs in, kicking Collins in the shins as he grabs the fleeing boys, trips over the tie table and receives a baseball in the cranium as they all escape toward the subway. Right on Collins' heels is the Police Captain (Donald MacBride, in another memorable turn as a confounded authority figure), who demotes him to duty "on 10th Avenue" for being out of uniform and failing to apprehend two peddlers and an illegal alien.

At the French Consulate, the boys, with Evey disguised as a boy, inquire about adoption requirements. Learning that Herbie must be married, have a "decent" home and an established business or job, they become flustered and botch their answers. When Herbie calls the "boy" Evey, she then speaks with Monsieur Duprez (Jean Del Val) in French, causing them to beat the retreat.

The trio rests on a park bench to formulate a plan. "Remember what that man said?" asks Slicker. "We've got to get married."

"*We* have to get married?" queries Herbie.

"Mmm hmm," mumbles Slicker.

"Oh, Slicker, you wouldn't marry me, would you?" Herbie innocently asks.

"Now don't get silly," he replies. "Did you ever hear of anyone marrying a man?"

"Yes, sir," affirms Herbie

"Who?" asks Slicker.

"My mudder," Herbie answers sincerely. (This punch line *may* still have worked in 1947.) This inane conversation ends with their decision to consult "Aunt Sylvia."

Much to Herbie's dismay, Sylvia is involved with Bill Gregory (Tom Brown), a promising midget car designer and racer, who needs $8,000 to get his prototype out of hock. Slicker offers their separation pay and possible G.I. loans in return for Gregory's promise of jobs for them both. Here, the boys and Beverly Simmons reprise the "marry a homely girl" routine from *Pardon My Sarong*. (It has been speculated that the originator of this joke was none other than Benjamin Franklin, so it *really* had grown a long beard by the time Bud and Lou began using it!)

Sylvia prepares a comfortable bed for Evey, who donates one of her pillows to her "Uncles," who are consigned to the bathroom. Herbie improvises "We're Going to Bed," his own version of "We're Going Home," singing, "Oh, tonight's the first night I'll really get some sleep" as he crawls into the tub. Slicker grabs him by the seat of the pants and spins him around, but he falls in, saying, "Thank you, Slicker. Thank you!"

"Get up out of there. Get up! *I'm* sleeping there," he insists in typical fashion.

"That's no way to treat a returned veteran," scolds Herbie, again referring to the uncaring attitudes he's experiencing back in his native land.

"When we were overseas, you didn't fire off a gun!" Slicker points out.

"I didn't have to," argues Herbie. "I did all my fightin' with a knife."

"With a *knife*?" asks Slicker.

"With a knife," echoes Herbie. "I had 6,382 to my credit."

"Enemies?" queries Slicker.

"No," replies Herbie. "Potatoes."

Slicker has had enough. "Oh, stop."

"And, furthermore," Herbie continues, "I was right where the bullets were the thickest."

"Where was that?" asks Slicker.

Herbie tells no lie: "Underneath the ammunition truck."

On his way out to sleep on the fire escape, Herbie falls down, making a mess of the floor coverings. "Straighten out that hooked rug!" orders Slicker.

"Hooked rug?" asks Herbie.

"That's what I said!" insists Slicker.

"Slicker, that's no way to talk about Miss Sylvia," scolds Herbie. "It's none of your business how she got it."

"Oh, go to bed!" Slicker commands. "Go to bed."

"Miss Sylvia," ponders Herbie, "hookin' rugs." (The censors at the Production Code Administration must have ignored this scene—or the reference simply may have flown over their heads—for this dialogue to survive in the final cut!)

Herbie fashions a hammock by pinning a blanket to a clothesline that reaches from Sylvia's fire escape to another on the adjacent apartment building. "Are you asleep yet, Herbie?" asks Slicker.

Perched several stories above the alley, Herbie answers, "Not yet, Slicker, but I'm about ready to *fall off*."

The next morning, the neighbor woman (Janna deLoos) begins to pull in her laundry, positioning Herbie directly above the middle of the alley far below. The waking man stretches and yawns, nearly falling out the side of his hammock "Slicker! Slicker!" he yells as the woman's husband (William Haade) emerges onto the fire escape, complaining of a "Clothesline Casanova." He and Slicker engage in a tug of war, until the husband threatens to cut the line. Herbie pleads with his pal not to coax the enemy, but Slicker replies, "You keep out of this. Here I am, standing up, fighting *your* battles, and what do you do? Lie down—take it easy. As far as he's concerned, he hasn't nerve enough to cut the line!"

Slicker climbs back in the window. Two clothespins pop off the hammock, leaving Herbie to hold onto the blanket, for dear life. The husband pulls out a pocket knife, saws through the line, and sends the screaming Herbie swinging through the window of an apartment one storey below. He crashes into a Murphy bed, which folds up into the wall. When it slams back to the floor, the little man finds himself in the sack with none other than Collins, who chases him into the street. Stumbling around outside in his underwear, he is met by—you guessed it—the Captain, who transfers him to an even worse beat. (This entire sequence is Bud and Lou's equivalent to the work of the great silent comics, particularly Buster Keaton, Harold Lloyd, and Laurel and Hardy. Though it really isn't needed, Universal chose to dub in a frantic Costello laugh at two different points in the scene; the giggle would later be re-used in *Abbott and Costello Meet Frankenstein*.)

"Priority" treatment for veterans again falls flat when the boys search for a place to live. One sign reads, "No vacancies until 1950," so they decide to spend their separation pay on their own home. "There hasn't been a house like this on the market since the war began," claims an agent from the Grant Realty Company (Lou's brother-in-law Joe Kirk making another appearance) who takes *Herbie's* $735, then yells, "Okay, Joe!" as his assistant tows away a false house front to reveal an old, broken-down *bus* behind. "I can't drive," admits Herbie.

At Mulroney's Garage, the boys inspect Gregory's midget racer, then set out for the Citizens Savings Bank, where they roll out the blueprints for the president. "Hey, Slicker, look," Herbie says, pointing to the office door, "'J. P. Quince—Private.' Serviceman." Addressing Quince, he asks, "Hiya, Buddy. When were you discharged?"

"Discharged?" replies Quince. "Why, I've been here six years."

"Six years and still a private," Herbie points out to Slicker. "This guy is dumber than me." As he attempts to demonstrate the workings of Gregory's midget car engine, the scale model backfires, sounding like a machine gun, as bank customers witness the silhouette on the frosted-glass office window. By all appearances, a violent armed robbery is being carried out. Two cops run in, a .45 is fired, and Herbie pretends that he's been shot. "They got me. They got me," he groans to his pal. "Slicker? Take care of Evey for me." He crawls across the floor, then pulls himself up by grabbing the barrel of a policeman's revolver, but is quickly dragged back into the room.

"Get out of here! Get out!" rages Quince.

"Without my G.I. loan?" Herbie asks.

"Get out!" repeats Quince, chalking up yet another denial for the "returned veteran." Herbie "double slaps" one of the cops and Quince with the blueprint before departing.

Miraculously, Sylvia has hired enough workmen (on credit) to have the entire bus remodeled in a single day. Before reaching their new home, Herbie spots a "MEN WANTED" sign, vows to "get a job," then comes running out, followed by men with syringes, just as the remainder of the banner—marked "TO JOIN THE ARMY"—is rolled out.

Celebrating at the bus, Herbie makes some lemonade, squirting himself in the face just as a knock is heard at the door. "I'm showering," he reveals, just as Collins walks in. As the renounced policeman sits down, he admits, "I'm sick of havin' the three of ya hang over my head," just before a framed photo of Slicker, Herbie and Evey falls from the wall above, knocking him unconscious. (A lobby card from the 1945 Universal thriller *Dead of Night* also adorns the wall.) The Captain arrives in the nick of time once more, this time taking his badge.

At the garage, Collins and two goons guard the midget racer. Outside, the boys arrive with Gregory, who—having raised the $8,000 from all his war buddies—pays off Mulroney (Eddie Dunn), who says, "If either of you is Herbie Brown, sounds like you're headed for the electric chair." A hilarious battle ensues, with Herbie tossing iron wrenches at the phony cops' heads, then playing hide and seek in several stacks of tires, at one point mimicking Bugs Bunny (a Warner Bros. property!) as he pops out of a stack, carrot in hand.

The three drive off, pulling the midget car on a trailer. Collins runs behind, throwing a

Buck Privates Come Home (1947). Inside the security of their new "bus home," Herbie Brown (Lou) safeguards little Evey (Beverly Simmons) from the ungainly Sergeant Collins (Nat Pendleton). His G.I. supporters include Whitey (Jimmie Dodd, third from left), Slicker Smith (Bud, third from right), Bill Gregory (Tom Brown, second from right) and Sylvia Hunter (Joan Shawlee, a.k.a. Fulton, far right) (original lobby card).

large hammer that crashes through the display window of a jewelry store across the street. The next day, a track announcer (Milburn Stone) calls the big race, which guarantees a $20,000 purse to the winner. Twelve prominent midget race car drivers appear in the scene as Slicker and Herbie serve as Gregory's pit crew. Unfortunately, the police arrive to take Slicker, Sylvia, Evey—and Bill—into custody, leaving no one but Herbie (who can't drive) to race the car!

The chase to end all Abbott and Costello chases ensues. The Captain commandeers the car of auto executive William Appleby (Russell Hicks)—who has two cars entered in the contest—and merrily pursues the would-be racer, who crashes out of the speedway, only to end up on the "wrong track" at the local horse races! Some Keystone Kops–style shtick unfolds, with policemen falling off motorcycles and Herbie cruising the midget car through a diner at the airport, where he also is menaced by a plane, receiving a landing-gear tire burn on his helmet, on the runway. (These incidents recall the torpedo chase scene in *Keep 'Em Flying*.)

While speeding down an urban street, Herbie is brained by a billboard that becomes a pair of wings, lifting the car into the air. The flight lasts only a few seconds, however, as the racer crashes into the side of a theater advertising a movie called "Romeo Junior" starring

Abbott and Costello! Originally, the sequence was to include a glimpse of Costello as Romeo, playing the balcony scene with Juliet (Betty Alexander), then stepping off the screen to punch Herbie, but the footage didn't make the final cut (although a humorous still survives).

Unlike the conclusion of Shakespeare's *Romeo and Juliet*, all's well that ends well: Appleby Motors purchases 20 midget cars and 200 engines, Bill and Sylvia are married and adopt Evey, and the boys get jobs as—policemen, under the command of good ol' Sergeant Collins. The film fades out after Herbie trips over his belt.

Universal encouraged exhibitors to play up the Army angle "for millions of G.I.s in civvies":

> Here is the first all-out laugh show aimed at the millions of ex–G.I.s, their families and their friends. That takes in just about the biggest potential movie audience in the U.S.A. Every returning vet has faced and is still facing the problem of readjustment to normal civilian life. "Buck Privates Come Home" offers every showman the golden opportunity of cashing in one this universal theme.... Start your campaign early and sell it for all it's worth. You have the ammunition. So load your guns for big business.[8]

The "ammunition" included tie-ins with local veteran's housing organizations, newspaper editors who might be persuaded to create a weekend supplement about "local buck privates who have come home," and Willys Agencies who could provide ads for vets who can't live without an Army Jeep. As a capper, Universal suggested that an "Abbott and Costello Trunk," plastered with "foreign travel labels," be displayed in the lobby:

> Contents of trunk when opened can be as varied and ingenious as the exhibitor's imagination. Here are some suggestions as a starter: (1) Hitler's moustache cup; (2) French post cards (censored, of course); (3) memo book of Paris telephone numbers; (4) French lingerie, garters and stockings; (5) piece of Eiffel Tower; (6) bottle of London fog; (7) dice and poker chips; (8) Costello's key to Madame from Amentieres' apartment; (9) piece of spaghetti from Mussolini's vest; (10) autographed photos of Parisienne lovelies.[9]

Buck Privates Come Home, released on April 4, 1947, was a critical and box-office success, transporting Bud and Lou from their recent story-driven "experimental" films to their solid formula involving the "wisecracking know-it-all" and the "dumb little fat guy." In fact, the *New York Times* noted that the film "doesn't make much sense—in fact, it doesn't make any sense at all—but the new Abbott and Costello comedy ... is a lot of fun ... find[ing] the roly-poly one and his straight man in the very best of form."[10]

Costello, again creating tangible chemistry with a costar—this time a six-year-old girl—stole the film. In fact, referring to this role, he later told an interviewer about Charles Chaplin's idea of directing him in the remake of *The Kid*.

15

COLD WAR MONSTERS

"[T]hey were important to the Forties and essential to the art of comedy."—Charles T. Barton[1]

"They weren't as carefree later on, you could tell. Their attitude was more like 'Let's get this done and get the hell out of here.'"—Sheldon Leonard[2]

In early 1947, Costello spent considerable cash on an authentic U.S. military purchase: an 80-foot Navy sub-chaser that he converted into a luxury yacht, which he christened *Lolly C* after his mother. On May 3, Bud and Lou, who had raised $350,000 during their personal-appearance tour, opened the Lou Costello, Jr., Youth Foundation in East Los Angeles. At first, enthusiastic donors helped fund the operation, but eventually Lou was providing most of the funding ($80,000 per year) from his own pocket, some of which came from wagering. Finally he was forced to turn over the center to the City of Los Angeles.

On March 20, Bud and Lou were both subpoenaed to appear before a Federal Grand Jury on April 1, to answer questions related to the income tax returns of Chicago nightclub owner Michael Potson. During 1940–43, the boys had given $85,000 in checks to Potson, who had leveled them in some of their notorious Hollywood poker games.

The boys' next Universal film, *The Wistful Widow of Wagon Gap* (1947), benefited from an excellent Robert Lees, Frederic Rinaldo and John Grant script loaded with classic B-Western clichés, plus the "delightful" Marjorie Main in the title role. Having scored a hit in her first appearance as "Ma Kettle," in *The Egg and I* (1946), Main immediately appealed to U-I executive Bill Goetz, who initially wasn't enthusiastic about Bud and Lou. Main's versatility, appealing bluster and crackerjack timing blended effortlessly with the boys' shtick, creating a trio not seen in an Abbott and Costello film since their teaming with Joan Davis in *Hold That Ghost*.

Originally intended for James Stewart, the film was inspired by a law enacted in 19th-century Montana that made the survivor of a gunfight responsible for the dependents and debts of the departed. Screenwriter D. D. Beauchamp had discovered the edict in an old law book, which he used as resource material for a short story, "The Widow of Wagon Gap," published by *Colliers* in May 1947.

The making of *Wistful Widow*, which began shooting on April 29, was a family affair. Bud's nephew, Norman Abbott, served as dialogue director, and Lou's father was allowed to visit the set, as he often did. On May 8, 1947, Lou saw to it that "Pop" availed himself of the studio barber shop and commissary. The following day, Sebastian, coughing heavily, collapsed on his sofa from a fatal heart attack. On the set, Lou tore into Eddie Sherman, who had called his father the previous evening, complaining about the uncooperative behavior of his client. Producer Robert Arthur called off shooting for the day. When the film was released on October 8, Sebastian Cristillo was listed in the opening credits as Associate Producer.

Enhanced by location footage shot at Vasquez Rocks and Iverson Ranch, *Wistful Widow* uses the familiar Western clichés as the basis for a non-stop parade of well-played gags. Gordon Jones (who later became Mike the Cop on the boys' TV show during its 1952–54 two-season run) is excellent as saloon owner Jake Frame, who *frames* Chester Wooley (Costello) for gunning down the drunken gambler husband of the Widow Hawkins (Main). Occasional Frankenstein Monster Glenn Strange also appears, initially as a member of the jury assigned to "try" Wooley (actually the lynch mob that had just attempted to string up Chester and his pal, Duke Egan [Abbott]!).

While working in Frame's saloon in an effort to pay off Hawkins' debt, Chester uses the reflective bottom of a spittoon to help Duke cheat at poker. In a reprise of Lou's gambling "ignorance" in *Buck Privates* and *Ride 'Em Cowboy*, the Widow claims no knowledge of cards but shuffles and deals like a pro. (The use of Main's double is obvious in these scenes.)

When an irate patron threatens Chester's life, he replies, "Go ahead and shoot me—and inherit this family." Throughout the remainder of the film, he carries a photo of the Widow and her brood to scare off similar villains. Soon, he is appointed Sheriff of Wagon Gap. The film concludes with a "shootout," during which the men of the town, having learned of the

The Wistful Widow of Wagon Gap (1947). Widow Hawkins (Marjorie Main), Duke Egan (Bud), "Sheriff" Chester Wooley (Lou) and Juanita Hawkins (Audrey Young) (original lobby card).

Widow's forthcoming receipt of railroad money, attempt to whack Wooley. Dressed in drag, Chester saunters down the street, leading the women, who end the conflict by furiously bludgeoning the gunmen with clubs. The Widow accepts the marriage proposal of Judge Benbow (George Cleveland); and the boys, heading for California, are chased into the final fadeout by a gang of "Indians." Released on October 8, 1947, *Wistful Widow* became Universal's fourth biggest box-office hit of the year.

In July, Bud and Lou again played the Roxy in New York, sharing the stage with such memorable acts as Maurice Rocco, Hermanos Williams and Amanda, Audrey Young, and the Gae Foster Roxyettes. In his *New York Times* column, critical curmudgeon Bosley Crowther wrote, "With Bud Abbott and Lou Costello as the stars of its stage show, the Roxy Theatre could be flashing the telephone directory on its screen and still draw the clamoring customers."[3]

While the boys were on the road, Universal announced that they soon would be appearing in a horror satire titled "The Brain of Frankenstein," a resurrection of their five-year-old idea to pit themselves against the Monster, Dracula, the Wolf Man—and the Mummy. The ace team of Robert Arthur, Charles T. Barton, Robert Lees, Frederic Rinaldo and John Grant were again on board and planned to begin production in October, as soon as Bud and Lou completed the independent project *The Noose Hangs High* (1948), to be released by Eagle-Lion Studios.

Universal had allowed their contract to expire after *Wistful Widow*. Studio suits Bill Goetz and Leo Spitz were clueless when it came to comedy, but they appreciated the solid box-office returns generated by the Abbott and Costello films. Milton Feld and Charles Barton accompanied the boys on their excursion to Eagle-Lion, so it was only a matter of time before they went home again. However, before production began in August 1947, Feld died suddenly.

On August 14, a third daughter, Christine, was born via Caesarian section to Anne Costello. Everyone who knew Lou suspected that he was hoping for a boy, a new male heir to carry on the family name. Two days later, the boys began *The Noose Hangs High*, joining a solid cast of veteran character actors, including Joseph Calleia, Leon Errol, Mike Mazurki, Fritz Feld, Ben Weldon and Joe Kirk. This fast-moving rehash of overly familiar routines, directed by Barton from a John Grant-Howard Harris script, involves Bud and Lou in a standard gangster plot bearing similarities to *Hit the Ice*.

Seeing the boys perform variations on "Pack/Unpack" and "Mudder and Fodder" yet again proves that *The Noose Hangs High* was created primarily to keep the team working until Universal got its contractual act together. A nightclub sequence, during which Ted (Bud) and Tommy (Lou) deliberately run up an enormous tab in the hopes of being thrown in jail to escape the mob (led by the entertaining Calleia as the boss, Nick Craig), is pure filler, with the team running through a string of unrelated routines: "Mustard," "Hole in the Wall" and "You're 40, She's 10." Other familiar shtick includes Tommy's visit to a crazed dentist (the team's old pal Murray Leonard), an episode already familiar decades earlier via Chaplin, Laurel and Hardy, and W. C. Fields.

Having listed his late father as Associate Producer on *Wistful Widow*, Lou did the same for his mother, Lolly Cristillo (who shared the credit with Feld's widow, Shirley), this time around. The proverbial "Lolly C" also shows up as the racehorse on which the boys and Carol (Cathy Downs) bet all their dough in an effort to repay the 50 grand they owe to Craig and Julius Caesar McBride (Leon Errol). The funniest gag in the film, a relatively fresh one, opens the first scene: Attempting to pull his own tooth, Tommy ties it to a dog, then releases a cat.

The Noose Hangs High (1948). Ted Higgins (Bud), Carol Scott (Cathy Downs) and Tommy Hinch-cliffe (Lou) in the team's independent gangster spoof produced and directed by Universal cohort Charles T. Barton (original lobby card).

As the mutt frantically chases the feline, he repeatedly slams into a wooden fence, then crashes into the doghouse.

Bertram Millhauser, a veteran of Universal's Sherlock Holmes series, penned the original script for *Abbott and Costello Meet Frankenstein*, a mishmash which was then rewritten by Lees, Rinaldo and Grant, who changed the title back to "The Brain of Frankenstein." Costello didn't want to make the film under any title, thinking the screenplay terrible, but by the time Barton had finished directing the team alongside Bela Lugosi as Dracula, Lon Chaney, Jr., as the Wolf Man, and Glenn Strange as the Monster (plus the voice of Vincent Price as the Invisible Man), Universal had a comic masterpiece on its hands.

The film opens with animated titles similar to those first created for *Hold That Ghost*, as the Frankenstein Monster knocks on two coffins from which skeletal versions of Bud and Lou emerge to scream their skulls off. Cartoon images of Dracula and the Wolf Man also join the Monster as the names of Lugosi, Chaney and Strange appear on the screen. The entire film benefits from terrifically atmospheric music by Frank Skinner, whose work here rivals his landmark score for Universal's *Son of Frankenstein* (1939).

Inspired by the marvelous material, Bud and Lou (as railroad baggage clerks Chick Young and Wilbur Gray) give their best team performance of the postwar era. Costello enjoys

Abbott and Costello Meet Frankenstein (1948). La Mirada, Florida, baggage porters Chick Young (Bud) and Wilbur Grey (Lou) meet the ultimate Monster (Glenn Strange) at McDougal's House of Horrors in the film many consider the team's cinematic zenith (original lobby card).

every opportunity to work in exceptional pantomime whenever Wilbur is frightened by the three monsters. Of course, only *he* sees them during the film's first half, and his attempts to convince his pal of their existence provoke only disbelief and disgust. Having blundered into the cavernous cellar of "the House of Dracula," Wilbur encounters the vampire and the Monster, then tries once again to inform Chick, who threatens, "If I don't find anything, I'm going to *beat your ears off!*"

After his harrowing experience, Wilbur sits silent in a chair as Chick paces, considering their next move. Here Costello arguably contributes one of the funniest moments in the history of film, as Wilbur, still silent, staring straight ahead, and swallowing nervously, jumps up from his seat, yelling loudly.

"Who screamed?" he asks Chick.

"*You* did," his pal replies.

"*I* did?" he puzzles. Emitting an uneasy laugh, he then sits back down to resume his previous state.

Released on August 20, 1948, *Abbott and Costello Meet Frankenstein* (1948) was one of their best films since *Hold That Ghost* (Lou's mother considered it *the* best), bringing them back into the studio's good graces (the box-office take was the boys' best since *Buck Privates* and *In the Navy*) and on to further "monster spoofs" blending the team's shtick with straightforward "horror" incidents that offer some genuine chills.

Chaney is particularly effective as the long-suffering Larry Talbot, who, when not in his hirsute lycanthropic mode, attempts to enlist the boys in foiling Dracula's plan to transplant Wilbur's brain into the Monster! In her first of two films with Bud and Lou, Lenore Aubert is sensuously sinister as Wilbur's bogus girlfriend, Sandra Mornay, who becomes the Count's vampire minion. Making his second and final screen appearance as Dracula, Lugosi literally sinks his teeth into his last great role. Eight years later, his descent into professional and personal oblivion would mercifully culminate with his death on August 16, 1956.

Charles Barton had began shooting *Mexican Hayride* (1948) on June 11. Supposedly based on a 1944 Cole Porter musical, the film benefits primarily from Lou's primo performance as Joe Bascom, a.k.a. Humphrey Fish, the victim of a stock swindle engineered by his former pal, Harry Lambert (Bud). Having "danced the samba for sixty-eight hours straight" in a marathon, Bascom immediately reverts to hoofing whenever the rhythmic music is within earshot.

The usual Costello nepotism was even more apparent during production of this film,

Mexican Hayride (1948). In this candid shot, Lou, Bud and costar John Hubbard entertain some guests (seated) to the set. A lucky Universal visitor that day obtained the team's autographs (middle left).

which features his brother, Pat, in an actual speaking role. As Tim Williams, one of the detectives who plans to provide restitution to Bascom's swindled "friends in Iowa," Pat—who had doubled for Lou so often in past films—now engages in a hilarious repartee with him.

WILLIAMS:
This guy adds up to Joe Bascom. Joe Bascom is short
and dumpy.

BASCOM:
Like you?

WILLIAMS:
Like me. And he's got a roly-poly face.

BASCOM:
Like you?

WILLIAMS:
Like me. And he's got short, fat, stumpy legs.

BASCOM:
Like you?

WILLIAMS:
Yeah! Like me!

BASCOM:
Officer! Arrest that man!

The boys' pal Sidney Fields again appears in a supporting role, a fast-talking interviewer who exasperates Bascom after he accidentally becomes the "Amigo Americana" at the hands of former flame, Montana (Virginia Grey), now a "lady bullfighter." Of course, writers Oscar Brodney and John Grant couldn't resist including a bullfight in the script, and the scene bears strong similarities to 20th Century–Fox's *The Bullfighters* (1945), a dreadful Laurel and Hardy programmer released three years earlier. Briskly directed and played by a fine cast (including Pat Costello, who claimed to be terrified at having to speak dialogue), this film fiesta was released on December 27, just in time for the 1948 holiday season.

Even while making *Meet Frankenstein*, the film being hailed as the team's masterpiece, Lou was preoccupied with "10,000 Kids and a Cop" (1948), a 20-minute promotional short about the Lou Costello, Jr., Foundation, starring William Bendix, who, since sharing scenes in *Who Done It?*, had become one of his closest friends. Charles Barton donated his services as director, and James Stewart signed on to narrate the opening sequence.

This film was the first Lou Costello project distributed by "Nassour Studios," an independent firm operated by Edward Nassour. Pat Costello co-wrote the screenplay, and William Clothier signed on as director of photography, while Jan Garber offered the services of his orchestra, who played a sprightly version of "On the Sunny Side of the Street" behind the opening credits. *All* the Hollywood Unions supported the effort: the Screen Actors Guild, followed by the Screen Extras Guild, the Screen Directors Guild, the Theatrical Stage Employees—IATSE, A.F. of I—the American Federation of Musicians, the American Federation of Labor, and the Script Supervisors Guild. Not wanting to be outdone by the workers, some liberal-minded production companies, studios and distributors also climbed aboard: Monogram, Pacific Title and Art, Pathe, R.C.A. Sound, and (not wishing to be embarrassed) Universal-International.

Mexican Hayride (1948). Con artist Harry Lambert (Bud) and "Amigo Americana," Joe Bascom, alias Humphrey Fish (Lou), who dances the samba "for sixty-eight hours straight" (original lobby card).

In "10,000 Kids," William Bendix plays Officer Bill Powell, a beat cop persuaded to visit the Foundation for "a half an hour." He ends up spending the entire day observing would-be wayward youth playing baseball and swimming who "no longer have time for mischief." The boys play themselves, initially appearing in a baseball game, with Bud as the catcher and Lou swinging the bat, knocking some easy flies out to the kids.

Powell approaches the boys, who readily shake hands (and, for 1948, pitch their bold, then-liberal, fast balls). The cop stands at home plate, asking, "This place is open to all kids—no race or religious distinction?"

Lou offers up:

> Tony Gonzales, first base;
> Willie Johnson, left field;
> Mike McNulty, short stop;
> Irving Rosenberg, center field;
> Charlie Lung, right field;
> Pete Pelligrinni, second base;
> Joe Wyriceck, second base;
> Olaf Swenson, catcher;
> Carl Ludwig, pitcher.

"You know, this is marvelous," the cop replies. "I still can't believe it."

During a swatting contest on the ball field, "officer" Bendix serves as umpire, but an underhanded pitcher sends his first batter to the clinic with a wild ball to the ankle.

The true highlight of "10,000 Kids" is a scene in which Officer Bill visits the hobby shop, where boys are there, "from morning until night, making things for themselves and presents for others."

Bud and Lou couldn't resist doing a bit for the Foundation flick. At the end of the tour, they added a scene in which the "director" of the Foundation leads the cop into the Holy of Holies, the office of Bud and Lou themselves.

Inside are "Uncle Lou" and a tiny blonde girl attempting to sing the "Too Fat Polka."

"What does Uncle Lou say to Uncle Bud, every Saturday morning, on the kiddy show?"

"Heyyyyyyyyyyyyyyyy, Abbott!" replies the kid.

After this philanthropic effort, Lou owed a "real" Abbott and Costello film to Nassour Studios. Shooting *Africa Screams* (1949) for Edward Nassour was often a pain for all concerned, including Shemp Howard (as a severely nearsighted marksman) and Joe Besser, but Bud again was pleased to have his nephew, Norman, aboard as dialogue director. Directed by Charles Barton, this freewheeling, nearly plot-less parody of the "jungle genre"—originally titled "Don't Bring 'Em Back Alive," but re-titled to cash in on the popularity of *Africa*

Africa Screams (1949). Harvey Livingston (Lou) is manhandled by the Baer brothers: Buddy and Max playing Boots Wilson and Grappler McCoy (original lobby card).

Speaks (1947)—marked the team's first collaboration with sophisticated, statuesque Hillary Brooke, who plays a con woman intent on stealing diamonds from an African tribe. Filmed in late 1948, the film, which features lion tamer Clyde Beatty and explorer-filmmaker Frank Buck as themselves, was faulted for its unfavorable stereotypes of Blacks. Like all the team's independent productions, this effort could have benefited from a tighter screenplay and less free improvisation.

On January 19, 1949, Bud and Lou performed at the Inaugural Gala of President Harry S. Truman in Washington, DC. Though Costello was now a Republican, his love of country went beyond politics, and his support for the wartime policies of Franklin Roosevelt carried over into his thoroughly professional approach to performing for FDR's successor.

Liberal labor activist Boris Karloff claimed that Bud and Lou were "nice chaps to work with," but he initially balked at appearing in *Bud Abbott and Lou Costello Meet the Killer, Boris Karloff* (1949). In the first place, he *isn't* "The Killer," and, worse yet, appears only briefly in a few scenes. Universal had a perfectly logical reason for this, however. Tentatively titled *Abbott and Costello Meet the Killers*, the screenplay was altered at the 11th hour to work "The King of Horror" into the plot. Originally written for a *female*, his character, "Swami Talpur," enjoys only one full scene, during which he unsuccessfully attempts to mesmerize Lou's moronic bellboy, Freddie Phillips, into committing suicide.

Abbott and Costello Meet the Killer, Boris Karloff (1949). House detective Casey Edwards (Bud) and bumbling bellhop Freddie Phillips (Lou) are "mesmerized" by phony Swami Talpur (Boris Karloff) (original lobby card).

The "fake swami from Brooklyn" (with a British accent) suggests shooting, hanging, and jumping out a window, but nothing works. "You're going to commit suicide if it's the *last thing* you do!" he insists. No other actor could have spoken this line in quite the same way; and Karloff also delivers the funniest one-liner of all: "Amazing," he admits, "even under hypnosis, the will of an idiot to cling to life." Trying one last method of self destruction, Talpur orders Freddie to look at his reflection, then "plunge the knife into the heart of the man in the mirror." Of course, Freddie sees the Swami, whom he tries to impale.

On February 10, 1949, Charles Barton began directing *Meet the Killer*, which proved to be his Abbott and Costello swansong at Universal. During shooting, Lou was continually dogged by the stress of trying to raise funds for the financially strapped Youth Foundation, but still gave a hilarious performance, turning a brief hotel-desk bit with the doomed Amos Strickland (Nicholas Joy) into a comic tour-de-force, smashing the old man's eyeglasses and dumping a bag of golf clubs on his feet before stumbling over suitcases to crash down on the lobby floor.

After the *Africa Screams* fiasco, *Meet the Killer,* an obvious follow-up to *Meet Franken-stein*, at least offered the boys an actual plot (though one with several unresolved loose ends) and a first-rate supporting cast, including Lenore Aubert (reprising her role as Lou's bogus girlfriend), James Flavin (in his usual police detective mode), and Percy Helton (as the slimy wolf, Abernathy, who tries to put the make on Freddie while he's in drag as a chambermaid!). One of Lou's favorite hangers-on, Joe Bozzo, a pal from Paterson, even turns up in a steam-room scene during which the *real* killer tries to cook Freddie's goose.

Karloff begrudgingly had posed for a few Universal publicity photos, pretending to stand in line for a ticket to *Meet Frankenstein*, but now his name alone brought throngs of fans into theaters across the nation when *Meet the Killer* was released on August 22. For his small role, Boris earned $20,000, while the boys landed $113,750 for their shenanigans. The investment paid off well for Universal, and the studio suits were doubly pleased when Bud and Lou were ranked third on the *Motion Picture Herald*'s Top 10 box-office attractions of 1949, right behind Bob Hope and Bing Crosby.

Abbott and Costello in the Foreign Legion was the sole project the team made for Universal during 1950. At this point, the market had become saturated with their films, both new productions and re-releases of their earlier wartime efforts. The studio believed that the core Abbott and Costello audience would buy tickets simply to see the team, so little imagination was lavished on the new script. Nonetheless, the film includes some hilarious scenes, including a lengthy desert section during which the exhausted boys are inundated with mirages. Director Charles Lamont had planned to begin shooting in December 1949, when Lou was hospitalized to undergo emergency gallbladder surgery, but production finally began on April 28, 1950.

Back at the studio, Lou scoffed at using a stunt double in the wrestling scenes, opting to take on William "Wee Willie" Davis and (future Ed Wood favorite) Tor Johnson himself, resulting in a painful arm injury. British actress Patricia Medina (then married to Richard Greene; later to Joseph Cotten), who plays the "French" female lead, Nicole Dupre, was warned by friends to be wary of Lou's practical jokes:

> That was very unnerving. But nothing like that ever did happen. He was a gentleman at all times and the greatest comedian I have ever seen. You cannot be the kind of performer that Lou Costello was without being a true sophisticate. He was that. Most children are very sophisticated and Lou was definitely a sophisticated child.[4]

Foreign Legion combines elements from their earlier service pictures with yet another go-round with Lou in the wrestling ring, this time casting him and Bud as Brooklyn promoters who follow "Abdullah the Assassin" (Davis), the "champion of all North Africa," to Algiers after he is insulted by their suggestion that he lose a contest with a local grappler. *Hold That Ghost* and *Hit the Ice* veteran Marc Lawrence again appears as a mobster, here insisting that the boys track down Abdullah to recoup the five Gs the syndicate had invested in the sham enterprise.

Though much of the film is a rehash of Laurel and Hardy's *Beau Hunks* (1931)—including a scene in which Lou resurrects Stan Laurel's old shtick by replying, "Yes, Ma'am" to Sergeant Axmann (the ever-sleazy Walter Slezak)—the desert section includes some truly exceptional moments. At one point, Lou imagines that he runs into a Brooklyn newsboy (David Gorcey, younger brother of "*Dead End* Kid" Leo Gorcey, and an "East Side Kid" in his own right), who dryly explains, "Can I help it if they gave me a *bad corner*?" before he disappears into the heat and sand.

One "mirage" that turns out to be real involves Bud and Lou discovering an oasis, complete with a pond full of fish. Moments before their arrival, an Arab, leaning down to get a drink of water, had lost his false teeth, which were quickly snapped up by an ornery catfish! While attempting to "clean up" the small fry caught by his pal, Lou loses them to the cat, which thrice jumps up to clamp down on them with his new choppers. The film concludes

Abbott and Costello in the Foreign Legion **(1950). Brooklyn wrestling promoters Bud Jones (Bud) and Lou Hotchkiss (Lou) pursue their star grappler to the point of joining the infamous desert legion (original lobby card).**

with a wrestling bout between Bud, Lou, Abdullah, and Abu Ben (Johnson)—during which they utilize the "Paterson routine"—followed by a furious desert chase and the heroic Brooklynites' honorable discharges.

Now represented by the William Morris Agency, Bud and Lou were making far less per year ($800,000) than they had previously ($2 million, plus 20 percent of the profits). Even though Lou had railed against the greed of Eddie Sherman, he and Bud decided to re-hire him, purely for business reasons.

In 1950, Lou bought two acres in North Hollywood he called the "L.C. Ranch," where he began to raise his own thoroughbred racehorses. The property included a two-bedroom house, where his new caretakers, Russ and Ruth Grose, moved in with their two children. Lou then requested a new barn, which Russ designed and built to house the horses, which eventually included "Bazooka," "Lolly C" and "Blue Baby."

Lou had Bazooka shipped from Ireland, the beginning of a costly training and racing endeavor that never paid off. Accompanied to the track by Universal producer Robert Arthur, he often dropped enormous sums on long shots—and his own horse was one of them. His breeding efforts resulted in a "son," "Bold Bazooka," who actually won some races. After taking first place in the Starlet Stakes at Hollywood Park, Bold Bazooka ran in the New Jersey Garden Stakes, a contest that cost Lou $35,000 just to fly the horse and a new trainer (a replacement for his late father) from California. But the expense was secondary to Lou's dream of entering the horse in the Kentucky Derby. Bold Bazooka led through the first half of the Garden Stakes race, but an undiagnosed weak shin prevented him from finishing. Lou was devastated, and the horse never was able to race again.

After extensive preparations, Bud and Lou, accompanied by a large contingent of associates, friends and family, sailed aboard the *Queen Mary* from New York to Southampton, England, where they were greeted by an enormous crowd of fans. Following a series of standing-room-only shows at the London Palladium, they continued with dates in Europe, including performances in Rome, where Lou was followed through the streets by enthusiastic admirers, and appearances at U.S. Army camps in Italy, Germany and France.

Back in the States, Lou became livid upon learning that Universal was distributing bootleg 16mm prints of their films. Holding the rights to this format, Lou, supported by Bud, wrangled with Eddie Sherman—who he assumed was getting a piece of the illegal action—then sued the studio, eventually settling for $2 million and a guarantee of future payments.

After wrapping *Foreign Legion*, Robert Arthur signed a contract with Warner Bros., and producer Howard Christie took over the Abbott and Costello production reins. Filmed between October 3 and November 6, 1950, *Abbott and Costello Meet the Invisible Man* (1951) rivals *Hit the Ice* as the team's best Charles Lamont–directed film, an atmospheric and funny murder mystery based on Universal's earlier *The Invisible Man Returns* (1940), starring Vincent Price.

The boys' characters in the film—Bud Alexander and Louis Francis—feature monikers based on their actual names. Relying on few burlesque gags, they benefit from another "monster" script by Robert Lees and Frederic Rinaldo, although it's actually a gangster plot involving racketeering in the boxing ring. The boys begin as graduates of DDT—Dugan Detective Training—and, as they immerse themselves in the case of Tommy Nelson (Arthur Franz), a framed pugilist who quaffs the invisibility serum invented by Jack Griffin (a photo of Claude Rains from James Whale's 1933 *The Invisible Man* makes a cameo appearance) to unmask the true killer of his manager, Lou becomes "Louie the Looper," the opponent of Rocky Hanlon, the mob's stooge in the ring.

Abbott is particularly good, trying to talk tough as a detective and playing a sham drunk scene laced with Shakespearean lines from *Hamlet* and *Richard III*, while Costello returns to his boxing roots, giving a remarkable physical performance in the ring. He is completely convincing as the Looper pulls his punches, allowing the Invisible Man to pummel Rocky with bare, unseen fists. The dialogue—again bolstered by the contributions of John Grant—is memorable.

"Tommy, do I have to go into the ring with Rocky Hanlon?" asks Lou.

"What are you worrying about?" the invisible Tommy replies. "I'll be in there with you every minute, dyin' to take a crack at Rocky."

"And I'll be in there, *just dyin'*," adds Lou.

After wearing nothing but trunks in the ring, Lou dons a hospital sheet folded into a giant diaper in the final scene. Having given a blood transfusion to save Tommy, he receives some of the invisibility serum in return. When he materializes, he wraps the diaper around himself as his legs reappear—backwards. "The End" zooms at the viewer as he crashes through a hospital window.

The supporting actors are perfectly cast. Soon to attain television immortality in *I Love Lucy*, William Frawley is a curmudgeonly delight as Lieutenant Roberts, who calls Lou a "psycho" yet ends up on the precinct psychiatrist's couch himself. Sheldon Leonard returns

Abbott and Costello Meet the Invisible Man (1951). **Louis Francis (Lou) and Bud Alexander (Bud) comfort their invisible pal, in the company of his fiancée, Helen Gray (Nancy Guild), and physician, Dr. Philip Gray (Gavin Muir) (original lobby card).**

in prime mob-boss form as Morgan, who had ordered the hit on Tommy's manager; and Adele Jergens plays the mob moll who attempts to steam up the Looper while suggesting that he take a dive during his bout with Rocky.

On top of their usual 10-percent of the take, Lou also earned additional returns by purchasing a 30-percent interest in *Meet the Invisible Man*. The premiere was a gala benefit for the Los Angeles *Examiner*'s Fund for Wounded Veterans of the Korean War, and included a live show that also featured Dean Martin and Jerry Lewis, Jerry Colonna, Lena Horne, Allan Jones, Danny Thomas, the Weire Brothers, and the Nat Young Orchestra.

Bud and Lou made their official television debut on January 7, 1951, as guest hosts of *The Colgate Comedy Hour*, an hour-long NBC variety program that was the first commercial series to originate in Hollywood rather than New York. Many popular comics, including Martin and Lewis, Bob Hope, and Jimmy Durante, hosted the show, which was created as competition for CBS's blockbuster *Ed Sullivan Show*. Though critics faulted Bud and Lou for relying on overly familiar routines, they consistently scored high ratings, hosting for three years.

Initially Bill Goetz and Leo Spitz had scoffed at the "low" comedy of Abbott and Costello, but now could care less as profits rolled in from Universal's homespun "Ma and Pa Kettle" series. From January 15 through February 12, 1951, the boys filmed the stereotype-ridden

Comin' Round the Mountain (1951). Wilbert, a.k.a. "Squeezebox McCoy" (Lou), and Al Stewart (Bud, at Lou's left) venture into the Kentucky mountains for a hillbilly feud (original lobby card).

Comin' Round the Mountain, which follows the exploits of Dorothy McCoy (Dorothy Shay), the "Manhattan Hillbilly," and show-biz mavens Al Stewart (Bud) and Wilbert (Lou) as they attempt to claim a hidden fortune in the Kentucky hills.

Dorothy, who convinces Wilbert that he is the grandson and heir of "Squeezebox" McCoy, becomes his unwitting love interest as an age-old feud is rekindled with the rival Witfield clan led by Devil Dan (former Frankenstein Monster Glenn Strange), a mountain man who pursues the new "Squeezebox," continually shouting, "W*ee*lbert!" into his frightened pan. Every cliché is intact, with Granny McCoy (Ida Moore) pulling a shootin' iron from her handbag to blast the bowl off the corncob pipe of anyone misfortunate enough to insult her or the clan.

Though running only 77 minutes, the film seems much longer, with several scenes of musical filler slowing the pace. Unlike the songs peppered throughout the wartime films, these numbers detract from, rather than enhance, the period atmosphere. The film's few highlights include Margaret Hamilton as the scary Aunt Huddy, a parody of her *Wizard of Oz* wicked witch, and a scene of gallows humor during which Wilbert, overhearing Kalem McCoy (Joseph Sawyer) describe the upcoming slaughter and roasting of a pig, assumes the carnage is meant for him. Briefly gracing the supporting cast are two familiar down-home faces from the John Ford stock company: Hank Worden as a referee at the "turkey shoot" and Russell Simpson as the judge who attempts to marry several potential couples after they all swig a love potion prepared by Huddy.

Bud and Lou's old Universal pal, Lon Chaney, Jr., joined them on the March 11, 1951, *Colgate Comedy Hour*, which they opened by performing yet another version of "Who's on First?" During a performance of the opera "Don Juan Costello," Chaney briefly emerged as the Frankenstein Monster to dance with Lou.

One of Costello's best business decisions was developing an independent television program to showcase the team's talents. NBC president Pat Weaver supported the idea, providing financing for a 26-episode season, which began filming at the old Hal Roach Studios in Culver City in May 1951. *The Abbott and Costello Show* ran for two seasons, making its broadcast debut on December 5, 1952, on CBS. Taking a page from his friend Lucille Ball, Lou wisely shot all the episodes on film rather than performing live, and made certain that his own production company, Television Corporation of America (TCA), owned the copyrights, insuring that the classic burlesque routines were preserved as Abbott and Costello material and providing future financial support for his family. The first season episodes are chock full of gags previously used in their films made at Universal—including the drill routine from *Buck Privates*—and MGM.

Their pal Sid Fields plays the cranky, slow-burn landlord of the boarding house in which they live, and the majority of the supporting cast were also old buddies: Joe Besser (as the extremely annoying "Stinky" Davis, an androgynous 40-year old in a Little Lord Fauntleroy suit), Lou's brother-in-law, Joe Kirk, as Italian merchant Mr. Bacciagalupe, Gordon Jones as Mike the Cop, and the ubiquitous Bobby Barber in a series of bit parts. The lovely Hillary Brooke, an American who spoke with a slight British accent, also costarred as the boys' neighbor whom Lou considered his girlfriend. During the second season, Besser was replaced by the even more irritating "Bingo the Chimp," who was "fired" after he bit Costello, whom the simian absolutely detested. (The early shows, which eschew coherent plots for constant, often disconnected hilarity, have repeatedly been cited by Jerry Seinfeld as a major influence on his own popular TV show.)

Sid Fields, Joe Kirk, Bobby Barber and Gordon Jones also guested with Bud and Lou on

The Colgate Comedy Hour. The legendary Louis Armstrong, one of the few African American performers to appear on television regularly throughout the 1950s, added some musical power to the November 18, 1951, episode. During a variation on the boys' *Buck Privates* shtick, Lou's friend George Raft appeared as a violent drill sergeant, and Armstrong donned military khaki to swing "Basin Street Blues," then riff reveille before ripping into another swinging solo at an Army training camp.

The second season of *The Abbott and Costello Show*, shorn of Hillary Brooke (except for one episode) and Joe Besser, was more ambitious plot-wise, with more focus on situations often resembling the classic Hal Roach shorts of Laurel and Hardy. For longtime fans, this season is more satisfying, giving them another 26 "films," often including top-notch improvised material, to enjoy. Chris Costello recalled:

> The shows were not making any money, so I don't know who opted to pull the plug. Back then, they had to have sponsors ... it could have been that it wasn't the right timing for it.... Dad probably not wanting to put any more money into it. Twenty-some years later, Bingo! The show sees a revival. I wish he were here to see that. Of course, he is....[5]

Lou's success with *The Abbott and Costello Show* gave him the courage to establish another company, Cosman Productions, to create a 26-episode series for George Raft, but the decision of MCA (who now owned Universal) to market *I Am the Law* as a syndicated product doomed it to failure. Raft, who played NYPD Lieutenant George Kirby on the show, later said:

> They should've sold the series to a network. In those days if you weren't on the network, what good was the show? I think Lou had bad advice.... To me, the only thing wrong with the show was the scripts. Lou had hired a director who employed radio writers, who wrote as if they were still in radio. Too much dialogue and not enough action.... It got so I was having arguments every day up at Lou's offices with the writers. If I had known it was going to be that way when Lou first asked me, I would never have done the series.[6]

Working constantly for the small screen, Bud and Lou also starred in several films (which, not surprisingly, rank among their worst): the independently made *Jack and the Beanstalk* (produced by a third Costello company, Exclusive Productions) and *Abbott and Costello Meet Captain Kidd* —both released by Warner Bros. in 1952; and *Lost in Alaska* (1952) and *Abbott and Costello Go to Mars* (1953) [a project initially envisioned by none other than Charles Chaplin during his visit to the ailing Lou in 1943] for Universal.

Pat Costello supplied the story and served as executive producer for *Jack and the Beanstalk*, a musical fantasy produced by Alex Gottlieb and featuring songs by Bob Russell and Lester Lee. Aping *The Wizard of Oz* (1939), the "modern story" is presented in sepia, while the fantasy scenes are rendered in "Super Cinecolor" (by an excellent cinematographer from the Universal days, George Robinson).

When unruly young "problem child" Donald Larkin (David Stollery) and his infant sister require a babysitter, the eldest sibling, Eloise (Shaye Cogan), calls the Cosman Employment Agency, who send over Dinklepuss (Bud) and Jack (Lou), who attempts to read the English fairytale *Jack and the Beanstalk* to the boy. (The more literate child winds up reading the "novel.")

The sepia scenes, featuring suitable Abbott and Costello half-improvised shtick, supply the film's funniest moments (Lou does some impressive pratfalls); but when the storybook

Jack and the Beanstalk (1952). Preparing to climb the beanstalk, Jack (Lou) is aided by Dinkle-puss (Bud) (original lobby card).

material (cramped studio shots inter-cut with occasional stock footage) takes over, the entire enterprise lapses into unremitting childishness. The sight of a three-strip-color Lou Costello roasting on an open fire for the forthcoming feast of Buddy Baer's (badly acted) Giant is *not* funny, and any viewer of this unfortunate fairytale will wish quickly to return to more familiar shenanigans in a sepia world. (Baer's repeated Frankenstein Monster–like growling may be *the most* insufferable element in a very obnoxious film.)

Having helmed *Beanstalk*, Jean Yarbrough migrated with the boys back to Universal for *Lost in Alaska*, which has the visual style, comic pacing and staginess of the television show. Opening in San Francisco, the film features some rather downbeat humor in the form of repeated suicide attempts and threats by Nugget Joe (Tom Ewell), who is obsessed with Rosette (Mitzi Green), a rather unattractive canary in cahoots with saloon owner Jake Stillman (Bruce Cabot) in Skagway. After saving Joe's life, Tom Watson (Bud) and George Bell (Lou) follow him into the freezing Yukon to escape the authorities who believe they murdered the gold prospector. In Skagway they are nearly gunned down by Joe's former partners, who have been made the joint beneficiaries of his will.

As Joe slowly recovers from his intentional attempt at drowning, the boys perform some dining-table shtick in an attempt to cheer him up. (The funniest element of the scene is the team's attempt to deliver the jokes with bad timing.)

"This'll kill ya," Tom assures Joe.

"Good. I want to die," he replies.

Most of the film is comically dead, as well. Among the tried-and-true gags is a labored scene in which Tom prevents George from getting any sleep. Announcing they will alternate two-hour slumber shifts in order to stand suicide watch, Tom moves the hands of the clock ahead two hours each time his pal climbs into bed. When George glances out the window at "eight o'clock," it's still pitch black. Later he passes out on a neighbor's doorstep and is carried home by the Skagway ship's captain.

Told that the current time is 7 A.M., George says, "Wait a minute. Only seven? Two hours ago it was nine o'clock."

"Well, what's two from nine?" Tom asks.

"Seven," replies George.

"That's what time it is," assures Tom.

The remainder of the plot is padded with chases through the cornflake-covered soundstage approximation of the frozen tundra and the stilted singing of Mitzi Green. However, the score features some quality contributions from (an un-credited) Henry Mancini.

The film becomes most entertaining when the boys finally get *lost in Alaska*, improvising some funny moments as they attempt to survive by ice fishing (George thinks an intruding seal is a dog), then using fish as projectiles, launched from a huge, makeshift slingshot which sends them slamming into the faces of Stillman and his henchmen. One gag involves Tom asking about the gloves worn by George, whose hands have merely turned blue from frostbite. After they freeze solid in a snowstorm, they are thawed out by some "Eskimos," including Kanook (Iron Eyes Cody, who engages in a funny "sign language" gag with Costello).

Having menaced the boys on the *Lost in Alaska* set, Bruce Cabot guest starred with Errol Flynn and Rhonda Fleming on the January 13, 1952, *Colgate Comedy Hour*. Flynn played his familiar role of the articulate, suave cowboy, but slapped Costello silly while resurrecting the old "Niagara Falls/Slowly I Turned" routine that Murray Leonard had unleashed as "Pokomoko" in *Lost in a Harem*. Flynn later returned as Black Pedro, a Mexican gunslinger who kills a cowpoke who tries to molest Fleming. Though his "accent" came and went, Errol demonstrated his talent for improvisational comedy by pulling off his false mustache before planting a furious kiss on Rhonda. Lou then entered the saloon as the inept sheriff, followed by a coin-tossing George Raft, who terrified him even further.

Alex Gottlieb repeated his role as independent producer for *Abbott and Costello Meet Captain Kidd*, another Super Cinecolor production, shot on cramped studio sets by veteran cinematographer Stanley Cortez. Charles Laughton, a formidable actor and major Abbott and Costello fan, was more than happy to sign on for the project. Taking a page from the boys' book, he ignored much of the script and approached the project with an over-the-top improvisational style. Though he had enjoyed a long film career—including a Best Actor Oscar in 1933 for *The Private Life of Henry VIII*—he was really hamming it up by the early 1950s. Captain Kidd (a character he first played on the screen in 1945) may not be his most blatant example of scenery chewing (his utterly slobbering nobleman in Universal's *The Strange Door* [1951] takes the cake), but it comes close to winning the prize ham.

Meet Captain Kidd is a nearly plot-less musical with cast-wide overacting and anachronistic songs by Bob Russell and Lester Lee. Howard Dimsdale supplied the "story" dialogue, while John Grant recycled old gags from *Hold That Ghost*, *Pardon My Sarong* and *Who Done It?* While trying to "work [their] way back to America" from Tortuga, Rocky Stonebridge

UNIVERSAL-INTERNATIONAL presents

BUD LOU
ABBOTT·COSTELLO LOST IN ALASKA

It's ALL NEW and a RIOT TOO!

CO-STARRING
MITZI GREEN
TOM EWELL with BRUCE CABOT

Directed by JEAN YARBROUGH
Screenplay by MARTIN A. RAGAWAY and LEONARD STERN
Produced by HOWARD CHRISTIE

Abbott and Costello Meet Captain Kidd CHARLES Laughton IN SUPER CINE COLOR

WARNER BROS.

(Bud) and Oliver "Puddin' Head" Johnson (Lou), become unwitting members of Captain Kidd's crew, which includes Captain Bonney (Hillary Brooke) and first mate Morgan (Leif Erickson, singing and reprising some of his *Sarong* shtick while menacing the boys). By the time this ridiculous maritime mess reaches "The End," Lou is impersonating Laughton as captain of the ship.

Production on *Meet Captain Kidd* wrapped on March 25, 1952, but Charles Laughton couldn't quit the boys just yet. On the April 6 *Colgate Comedy Hour*, he recited a portion of Lincoln's Gettysburg address amidst Bud and Lou's frantic mugging. The great actor's earnest recitation was so powerful that Lou was genuinely moved; but the master comic instantly shifted back into slapstick mode as soon as the oration ended. References to other Abbott and Costello projects popped up throughout the show, including Bobby Barber playing a character called "Stinky," Joe Kirk appearing as Mr. Bacciagalupe, and a poster advertising the fact that *Jack and the Beanstalk* was to open the next day.

On October 30, 1952, Bud, Lou and Universal signed the Eleven Picture Participation Contract, which gave the team an interest in further profits made by *One Night in the Tropics*, *Buck Privates*, *In the Navy*, *Hold That Ghost*, *Keep 'Em Flying*, *Ride 'Em Cowboy*, *Pardon My Sarong*, *Who Done It?*, *It Ain't Hay*, *Hit the Ice* and *In Society*. These wartime titles provided for the future of their families, with the share divided as follows: 40.5 percent for Bud and 49.5 percent for Lou, leaving the customary 10-percent agent fee for Eddie Sherman.

Although the film is called *Abbott and Costello Go to Mars*, the boys never actually land on the angry red planet. Instead, they accidentally fly a rocket ship to New Orleans during the Mardi Gras, then to Venus, where they encounter a bevy of beauties (actually 1953 Miss Universe contestants) led by the man-hating Queen Allura (Mari Blanchard), who briefly tolerates Orville (Lou) as her King. Despite a respectable budget (used primarily for special effects and sets that were later recycled by Universal for *This Island Earth* [1955]), this inferior effort remains overlong (at 77 minutes) and often unfunny. Brother-in-law Joe Kirk makes another of his frequent supporting appearances, here as Dr. Orvilla, who becomes involved in a slapstick identity mix-up with Orville.

Following a second European tour in 1953, Bud and Lou returned to California to find themselves being audited by the Internal Revenue Service. Lou, in particular, had made and spent a lot of cash for which no receipts existed. To make matters worse, he had fallen prey to a dishonest and incompetent accountant who had both embezzled from the accounts and failed to file his taxes on several occasions—a fate that has befallen many entertainers. Income had not been claimed, and many substantial legitimate deductions could not be supported by documentation. Arthur Manella, Costello's defense attorney, said:

> I had doubts of my own—until I got to know Lou Costello. Then, in my heart, I knew Lou was innocent and totally unaware of what was going on with his finances. He was too patriotic to cheat the government. Perhaps that sounds corny, but that's the type of man Lou was.[7]

Eventually Manella's negotiations resulted in a 50-percent reduction in Lou's back taxes from $750,000 to $375,000. But when the IRS confiscated a $20,000 purse won by Bold

Opposite, top: Lost in Alaska (1952). Tom Watson (Bud) and George Bell (Lou), stranded with a dog-less sled, in the frozen tundra (original lobby card). *Bottom: Abbott and Costello Meet Captain Kidd* (1953). Motley crew: Morgan (Leif Erickson), Rocky Stonebridge (Bud), Oliver "Puddin' Head" Johnson (Lou), Captain Kidd (Charles Laughton) and Captain Bonney (Hillary Brooke) (original lobby card).

Abbott and Costello Go to Mars (1953). Mars-bound spacemen Orville (Lou) and Lester (Bud) explore the outskirts of New Orleans! (original lobby card).

Bazooka, Manella explained that Lou needed it to finance the horse's transportation to the Garden Stakes, a race that could provide him with a way to pay off some of the tax debt. Unfortunately, the horse was injured and the money was lost. Manella said, "The funny thing is, in actuality when the government turned that money over to Lou, they were in essence placing a twenty-thousand-dollar bet on a horse."[8]

Indeed, Lou didn't allow the IRS to cramp his gambling style. The boys had played Las Vegas in 1947 (at the Flamingo, shortly before the whacking of infamous proprietor Benjamin "Bugsy" Siegel, who was irritated by Costello's tendency to rip off the corners of $100 bills), and now returned for an engagement at the El Rancho Vegas. While off stage, Lou dropped loads of dough at the tables, but insisted that he have his picture taken every time he won. What better proof could he have?

The tap dancing interludes from the early wartime films were recalled during the December 14, 1952, *Colgate Comedy Hour* when the powerhouse duo of Harold and Fayard Nicholas burned the floor for the boys. Bud, who was obviously impressed, gave the duo a bow, then introduced Irving Berlin's "White Christmas," which was sung—in Jolson style—by none other than Lou himself.

Boris Karloff was convinced to costar in another film with the boys, *Abbott and Costello Meet Dr. Jekyll and Mr. Hyde* (1953), this time being given an actual character to play. Charles

Abbott and Costello Meet Dr. Jekyll and Mr. Hyde (1953). Slim (Bud) and Tubby (Lou), American cops in London, provide "protection" for none other than Robert Louis Stevenson's Dr. Henry Jekyll (Boris Karloff, in his second—reluctant—appearance with the boys) (original lobby card).

Lamont closely followed the pattern established by Charles Barton in *Meet Frankenstein*, with musical supervisor Joseph Gershenson simply recycling Frank Skinner's superb score from the earlier film.

Sid Fields collaborated with Grant Garrett on the original treatment, which was expanded by screenwriters Lee Loeb and John Grant. The film maintains a respectable Victorian setting, opening with an unusual scene involving a altercation between London working men and a group of radical suffragettes led by Vicky Edwards (Helen Westcott). The boys play Slim and Tubby, two American police officers studying British crime control methods, who arrive in an *attempt* to quell the row, but also are thoroughly brained by the brawling broads. This scene offers an atypical "political" element in a postwar Abbott and Costello picture.

The plot features an interesting variation on earlier cinematic adaptations of Robert Louis Stevenson's classic depiction of the dual personality. The discovery of "what makes men evil," according to Dr. Jekyll, will bring lasting world peace. However naïve his belief may be, it is quite lofty for an Abbott and Costello film.

The most charming scene involves Tubby metamorphosing into a giant mouse after he quaffs some "funny tasting water"—actually a transformational drug prepared by Jekyll's hulking, mute assistant, Batley (John Dierkes)—and frightening some drunks in a local pub. Abbott once again is allowed to demonstrate his comic prowess, nearly upstaging his partner, when Slim first sees the bowler-wearing rodent. While chewing some bar pretzels, he first does a flawless spit-take, then registers the best double take of his film career as he collapses on the floor.

Boosted by the presence of Boris—who plays his scenes with complete conviction—*Meet Dr. Jekyll and Mr. Hyde* proved a box-office hit, but the interest accruing on Lou's back taxes forced him to sell the family home nonetheless. He had recently moved his race horse operation to a larger "L.C. Ranch," located on 22 acres in the San Fernando Valley's Canoga Park, and needed the cash. Anne Costello hated the unfamiliar environment, which led to further depression and more self-medicating with alcohol, while Lou, working less in Hollywood, spent more time with his daughters.

In between Universal projects, the boys continued to host *The Colgate Comedy Hour*, welcoming Hoagy Carmichael and Teresa Brewer to the April 26, 1953, episode, during which Bud, Lou and an entire dancing chorus plugged *Abbott and Costello Go to Mars*. The inimitable Carmichael sang "Old Buttermilk Sky," then offered a medley including a few bars from "Rocking Chair," "Lazy Bones" and "In the Cool, Cool, Cool of the Evening," all bridged with some dry witticisms. Another notable musical combination, Les Paul and Mary Ford, guested on the March 21, 1954, episode, offering guitar and vocal harmonies on "I Really Don't Want to Know," "There's No Place Like Home" and "Hold That Tiger."

Lou's daughter Carole, who had acting aspirations, was given a cameo role as the theater cashier in *Abbott and Costello Meet the Keystone Kops*, filmed from June 7 to July 9, 1954, at Universal. Charles Lamont, who had begun his career making two-reelers with Mack Sennett, was truly in his element during the shoot. After developing the idea—facing some opposition from Universal, who believed no one would remember the Keystone Kops—he called Sennett, who agreed to make a cameo appearance in one scene, during which he hits Abbott in the face with a pie. Fortunately, the great comic pioneer had recently finished his memoirs, *The King of Comedy*, and his early films, including the Kops comedies, were now being shown on television.

Bud and Lou play Harry Pierce and Willie Piper, two innocent victims of a swindle engineered by Joe Gorman (Fred Clark), who "sells" them Thomas Edison's original movie studio in West Orange, New Jersey, then accidentally becomes their director at Amalgamated Pictures in Hollywood while masquerading as "famous" Russian filmmaker Sergei Toumanoff. When Gorman's stooge, Hinds ("Slapsie" Maxie Rosenbloom) convinces him to rob the studio safe, Pierce and Piper grab the Keystone Kops and run the burglars to ground. Unfortunately, Willie opens the satchel, allowing all the cash to blow away in the gale generated by an airplane's propeller.

Released on January 31, 1955, *Meet the Keystone Kops*, like *Dr. Jekyll and Mr. Hyde*, was a major improvement on the team's three previous Universal efforts. Lou was pleased that a dialogue exchange with his daughter actually survived the final cut. Early in the film, after Willie is thrown out of the movie theater because of excessive *crying* (during the famous ice-flow sequence in D. W. Griffith's melodrama *Way Down East* [1920]), Carole looks at Lou and remarks, "You're silly."

"So's your old man," Lou replies, then walks off.

John Grant remained as a major writer through the final Universal release, the very funny *Abbott and Costello Meet the Mummy* (1955), filmed from October 28 to November 24, 1954. Reportedly, his relationship with Lou had soured a bit after he contributed "addi-

Abbott and Costello Meet the Keystone Kops (1955). Would-be silent movie moguls Willie Piper (Lou) and Harry Pierce (Bud) reduced to bindle-stiff status (original lobby card).

tional dialogue" (including recycled material from *Buck Privates*) to the Martin and Lewis military opus *Sailor Beware!* (1952).

Meet the Mummy allowed the boys to riff a new variation on the "Mudder Fodder" routine. As two "adventurers" in Egypt who sign on to accompany someone's "Mummy" back to the States, they engage in some classic gender-confusion before becoming mixed up with criminals, cultists, linen-bound zombies, and a giant iguana! For his final film with the boys, Charles Lamont created an exotic atmosphere recalling the "monster" mood first established by Charles Barton in *Meet Frankenstein*. The excellent musical score again features contributions from Henry Mancini.

For the first (and last) time on screen, Lou yells, "*Hey*, Abbott!" as he runs from the first sight of the mummy, Klaris (Eddie Parker). Though the screenplay assigned them the character names of Pete Patterson and Freddie Franklin, they freely use their real names throughout the film.

"The sacred medallion is missing," remarks one of the "followers of Klaris" after cultists steal the mummy from the home of Dr. Gustav Zoomer (Kurt Katch), who gets a fatal poison dart for his part in the ancient affair. The followers, led by the high priest Semu (Richard Deacon), go to extremes to recover the medallion, especially after Lou eats it (as an accidental condiment on his hamburger)! Carole Costello again appears in a bit part, as a flower

Abbott and Costello Meet the Mummy (1955). Freddie Franklin (Lou) and Pete Patterson (Bud), imperiled by the very embodiment of "The Curse of Klaris!" in the team's final Universal film (original lobby card).

seller who hands the cursed medallion back to Lou after he attempts to hide it in one of her bouquets.

Universal's final "sequel" to the Boris Karloff classic *The Mummy* (1932), *Meet the Mummy* features more sinister atmosphere than all the previous "Kharis" films (starring Lon Chaney, Jr., and his stunt doubles) of the 1940s combined. The gang of treasure hunters intent on foiling Semu's plans includes Madame Rontru (Marie Windsor) and Charlie (Michael Ansara), who intently delivers such choice lines as "Watch out for the baby-face guy. He's a *killer*."

The conservative Costello had supported the liberal FDR because he was *the* wartime President. When the Cold War arrived, Lou became a hard-line anti–Communist and supporter of Joseph McCarthy. Chris Costello explained:

> Dad was thoroughly convinced that there was a Communist conspiracy to infiltrate the film industry.... Dad was an old-fashioned patriot, of a sort far more prevalent then than now.... Dad, among many other zealous conservatives, actually went so far as to carry petitions around to the studios, asking his fellow stars and anyone else working in the industry to sign, swearing they had no part in any Communist work or organization.[9]

Though Lucille Ball, who greatly admired Lou, turned down his solicitation, he supported her when she was accused of being a Communist by the House Committee on Un-American Activities (HUAC). However, Chris' contention that John Grant was sacked when he "took exception" to her father's "ultimatum" that he sign a petition to prove he was "a red-blooded American" is a myth. Chris continued:

> "I guess I'm not going to be writing for Abbott and Costello anymore," John said, getting up and starting for the door in Dad's office.
>
> "Does that mean you're quitting?"
>
> "That means I guess I'm fired," Grant replied.
>
> As the door shut behind him, Dad said, lowering his voice to a whisper, "Damn right it does." But he knew he'd gone too far. Dad never thought John was anything other than a good gag writer who loved his work, his wife, and his country, but each man had too much pride to restore the relationship. Dad missed John and later said to my mother, "Now why did John have to be so hardheaded?"[10]

Chris Costello fails to cite the source of this information, which could have been based on an actual incident; but, by the time she wrote her book nearly three decades later, whatever truth existed had become buried in an embellished account. The truth is that John Grant never stopped contributing to the work of Abbott and Costello, and wrote or co-wrote seven of their eight Universal films directed by Charles Lamont and released during the 1950s. Only his death ended the collaboration. On November 19, 1955—less than six months after the premiere of *Meet the Mummy*—he passed away at the age of 63 in Palm Desert, California.

The inevitable split of the team was apparent during the filming of *Meet the Mummy*. Lou had suffered another bout with rheumatic fever, and Bud's drinking was beginning to make him look heavier than his partner. While Charles Lamont kept the cameras rolling, they gave it all they had, but when "cut" was called, they went their separate ways between set-ups. Universal didn't renew their contract.

The boys made their final *Colgate Comedy Hour* appearance on May 15, 1955. Lou, the Republican patriot, was more than pleased to share the spotlight with none other than President Dwight D. Eisenhower. The following year, the chief executive, who frequently appeared on the small screen, won the Emmy "Governor's Award" for his "use and encouragement of" television.

Produced independently for a United Artists release, *Dance with Me, Henry* (1956) became their cinematic swan song. Completely free of burlesque material, the screenplay by Devery Freeman (a veteran of five Red Skelton films) was based on an original story by William Kozlenko and Leslie Kardos. The usual shtick contributed by John Grant was absent for the simple fact that the team's faithful "third member" was no longer on the planet.

Freeman approached the project with a *serious* intent, believing that comic situations arise naturally from real challenges. Costello appreciated this slant, specifically the idea of his playing Lou Henry (aka "Popsie"), proprietor of the Kiddyland amusement park and faithful foster father to orphans from a neighboring home, who has a full heart but a half-empty head. When his pal, Bud Flick, an inveterate gambler (no stretch for Abbott) gets over his head with the local mob, Lou's conflict with Miss Mayberry (Mary Wickes, Costello's old *Who Done It?* "paramour"), a local welfare agent, escalates, until he makes a desperate call to District Attorney Proctor (Robert Shayne), offering information on the mob's "First National job" in exchange for due consideration.

When the D.A. is gunned down by Mushie (Richard Reeves), henchman of Big Frank (Ted DeCorsia), the mob mastermind, Lou is framed for the whack. Not until the orphans,

BUD **ABBOTT**
and
LOU **COSTELLO** DANCE WITH ME, HENRY!

Dance with Me, Henry (1956). In the team's final film together, the local D.A. is gunned down. The patsy: Lou Henry (Lou), who is framed for the whack (original lobby card).

including his "kids," Shelly (Gigi Perreau) and Duffer (Rusty Hamer), along with little Bootsy (Sherry Alberoni), menace the mobsters with toy guns, darts and baseball bats (during the obligatory Abbott and Costello chase), does the local police force get wise.

Though United Artists' trailer for *Dance with Me, Henry* opens with the boys improvising on "Who's on First," no such shtick appears in the film, which is essentially a reflection of Bud and Lou's actual personalities, a heartfelt half-statement to crown their final cinematic collaboration. But their performances are wholehearted, and well supported by Mary Wickes, who finally re-teamed with them after several proposed reunions; Ted DeCorsia, whose Brooklyn demeanor typecast him as thugs, including "Big Jim" Harrington in two episodes of *The Untouchables* (1959–62) television series; prolific character actor Frank Wilcox as Father Mullahy; Ron Hargrave as Ernie, the stereotypical 1950s bopper; and the kids: Perreau had made her film debut at 18 months in MGM's *Madame Curie* (1943); and Hamer, a prodigiously talented child actor, found stardom on the small screen in *Make Room for Daddy* (1953–1965), but then hit the skids (eventually shooting himself to death at the age of 42 in 1990).

When Lou took his family to see the film in Canoga Park, the theater manager introduced him as the town's honorary mayor to the throng of children packing the seats. Unable to resist cracking up the kids, Lou began to walk toward the stage, tripping and doing a pratfall along the way.

Contemporary critics were decidedly lukewarm; but, in retrospect, *Dance with Me Henry* is arguably one of Bud and Lou's best films of the 1950s. (The same assessment has been unconvincingly leveled on the swansongs of other comedy teams—i.e. Laurel and Hardy's positively moribund *Utopia* [1951], which no amount of revisionism can rescue from the list of "Films That Never Should Have Been Made.")

On November 21, 1956, host Ralph Edwards surprised Lou by making him the subject of the *This Is Your Life* television program. A bittersweet trip down memory lane, the tribute ended on an emotional note when children from the Lou Costello, Jr., Youth Foundation gave him the gift of a gold watch, inscribed, "Thanks for sharing your life with ours." Later, Edwards mentioned, "Lou's jolliness and his tremendous concern for others. It was as though he had a mission to make other people happy."

Both Bud and Lou were highly honored when "Who's on First" was inducted into the Baseball Hall of Fame in Cooperstown, New York. While appearing nationwide on NBC's *The Steve Allen Show*, they presented a gold record to the Hall of Fame on the 20th anniversary of the routine.

On July 14, 1957, papers across the nation reported news of the official break-up of Abbott and Costello. After two decades of teamwork, there were a myriad of reasons for the split. No longer under contract to a movie studio, their classic form of burlesque comedy was now viewed as hopelessly old-fashioned by some. (More decades would need to pass before their collective comic genius would be viewed as being timeless.) But the reasons were just as personal as they were professional. Abbott's escalating alcohol use was a major factor, a problem borne out during their final Las Vegas engagement at the Sahara in December 1956, when Bud, having played an excellent early show, later returned to the stage after gambling and drinking, unable to remember the routines and missing cues from his partner.

Costello's dream of becoming a dramatic actor also fueled his decision to end the collaboration. He had definite plans to take to the legitimate stage, including a major part as Fiorello LaGuardia on Broadway. He also dreamed of portraying Sancho Panza in *The Man of La Mancha*. On television, he made his dramatic debut in "Blaze of Glory" on the *General Electric Theater*.

Produced by his old friend Howard Christie, "The Tobias Jones Story," the October 22, 1958, episode of the popular series *Wagon Train*, features what is arguably Lou's finest performance, his brilliant, touching turn as a drunk accused of murder. During production, when forgetting his lines during a poignant exchange with star Ward Bond, Lou sent everyone rolling with laughter by maintaining a dramatic demeanor while improvising some humorous dialogue. Tobias' touching relationship with a young orphan girl, Midge (Beverly Washburn), reflected Lou's own values; and the scene in which he sits on horseback, unshaven, with a large noose around his neck, provides a solemn parallel to the humorous near-hanging that he and Bud experience in *The Wistful Widow of Wagon Gap*.

Lou also guested eight times on *The Steve Allen Show*, recreating some of the classic burlesque routines with Louis Nye and Tom Poston. Bud sent him a telegram, claiming he'd be watching to make sure his former partner was in top form.

Lou returned to Las Vegas to star in *Minsky's Follies of 1958* at the Dunes Hotel. Recreating the atmosphere of classic burlesque, he performed some of the best routines with his old pal Sid Fields, who ably filled in for Bud. The engagement, which sold out every night for six weeks, was Lou's last. In December, he starred in his only film without Bud, *The 30 Foot Bride of Candy Rock* (1959), a parody of contemporary science-fiction fare such as *The Amazing Colossal Man* (1957), but he didn't live to see its release.

On February 26, 1959, Lou suffered a heart attack while in bed at home. He was taken to Doctors Hospital in Beverly Hills, where he showed enough signs of improvement to allow visitors, including Anne and his two older daughters, Bobby Barber, and Eddie Sherman, who was the only friend present on the morning of March 3. Lou struggled to ask his nurse to turn him over on his side, but then slouched back onto his pillow, dying from a second heart attack. Anne had to receive the news from Lou's physician, Dr. Immerman, over the telephone.

On her way back to the hospital, Carole learned of her father's death from a radio announcement, then became livid when she discovered Sherman, sitting beside Lou's sheet-covered corpse, giving gossip columnist Louella Parsons all the details over the telephone. He had promised Anne that he would call if Lou appeared to be in distress, but chose to drum up publicity instead.

Bud, who also was ill, had not been told of the hospitalization. "My heart is broken," he told Lou's mother after hearing the news. "I've lost the best pal anyone ever could have."[11] During the funeral at Saint Francis de Sales Church, where 500 mourners had crowded in, Bud led the pallbearers, who also included the beloved Bobby Barber, Howard Christie, Bud's nephew, Norman Abbott, and Eddie Sherman (whose later erroneous claims about the team would anger the Costello children). At Calvary Cemetery in East Los Angeles, Lou was interred in the mausoleum, next to the remains of little "Butch."

On the occasion of Lou's passing, one Los Angeles newspaper reported that he was a "clown with a heart as big as his girth." Lewis Rachmil, who produced the mediocre *The 30 Foot Bride of Candy Rock* for a Columbia release, recalled:

> Lou ... said, "Lewis, I've never acted alone before" ... I stayed on the set during much of the filming and watched Lou. He could get so wound up, but then could also sink into tremendous lows. He seemed to lack the confidence he'd always shown before. He missed Bud.[12]

Anne Costello had become inconsolable upon hearing of her husband's death. She had been all but ignored following the tragic passing of her baby son, and now the experience was repeated all over again, made even worse by the continual escalation of her alcohol abuse. Christmas had always been Lou's favorite time of year, and fate made certain that Anne didn't have to attempt the celebration without him. Just before Yuletide—a little more than six months after his demise—she followed him to the grave.

In 1965, Universal released *The World of Abbott and Costello*, a compilation of scenes from 18 of the 28 films made at their home studio. Though some of the choices are poor, clips from the wartime films represent *Buck Privates* (the drill routine), *In the Navy, Ride 'Em Cowboy, Who Done It?, Hit the Ice, In Society, The Naughty Nineties* (Who's on First?), *Little Giant* and *Buck Privates Come Home*. Not surprisingly, their later masterpiece, *Abbott and Costello Meet Frankenstein*, is well covered, but their 1941 gem, *Hold That Ghost*, is conspicuously absent. Inspired by the comedy compilations of Robert Youngson (*When Comedy Was King* [1960] and *MGM's Big Parade of Comedy* [1964], which includes the washing machine sequence from *Rio Rita*), Universal jumped on the band wagon. The film was a box-office hit, appealing to audiences anxious to relive classic comedy moments or discovering the magic of the boys for the first time.

Opposite, top: **The World of Abbott and Costello** (1965). **The classic drill routine from** *Buck Privates* **featuring (front row) Nat Pendleton, Bud and Lou (original lobby card).** *Bottom:* **The World of Abbott and Costello** (1965). **"Who's on First" from** *The Naughty Nineties* **(original lobby card).**

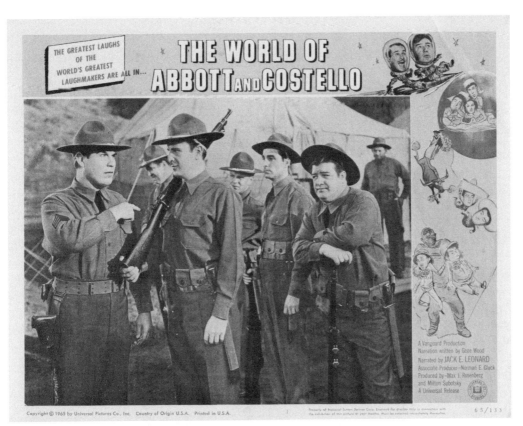

Bud had been hospitalized after suffering a mild stroke in 1964, but began working again when Hanna-Barbera produced a series of 156 color cartoons during 1966–1968. Bud provided the voice for his animated version, while the Lou character was voiced by Stan Irwin.

A few years later, Bud suffered two falls, resulting in a broken hip and left leg. Confined to a wheelchair, he endured a series of further strokes. As his health worsened, he was diagnosed with inoperable prostate cancer. He spent his last days in a hospital bed that had been moved into his Woodland Hills dining room, and was surrounded by friends and family, including his two adopted children, Bud, Jr., and Victoria, and wife, Betty, who was able to help celebrate their 55th wedding anniversary before he passed away on April 24, 1974. Newspaper reports predictably focused on (and exaggerated) his battles with the IRS.

Art doesn't always imitate life. In the case of Abbott and Costello, their art—yes, it deserves to be addressed as such—helps us laugh in the face of life's usually challenging, often grim pageant. While the team's three "service pictures" feature patriotic propaganda, and *Rio Rita* includes the requisite MGM pseudo-Nazis, the Abbott and Costello wartime films, in particular, follow the USO's mandate not to "wave the flag," but to provide escapism for folks facing arduous circumstances. As Maxene Andrews recalled, a USO provision explained, "The men you're playing to don't need pep talks. They'll do the fighting. You do the entertaining."[13]

Lou's daughter Paddy recalled:

> I think being together for 26 years, they had accomplished what they had set out to do, and probably reached a point where they figured that was as far as they could go. Dad wanted to go on to other things. He had a dramatic streak in him that he wanted to explore ... and that didn't leave room for Bud—but I think Bud ... was satisfied with that....
>
> Dad was adventurous, somewhat, and wanted to go into different fields of entertainment.... I think he liked some of the work behind the scenes ... producing. I never did hear him talk about directing, as such, but he wanted to have some hand at putting things together.
>
> Bud was the more mild mannered of the two, which kind of surprises people. Dad— you could just see that he was more goal oriented. And it's so sad that he passed away so young, because he didn't really get to do the things he wanted to do.... He did do some great things, but he could have done ... *greater* things.[14]

APPENDIX: THE FEATURE FILMS OF ABBOTT AND COSTELLO

One Night in the Tropics (Universal; November 15, 1940)

Director: A. Edward Sutherland; Producer: Leonard Spigelglass; Screenplay: Gertrude Purcell, Charles Grayson; Adaptation: Kathryn Scola, Francis Martin; Based on the novel *Love Insurance* by Earl Derr Biggers; Director of Photography: Joseph Valentine; Art Director: Jack Otterson; Musical Director: Charles Previn; Orchestrations: Frank Skinner; Film Editor: Milton Carruth; Songs: Jerome Kern, Dorothy Fields, Oscar Hammerstein II; Sound Supervisor: Bernard B. Brown; Assistant Director: Joseph A. McDonough; Running Time: 82 minutes.

Allan Jones, Robert Cummings, Nancy Kelly, Mary Boland, Bud Abbott, Lou Costello, Peggy Moran, William Frawley, Leo Carrillo, Don Alvarado, Theodore Rand, Mina Farragut, Richard Carle, Edgar Dearing, Barnett Parker, Francis MacDonald, Jerry Mandy, Eddie Dunn, Vivian Fay, Eddie Acuff, Frank Penny, William Alston, Charles B. Murphy, Charlie Hall.

Buck Privates (Universal; January 31, 1941)

Director: Arthur Lubin; Producer: Alex Gottlieb; Screenplay: Arthur T. Horman, John Grant; Directors of Photography: Milton Krasner, Jerome Ash; Songs: Hughie Prince, Don Raye; Musical Director: Charles Previn; Vocal Arrangements: Vic Schoen; Film Editor: Philip Cahn; Art Director: Jack Otterson; Dance Director: Nick Castle; Sound Supervisor: Bernard B. Brown; Gowns: Vera West; Set Decorator: R. A. Gausman; Assistant Director: Gilbert J. Valle; Military Advisor: Jack Voglin; Running Time: 82 minutes.

Bud Abbott, Lou Costello, Andrews Sisters, Lee Bowman, Alan Curtis, Jane Frazee, Nat Pendleton, Don Raye, Don Clemant, J. Anthony Hughes, Hughie Prince, Leonard Elliott, Jeanne Kelly, Elaine Morey, Kay Leslie, Harry Strang, Frank Cook, Samuel S. Hinds, Shemp Howard, James Flavin, Mike Frankovich, Jack Mulhall, Nella Walker, Douglas Wood, Charles Coleman, Selmer Jackson, Tom Tyler, Harold Goodwin, Bud Harris, Al Billings, Frank Penny, Frank Grandetta, Bob Wayne.

In the Navy (Universal; May 27, 1941)

Director: Arthur Lubin; Producer: Alex Gottlieb; Screenplay: Arthur T. Horman, John Grant; Original Story: Arthur T. Horman; Director of Photography: Joseph Valentine; Songs: Gene de Paul and Don Raye; Musical Director: Charles Previn; Musical Numbers: Nick Castle; Vocal Arrangements: Vic Schoen; Special Effects: John P. Fulton; Art Director: Jack Otterson; Sound Supervisor: Bernard B. Brown; Set Decorator: R. A. Gausman; Assistant Director: Philip P. Karlstein; Technical Advisor: H.E. Harris, USN; Film Editor: Philip Cahn; Running Time: 85 minutes.

Bud Abbott, Lou Costello, Dick Powell, Claire Dodd, Andrews Sisters, Dick Foran, Shemp Howard, Billy Lenhart, Kenneth Brown, Condos Brothers, William B. Davidson, Thurston Hall, Robert Emmet Keane, Edward Fielding; Don Terry; Sunnie O'Dea, Eddie Dunn, Ralph Dunn, Dick Alexander, Loren Raker, Frank Penny, Pat Gleason, Jack Mulhall, Mickey Simpson, Lyle Latell, Chuck Morrison, Lee Kass, James Sullivan, Edna Hall, Claire Whitney, Joe Bautista, Doris Herbert, Charles Sullivan.

In the Navy (1941). The Andrews Sisters bid you a "Hula Ba Luau" (original lobby card).

Hold That Ghost (Universal; August 6, 1941)

Director: Arthur Lubin; Producer: Alex Gottlieb; Associate Producers: Burt Kelly, Glenn Tryon; Screenplay: Robert Lees, Frederic I. Rinaldo, John Grant; Original Story: Robert Lees, Frederic I. Rinaldo; Director of Photography: Elwood Bredell; Musical Direction: Hans J. Salter; Musical Numbers: Nick Castle; Film Editor: Philip Cahn; Art Director: Jack Otterson; Assistant Director: Gilbert J. Valle; Sound Supervisor: Bernard B. Brown; Gowns: Vera West; Set Decorator: R. A. Gausman; Running Time: 86 minutes.

Bud Abbott, Lou Costello, Richard Carlson, Evekyn Ankers, Joan Davis, Andrews Sisters, Ted Lewis, Mischa Auer, Marc Lawrence, Milton Parsons, Frank Penny, Edgar Dearing, Don Terry, Edward Pawley, Nestor Paiva, Russell Hicks, William B. Davidson, Paul Fix, Howard Hickman, Harry Hayden, William Forrest, Paul Newlan, Joe LaCava, Bobby Barber.

Keep 'Em Flying (Universal; November 28, 1941)

Director: Arthur Lubin; Producer: Glenn Tryon; Screenplay: True Boardman, Nat Perrin, John Grant; Original Story: Edmund L. Hartmann; Director of Photography: Joseph Valentine; Aerial Photography: Elmer Dyer; Special Effects: John P. Fulton; Songs: Don Raye, Gene de Paul, Ned Washington, George Bassman; Musical Score: Frank Skinner; Musical Numbers: Edward Prinz; Film Edi-

Opposite, top: Buck Privates (1941). Patty Andrews, Lou, Laverne Andrews, Bud, Maxene Andrews. *Bottom: In the Navy* (1941). Bud and Lou.

tors: Philip Cahn, Arthur Hilton; Art Director: Jack Otterson; Sound Director: Bernard B. Brown; Set Decorator: R. A. Gausman; Gowns: Vera West; Assistant Director: Gilbert J. Valle; Technical Advisors: Major Robert L. Scott, Jr., Lieutenant David L. Jones; Running Time: 86 minutes.

Bud Abbott, Lou Costello, Martha Raye, Carol Bruce, William Gargan, Dick Foran, Truman Bradley, Charles Lang, William B. Davidson, Frank Penny, Loring Smith, Stanley Smith, James Horne, Jr., Charlie King, Jr., Regis Parton, Dorothy Darrell, Marsha Ralston, Doris Lloyd, Emil Van Horn, James Seay, William Forrst, Earl Hodgins, Harry Strang, Carleton Young, Harold Daniels, Dick Crane, Paul Scott, Virginia Engels, Dorothy L. Jones.

Ride 'Em Cowboy (Universal; February 20, 1942)

Director: Arthur Lubin; Producer: Alex Gottlieb; Screenplay: True Boardman, John Grant; Adaptation: Harold Shumate; Original Story: Edmund L. Hartmann; Director of Photography: John W. Boyle; Songs: Don Raye, Gene de Paul; Musical Score: Frank Skinner; Musical Direction: Charles Previn; Musical Numbers: Nick Castle; Film Editor: Philip Cahn; Art Director: Jack Otterson; Sound Supervisor: Bernard B. Brown; Set Decorator: Bernard B. Brown; Gowns: Vera West; Assistant Director: Gilbert J. Valle; Running Time: 82 minutes.

Bud Abbott, Lou Costello, Anne Gwynne, Samuel S. Hinds, Dick Foran, Richard Lane, Judd McMichael, Ted McMichael, Joe McMichael, Mary Lou Cook, Johnny Mack Brown, Ella Fitzgerald, Douglas Dumbrille, Jody Gilbert, Morris Ankrum, Charles Lane, Russell Hicks, Wade Boteler, James Flavin, Boyd Davis, Eddie Dunn, Isabel Randolph, Tom Hanlon, James Seay, Harold Daniels, Ralph Peters, Linda Brent, Lee Sunrise, Chief Yowlatchie, Harry Monty, Sherman E. Sanders, Carmela Cansino, Harry Cording.

Keep 'Em Flying (1941). Lou, William Gargan, Bud.

Rio Rita (MGM; March 11, 1942)

Director: S. Sylvan Simon; Producer: Pandro S. Berman; Screenplay: Richard Connell, Gladys Lehman, John Grant; Director of Photography: George Folsey; Songs: Harold Arlen, E. Y. Harburg, Harry Tierney, Joseph McCarthy; Musical Direction: Herbert Stothart; Special Effects: Warren Newcombe; Film Editor: Ben Lewis; Art Director: Cedric Gibbons; Set Decorator: Edwin B. Willis; Recording Director: Douglas Shearer; Running Time: 91 minutes.

Bud Abbott, Lou Costello, Kathryn Grayson, John Carroll, Patricia Dane, Tom Conway, Peter Whitney, Arthur Space, Joan Valerie, Dick Rich, Barry Nelson, Eva Puig, Mitchell Lewis, Eros Volusia, Julian Rivero, Douglass Newland, Lee Murray, Inez Cooper, Frank Penny.

Pardon My Sarong (Universal; August 7, 1942)

Director: Erle C. Kenton; Producer: Alex Gottlieb; Screenplay: True Boardman, Nat Perrin, John Grant; Director of Photography: Milton Krasner; Songs: Don Raye, Gene de Paul, Milton Drake, Ben Oakland, Stanley Cowan, Bobby North; Musical Direction: Charles Previn; Dance Director: Katherine Dunham; Film Editor: Arthur Hilton; Art Director: Jack Otterson; Sound Director: Bernard B. Brown; Set Decorator: R. A. Gausman; Gowns: Vera West; Assistant Director: Howard Christie; Running Time: 83 minutes.

Bud Abbott, Lou Costello, Virginia Bruce, Robert Paige, Lionel Atwill, Leif Erickson, William Demarest, Samuel S. Hinds, Orville Jones, Charles Fuqua, Bill Kenney, Deek Watson, Raymond Winfield, Sammy Green, Teddie Fraser, Irving Bacon, Nan Wynn, Marie McDonald, Elaine Morey, Susan Levine, Jack La Rue, Hans Schumm, Joe Kirk, Frank Penny, Charles Lane, Chester Clute, Tom Fadden, George Chandler, Eddie Acuff, Sig Arno, Jane Patten, Florine McKinney, Marjorie Reardon, Audrey Long, Teddy Infuhr, Sharkey the Seal.

Ride 'Em Cowboy (1941). Lou and Helen Thurston.

Pardon My Sarong (1942). Irving Bacon, Lou and Bud.

Who Done It? (Universal; November 6, 1942)

Director: Erle C. Kenton; Producer: Alex Gottlieb; Screenplay: Stanley Roberts, Edmund Joseph, John Grant; Original Story: Stanley Roberts; Director of Photography: Charles Van Enger; Musical Score: Frank Skinner; Film Editor: Arthur Hilton; Art Director: Jack Otterson; Set Decorator: R. A. Gausman; Costumes: Vera West; Assistant Director: Howard Christie; Running Time: 77 minutes.

Bud Abbott, Lou Costello, William Gargan, Louise Allbritton, Patric Knowles, Don Porter, Jerome Cowan, William Bendix, Mary Wickes, Thomas Gomez, Ludwig Stossel, Edmund MacDonald, Joe Kirk, Walter Tetley, Crane Whitley, Margaret Brayton, The Pinas, Milton Parsons, Edward Keane, Ed Emerson, Buddy Twiss, Gladys Blake, Eddie Bruce, Harry Strang, Frank Penny, Jerry Frank, Bobby Barber.

It Ain't Hay (Universal; March 19, 1943)

Director: Erle C. Kenton; Producer: Alex Gottlieb; Screenplay: Allen Boretz, John Grant; Original Story: Damon Runyon; Director of Photography: Charles Van Enger; Songs: Harry Revel, Paul Francis Webster; Musical Direction: Charles Previn; Orchestrations: Frank Skinner; Musical Numbers: Danny Dane; Film Editor: Frank Gross; Art Director: John B. Goodman; Sound Director: Bernard B. Brown; Set Decorator: R. A. Gausman; Gowns: Vera West; Running Time: 79 minutes.

Bud Abbott, Lou Costello, Grace McDonald, Eugene Pallette, Leighton Noble, Cecil Kellaway, Patsy O'Connor, Shemp Howard, Eddie Quillan, Dave Hacker, Richard Lane, Samuel S. Hinds, Harold De Garro, The Vagabonds, Andrew Tombes, Pierre Watkin, William Forrest, Ralph Peters,

Who Done It? (1942). Bud and Lou, a.k.a. "Muck" and "Meyer," with Patric Knowles (right).

Wade Boteler, Bobby Watson, James Flavin, Jack Norton, Tom Hanlon, Harry Harvey, Herbert Vigran, Ed Foster, Harry Strang, Mike Mazurki, Sammy Stein, Matt Willis, Harbert Hayes, Barry Macollum, Eddie Bruce, Paul Dubov, Charles Bennett, Rod Rogers, Janet Ann Gallow, Kate Lawson, Frank Penny, Fred Cordova, Spec O'Donnell, Stephen Gottlieb, The Four Step Brothers.

Hit the Ice (Universal; July 2, 1943)

Director: Charles Lamont; Producer: Alex Gottlieb; Screenplay: Roberet Lees, Frederic I. Rinaldo,, John Grant; Original Story: True Boardman; Director of Photography: Charles Van Enger; Songs: Harry Revel, Paul Francis Webster; Musical Direction: Charles Previn; Musical Numbers: Sammy Lee; Skating Number: Harry Losee; Film Editor: Frank Gross; Art Directors: John B. Goodman, Harold MacArthur; Sound Director: Bernard B. Brown; Set Decorators: R. A. Gausman, A. J. Gilmore; Gowns: Vera West; Running Time: 81 minutes.

Bud Abbott, Lou Costello, Ginny Simms, Patric Knowles, Elyse Knox, Joseph Sawyer, Marc Lawrence, Sheldon Leonard, Johnny Long, Joseph Crehan, Edward Gargan, Pat Flaherty, Eddie Dunn, Dorothy Vaughn, Minerva Urecal, Mantan Moreland, Bobby Barber, Wade Boteler, Ken Christy, Billy Wayne, Rebel Randall, Cordelia Campbell, Eddie Parker.

In Society (Universal; August 18, 1944)

Director: Jean Yarbrough; Producer: Edmund L. Hartmann; Screenplay: John Grant, Edmund L. Hartmann, Hal Fimberg, Sid Fields; Original Story: Hugh Wedlock, Jr., Howard Snyder; Director of Photography: Jerome Ash; Songs: Mann Curtis, Vic Mizzy; Musical Direction: Edgar Fairchild;

In Society (1944). Bud and Lou monkey around on the set with actress Alice Fleming.

Musical Numbers: George Dobbs; Film Editor: Philip Cahn; Special Photography: John P. Fulton; Art Directors: John B. Goodman, Eugene Lourie; Sound Director: Bernard B. Brown; Gowns: Vera West; Assistant Director: Howard DeHaven; Running Time: 75 minutes.

Bud Abbott, Lou Costello, Marion Hutton, Kirby Grant, Ann Gillis, Arthur Treacher, Thomas Gomez, George Dolenz, Steven Greay, Margaret Irving, Murray Leonard, Thurston Hall, Nella Walker, William B. Davidson, Elvia Allman, Milt Bronson, Don Barclay, Edgar Dearing, Ann Roberts, Ian Wolfe, Charles Sherlock, Al Thompson, Luis Alberni, Tom Fadden.

Lost in a Harem (MGM; August 31, 1944)

Director: Charles Riesner; Producer: George Haight; Screenplay: John Grant, Harry Crane, Harry Ruskin; Director of Photography: Lester White; Songs: Don Raye, Gene de Paul, Sammy Fain, Ralph Freed, Toots Camarata; Musical Supervision: Johnny Green; Musical Direction: David Snell; Film Editor: George Hively; Art Directors: Cedric Gibbons, Daniel C. Cathcart; Set Decorator: Edwin B. Willis; Recording Director: Douglas Shearer; Costumes: Irene; Makeup: Jack Dawn; Running Time: 89 minutes.

Bud Abbott, Lou Costello, Marilyn Maxwell, John Conte, Douglas Dumbrille, Jimmy Dorsey, Lottie Harrison, J. Lockhard Martin, Murray Leonard, Adia Kuznetzoff, Milton Parsons, Ralph Sanford, Bud Wolfe, Carey Loftin, Harry Cording, Eddie Abdo, Sammy Stein, Duke York, Katherine Booth, Frank Penny, Frank Scannell, Nick Thompson, Tor Johnson, Jody Gilbert, Tiny Newland,

Eddie Dunn, Sondra Rogers, Dick Alexander, Tom Herbert, Heinie Conklin, Ernest Brenck, Toni LaRue, Frances Ramsden, Margaret Savage, Jan Bryant, Margaret Kelly, Elinor Troy, Symona Boniface, The Pinas.

Here Come the Co-eds (Universal; February 2, 1945)

Director: Jean Yarbrough; Producer: John Grant; Screenplay: Arthur T. Horman, John Grant; Original Story: Edmund L. Hartmann; Director of Photography: George Robinson; Songs: Jack Brooks, Edgar Fairchild; Musical Direction: Edgar Fairchild; Musical Numbers: Louis Da Pron; Film Editor: Arthur Hilton; Special Photography: John P. Fulton; Art Directors: John B. Goodman, Richard H. Riedel; Sound Director: Bernard B. Brown; Set Decorators: R. A. Gausman, A. J. Gilmore; Running Time: 88 minutes.

Bud Abbott, Lou Costello, Peggy Ryan, Martha O'Driscoll, June Vincent, Lon Chaney, Jr., Donald Cook, Charles Dingle, Richard Lane, Joe Kirk, Phil Spitalny and His Band, Bill Stern, Anthony Warde, Dorothy Ford, Sammy Stein, Carl Knowles, Martha Garotto, Naomi Stout, June Cuendet, Muriel Stetson, Marilyn Hoeck, Margarey Eversole, Lorna Peterson, Ruth Lee, Don Costello, Rebel Randall, Maxine Gates, Dorothy Granger, Marie Osborn, Milt Bronson.

The Naughty Nineties (Universal; July 6, 1945)

Director: Jean Yarbrough; Producers: Edmund L. Hartmann, John Grant; Screenplay: Edmund L. Hartmann, John Grant, Edmund Joseph, Hal Fimberg, Felix Adler; Director of Photography:

Here Come the Co-Eds (1945). Peggy Ryan (left), Lou, June Vincent (fourth from left), Martha O'Driscoll (front, dark skirt) (original lobby card).

The Naughty Nineties (1945). Lou heads the off-camera "glee club."

George Robinson; Songs: Edgar Fairchild, Jack Brooks; Musical Direction: Edgar Fairchild; Musical Numbers: Jack Doyle; Film Editor: Arthur Hilton; Art Directors: John B. Goodman, Harold H. MacArthur; Sound Director: Bernard B. Brown; Set Decorators: R. A. Gausman, Leigh Smith; Gowns: Vera West; Makeup: Jack P. Pierce; Assistant Director: Howard Christie; Running Time: 76 minutes.

Bud Abbott, Lou Costello, Alan Curtis, Rita Johnson, Henry Travers, Lois Collier, Joe Sawyer, Joe Kirk, Jack Norton, Sam McDaniel, Billy Green, Bud Wolfe, Henry Russell, Ralph Jones, Bing Conley, Tony Dell, John Indrisano, Bud O'Connor, Charles Phillips, William W. Larsen, Dolores Evers, Jack Worth, Lillian Yarbo, Emmet Vogan, Milt Bronson, John Hamilton, Ed Gargan, Donald Kerr, Rex Lease, Jack Chefe, Torchy Rand, Ronnie Stanton, Sid Fields.

Abbott and Costello in Hollywood (MGM; August 22, 1945)

Director: S. Sylvan Simon; Producer: Marvin A. Gosch; Screenplay: Nat Perrin, Lou Breslow; Original Story: Nat Perrin, Marvin A. Gosch; Director of Photography: Charles Schoenbaum; Songs: Ralph Blane, Hugh Martin; Musical Direction: George Bassman; Orchestrations: Ted Duncan; Dance Direction: Charles Walters; Film Editor: Ben Lewis; Art Directors: Cedric Gibbons, Wade B. Rubottorn; Recording Director: Douglas Shearer; Set Decorator: Edwin B. Willis; Costumes: Irene; Makeup: Jack Dawn; Running Time: 84 minutes.

Bud Abbott, Lou Costello, Frances Rafferty, Robert Stanton, Jean Porter, Warner Anderson, Rags Ragland, Lucille Ball, Preston Foster, Robert Z. Leonard, Butch Jenkins, Mike Mazurki, Carleton G. Young, Donald MacBride, Robert Emmet O'Connor, Arthur Space, Katharine Booth, Edgar Dearing, The Lyttle Sisters, Marion Martin, Dean Stockwell, Bill Phillips, Chester Clute, Marie Blake, Harry Tyler, Skeets Noyes, Dick Alexander, Dick Winslow, Jane Hale, Frank Scannell.

Little Giant (Universal; February 22, 1946)

Director: William A. Seiter; Producer: Joseph Gershenson; Screenplay: Walter DeLeon; Original Story: Paul Jarrico, Richard Collins; Director of Photography: Charles Van Enger; Musical Score and Direction: Edgar Fairchild; Film Editor: Fred R. Feitshans; Art Directors: John B. Goodman, Martin Obzina; Sound Director: Bernard B. Brown; Set Decorators: R. A. Gausman, E. R. Robinson; Gowns: Vera West; Assistant Director: Seward Webb; Makeup: Jack P. Pierce; Running Time: 91 minutes.

Bud Abbott, Lou Costello, Brenda Joyce, Jacqueline De Wit, George Cleveland, Elena Verdugo, Mary Gordon, Pierre Watkins, Donald MacBride, Victor Kilian, Margaret Dumont, George Chandler, Beatrice Gray, Ed Gargan, Ralph Peters, Bert Roach, George Holmes, Eddie Waller, Ralph Dunn, Dorothy Christy, Chester Conklin, William "Red" Donahue.

The Time of Their Lives (Universal; August 16, 1946)

Director: Charles T. Barton; Producer: Val Burton; Executive Producer: Joseph Gershenson; Screenplay: Val Burton, Walter DeLeon, Bradford Ropes, John Grant; Director of Photography: Charles Van Enger; Musical Score and Direction: Milton Rosen; Special Photography: David S. Horsley, Jerome Ash; Film Editor: Philip Cahn; Art Directors: John B. Goodman, Richard H. Riedel; Sound Director: Bernard B. Brown; Set Decorator: Morgan Farley; Gowns: Rosemary Odell; Makeup: Jack P. Pierce; Assistant Director: Seward Webb; Running Time: 82 minutes.

Bud Abbott, Lou Costello, Marjorie Reynolds, Binnie Barnes, John Shelton, Jess Barker, Gale Sondergaard, Robert Barrat, Donald MacBride, Anne Gillis, Lynne Baggett, William Hall, Rex Lease, Selmer Jackson, Vernon Downing, Marjorie Eaton, Wheaton Chambers, Myron Healy, John Crawford.

Little Giant (1946). Lou and Mary Gordon.

Buck Privates Come Home (Universal; April 4, 1947)

Director: Charles T. Barton; Producer: Robert Arthur; Screenplay: John Grant, Frederic I. Rinaldo, Robert Lees; Original Story: Richard MacCauley, Bradford Ropes; Director of Photography: Charles Van Enger; Musical Score: Walter Schumann; Film Editor: Edward Curtiss; Art Directors: Bernard Herzbrun, Frank A. Richards; Special Photography: David S. Horsley; Sound Director: Charles Felstead; Gowns: Yvonne Wood; Makeup: Jack P. Pierce; Assistant Director: Joseph E. Kenny; Running Time: 77 minutes.

Bud Abbott, Lou Costello, Tom Brown, Joan Fulton (Shawlee), Nat Pendleton, Beverly Simmons, Don Beddoe, Don Porter, Donald MacBride, Lane Watson, William Ching, Peter Thompson, George Beban, Jr., Jimmie Dodd, Lennie Bremen, Al Murphy, Bob Wilke, William Haade, Janna deLoos, Buddy Roosevelt, Chuck Hamilton, Patricia Alphin, Joe Kirk, Charles Trowbridge, Russell Hicks, Ralph Dunn, John Sheehan, Cliff Clark, Jean Del Val, Frank Marlowe, Ottola Nesmith, Eddie Dunn, Harlan Warde, Lyle Lattel, Myron Healy, James Farley, Rex Lease, Ernie Adams, Milburn Stone, Knox Manning.

The Wistful Widow of Wagon Gap (Universal; October 8, 1947)

Director: Charles T. Barton; Producer: Robert Arthur; Screenplay: Robert Lees, Frederic I. Rinaldo, John Grant; Original Story: D. D. Beauchamp, William Bowers; Director of Photography: Charles Van Enger; Musical Score: Walter Schumann; Orchestrations: David Tamkin; Associate

Buck Privates Come Home (1947). Lou, Beverly Simmons, Bud.

The Wistful Widow of Wagon Gap (1947). Lou and Bud.

Producer: Sebastian Cristillo; Dialogue Director: Norman Abbott; Film Editor: Frank Gross; Art Directors: Bernard Herzbrun, Gabriel Scognamillo; Sound Directors: Charles Felstead, Robert Pritchard; Set Decorators: R. A. Gausman, Charles Wyrick; Makeup: Bud Westmore; Assistant Director: Joseph E. Kenny; Running Time: 78 minutes.

Bud Abbott, Lou Costello, Marjorie Main, Audrey Young, George Cleveland, Gordon Jones, William Ching, Peter Thompson, Olin Howlin, Bill Clauson, Billy O'Leary, Pamela Wells, Jimmie Bates, Paul Dunn, Diane Florentine, Rex Lease, Glenn Strange, Dewey Robinson, Edmund Cobb, Wade Crosby, Murray Leonard, Emmett Lynn, Iris Adrian, Lee Lasses White, George Lewis, Charles King, Jack Shutta, Harry Evans, Mickey Simpson, Frank Marlo, Ethan Laidlaw.

The Noose Hangs High (Eagle-Lion; April 5, 1948)

Director and Producer: Charles T. Barton; Screenplay: John Grant, Howard Harris; Adapted from a Screenplay by Charles Grayson and Arthur T. Horman; Original Story: Daniel Taradash, Julian Blaustein, Bernard Fins; Director of Photography: Charles Van Enger; Musical Score: Walter Schumann; Musical Direction: Irving Friedman; Associate Producers: Lolly Cristillo, Shirley Field; Film Editor: Harry Reynolds; Set Decorator: Arthur Marlowe; Makeup: Em Westmore, Russell Drake; Sound Directors: Leon S. Becker, Robert Pritchard; Running Time: 77 minutes.

Bud Abbott, Lou Costello, Cathy Downs, Joseph Calleia, Leon Errol, Mike Mazurki, Jack Overman, Fritz Feld, Vera Martin, Joe Kirk, Matt Willis, Ben Weldon, Jimmie Dodd, Ben Hall, Ellen Corby, Isabel Randolph, Frank O'Connor, Bess Flowers, Murray Leonard, Pat Flaherty, Elvia Allman, Lois Austin, Herb Vigran, James Flavin, Minerva Urecal, Russell Hicks, Arno Frey, Paul Maxey, Lyle Latell.

The Noose Hangs High (1948). Unidentified, Lou, Joseph Calleia, unidentified, Mike Mazurki, Bud.

Abbott and Costello Meet Frankenstein (Universal; August 20, 1948)

Director: Charles T. Barton; Producer: Robert Arthur; Screenplay: Robert Lees, Frederic I. Rinaldo, John Grant; Director of Photography: Charles Van Enger; Musical Score: Frank Skinner; Film Editor: Frank Gross; Art Directors: Bernard Herzbrun, Hilyard Brown; Special Photography: David S. Horsley, Jerome Ash; Sound Directors: Leslie I. Carey, Robert Pritchard; Makeup: Bud Westmore; Set Decorators: R. A. Gausman, Oliver Emert; Gowns: Grace Houston; Assistant Director: Joseph E. Kenny; Running Time: 83 minutes.

Bud Abbott, Lou Costello, Lon Chaney, Jr., Bela Lugosi, Glenn Strange, Lenore Aubert, Jane Randolph, Frank Ferguson, Charles Bradstreet, Howard Negley, Joe Kirk, Clarence Straight, Harry Brown, Helen Spring, George Barton, Carl Sklover, Paul Stader, Joe Walls, Bobby Barber, Vincent Price.

Mexican Hayride (Universal; Decmber 27, 1948)

Director: Charles T. Barton; Producer: Robert Arthur; Screenplay: Oscar Brodney, John Grant; Original Musical Play: Herbert and Dorothy Fields, Cole Porter; Director of Photography: Charles Van Enger; Musical Arrangements and Direction: Walter Scharf; Film Editor: Frank Gross; Special Photography: David S. Horsley; Art Directors: Bernard Herzbrun, John F. DeCuir; Set Decorators: R. A. Gausman, John Austin; Costumes: Yvonne Wood; Dance Director: Eugene Loring; Makeup: Bud Westmore; Sound Directors: Leslie I. Carey, Robert Pritchard; Running Time: 77 minutes.

Opposite, top: Abbott and Costello Meet Frankenstein (1948) (original title lobby card). *Bottom: Mexican Hayride* (1948). Bud and Lou.

Bud Abbott, Lou Costello, Virginia Grey, Luba Malina, John Hubbard, Pedro de Cordoba, Fritz Feld, Tom Powers, Pat Costello, Frank Fenton, Sid Fields, Chris Pin Martin, Flores Brothers Trio, Argentina Brunetti, Mary Brewer, Marjorie L. Carver, Lucille Casey, Toni Castle, Lorraine Crawford, Eddie Kane, Ben Chavez, Pedro Regas, Charles Miller, Harry Brown, Joe Kirk, Julian Rivero, Tony Roux, Roque Ybarra, Joe Dominguez, Felipe Turich, Alex Montoya, Julia Montoya, George Mendoza, Robert Elias, Rose Maria Lopez, Earl Spainard, Suzanne Ridgway, Cosmo Sardo.

Africa Screams (United Artists; May 4, 1949)

Director: Charles T. Barton; Producer: Edward Nassour; Associate Producer: David S. Garber; Screenplay: Earl Baldwin; Director of Photography: Charles Van Enger; Musical Score: Walter Schumann; Film Editor: Frank Gross; Art Director: Lou Creber; Special Effects: Carl Lee; Dialogue Director: Norman Abbott; Set Decorator: Ray Robinson; Assistant Director: Joe Kenny; Running Time: 79 minutes.

Bud Abbott, Lou Costello, Hillary Brooke, Max Baer, Buddy Baer, Shemp Howard, Joe Besser, Clyde Beatty, Frank Buck, Bobby Barber, Burton Weriland, Charles Gemora.

Abbott and Costello Meet the Killer, Boris Karloff (Universal; August 22, 1949)

Director: Charles T. Barton; Producer: Robert Arthur; Screenplay: Hugh Wedlock, Jr., Howard Snyder, John Grant; Original Story: Hugh Wedlock, Jr., Howard Snyder; Director of Photography: Charles Van Enger; Musical Score: Milton Schwarzwald; Film Editor: Edward Curtiss; Art Direc-

Abbott and Costello Meet the Killer, Boris Karloff (1949) (original title lobby card).

tors: Bernard Herzbrun, Richard H. Riedel; Special Effects: David S. Horsley; Makeup: Bud Westmore; Sound Directors: Leslie I. Carey, Robert Pritchard; Costumes: Rosemary Odell; Running Time: 94 minutes.

Bud Abbott, Lou Costello, Boris Karloff, Lenore Aubert, Gar Moore, Donna Martell, Alan Mowbray, James Flavin, Roland Winters, Nicholas Joy, Mikel Conrad, Morgan Farley, Victoria Horne, Percy Helton, Claire Du Brey, Harry Hayden, Vincent Renno, Patricia Hall, Murray Alper, Marjorie Bennett, Harry Brown, Beatrice Gray, Billy Snyder.

Abbott and Costello in the Foreign Legion (Universal; July 24, 1950)

Director: Charles Lamont; Producer: Robert Arthur; Screenplay: John Grant, Martin Ragaway, Leonard Stern; Original Story: D. D. Beauchamp; Director of Photography: George Robinson; Musical Direction: Joseph Gershenson; Film Editor: Frank Gross; Special Photography: David S. Horsley; Makeup: Bud Westmore; Art Directors: Bernard Herzbrun, Eric Orbom; Set Decorators: R. A. Gausman, Ray Jeffers; Sound Directors: Leslie I. Carey, Robert Pritchard; Running Time: 79 minutes.

Bud Abbott, Lou Costello, Patricia Medina, Walter Slezak, Douglas Dumbrille, Leon Belasco, Marc Lawrence, Tor Johnson, Wee Willie Davis, Sam Menacker, Fred Nurney, Paul Fierro, Henry Corden, Jack Raymond, Jack Shutta, Ernesto Morelli, Chuck Hamilton, Dan Seymour, Alberto Morin, Guy Beach, Ted Hecht, Mahmud Shaikhaly, Buddy Roosevelt, Charmienne Harker, David Gorcey, Bobby Barber.

Abbott and Costello Meet the Invisible Man (Universal; March 19, 1951)

Director: Charles Lamont; Producer: Howard Christie; Screenplay: Robert Lees, Frederic I. Rinaldo, John Grant; Original Story: Hugh Wedlock, Jr., Howard Snyder; Suggested by H. G. Wells'

Abbott and Costello in the Foreign Legion (1950). Henry Corden (far left), Lou and two unidentified actors.

Abbott and Costello Meet the Invisible Man (1951). Lou and Bud (original lobby card).

The Invisible Man; Director of Photography: George Robinson; Musical Direction: Joseph Gershenson; Film Editor: Virgil Vogel; Art Directors: Bernard Herzbrun, Richard H. Riedel; Special Effects: David S. Horsley; Set Decorators: R. A. Gausman, John Austin; Sound Directors: Leslie I. Carey, Robert Pritchard; Makeup: Bud Westmore; Running Time: 82 minutes.

    Bud Abbott, Lou Costello, Nancy Guild, Adele Jergens, Sheldon Leonard, William Frawley, Gavin Muir, Arthur Franz, Sam Balter, Sid Saylor, Bobby Barber, Billy Wayne, John Day, George J. Lewis, Frankie Van, Carl Sklover, Charles Perry, Paul Maxey, Ed Gargan, Herbert Vigran, Ralph Dunn, Herold Goodwin, Richard Bartell, Pere Launders, Edith Sheets, Milt Bronson.

Comin' Round the Mountain (Universal; June 18, 1951)

    Director: Charles Lamont; Producer: Howard Christie; Screenplay: Robert Lees, Frederic I. Rinaldo, John Grant; Director of Photography: George Robinson; Musical Direction: Joseph Gershenson; Film Editor: Edward Curtiss; Art Directors: Bernard Herzbrun, Richard H. Riedel; Special Photography: David S. Horsley; Set Decorators: R. A. Gausman, Joe Kish; Sound Directors: Leslie I. Carey, Robert Pritchard; Gowns: Rosemary Odell; Makeup: Bud Westmore; Assistant Directors: Fred Frank, Les Warner; Running Time: 77 minutes.

    Bud Abbott, Lou Costello, Dorothy Shay, Kirby Grant, Joe Sawyer, Margaret Hamilton, Ida Moore, Glenn Strange, Russell Simpson, Shaye Cogan, Robert Easton, Guy Wilkerson, Virgil "Slats" Taylor, O. Z. Whitehead, Norman Leavitt, Jack Kruschen, Peter Mamakos, Barry Brooks, Joe Kirk, William Fawcett, Harold Goodwin, Robert R. Stephenson, Sherman E. Sanders, Shirlee Allard, James Clay.

Comin' Round the Mountain (1951). Dorothy Shay and Lou (original lobby card).

Jack and the Beanstalk (Warner Bros.; April 9, 1952)

Director: Jean Yarbrough; Producer: Alex Gottlieb; Screenplay: Nat Curtis; Original Story: Pat Costello; Director of Photography: George Robinson (color); Musical Score: Heinz Roemheld; Music Supervision: Raoul Kraushaar; Choral Direction: Norman Luboff; Choreography: Johnny Conrad; Film Editor: Otto Lovering; Art Director: McClure Capps; Set Decorator: Fred McClean; Sound Directors: William Randall, Joe Moss; Costumes: Jack Mosser, Lloyd Lambert; Makeup: Abe Haberman; Special Effects: Carl Lee; Dialogue Director: Milt Bronson; Assistant Director: Alfred Weston; Running Time: 78 minutes.

Bud Abbott, Lou Costello, Buddy Baer, Dorothy Ford, Barbara Brown, David Stollery, William Farnum, Shaye Cogan, James Alexander, Joe Kirk, Johnny Conrad and Dancers.

Lost in Alaska (Universal; July 28, 1952)

Director: Yean Yarbrough; Producer: Howard Christie; Screenplay: Martin Ragaway, Leonard Stern; Original Story: Elwood Ullman; Director of Photography: George Robinson; Musical Direction: Joseph Gershenson; Musical Numbers: Harold Belfer; Film Editor: Leonard Weiner; Art Directors: Bernard Herzbrun, Robert Boyle; Set Decorators: R. A. Gausman, Ray Jeffers; Sound Directors: Leslie I. Carey, Harold Lewis; Costumes: Kara; Makeup: Abe Haberman; Running Time: 76 minutes.

Bud Abbott, Lou Costello, Mitzi Green, Tom Ewell, Bruce Cabot, Emory Parnell, Jack Ingram, Rex Lease, Joe Kirk, Minerva Urecal, Howard Negley, Maudie Prickett, Billy Wayne, Paul Newlan,

Lost in Alaska (1952). Lou, Bud, unidentified, Mitzi Green, Tom Ewell, Iron Eyes Cody (original lobby card).

Michael Ross, Julia Montoya, Iron Eyes Cody, Fred Aldrich, Donald Kerr, George Barton, Bobby Barber.

Abbott and Costello Meet Captain Kidd (Warner Bros.; December 27, 1952)

Director: Charles Lamont; Producer: Alex Gottlieb; Screenplay: Howard Dimsdale, John Grant; Director of Photography: Stanley Cortez (color); Songs: Bob Russell, Lester Lee; Musical Score: Raoul Kraushaar; Musical Numbers: Val Raset; Choral Arrangements: Norman Luboff; Film Editor: Edward Mann; Art Director: Daniel Hall; Sound Directors: Ben Winkler, "Mac" Dalgleish; Set Decorator: Al Orenbach; Dialogue Director: Milt Bronson; Special Effects: Lee Zavitz; Makeup: Abe Haberman; Assistant Director: Robert Aldrich; Running Time: 70 minutes.

Bud Abbott, Lou Costello, Charles Laughton, Hillary Brooke, Fran Warren, Bill Shirley, Leif Erickson, Sid Saylor, Frank Yaconelli, Rex Lease, Bobby Barber.

Abbott and Costello Go to Mars (Universal; April 6, 1953)

Director: Charles Lamont; Producer: Howard Christie; Screenplay: D. D. Beauchamp, John Grant; Original Story: Howard Christie, D. D. Beauchamp; Director of Photography: Clifford Stine; Musical Direction: Joseph Gershenson; Film Editor: Russell Schoengarth; Special Photography:

Opposite, top: Abbott and Costello Meet Captain Kidd (1953). Lou, Charles Laughton, Bud, Leif Erickson. *Bottom: Abbott and Costello Go to Mars* (1953). Bud, Lou, Horace McMahon (above), Jack Kruschen (original lobby card).

BUD ABBOTT and LOU COSTELLO GO TO MARS

WITH
MARI BLANCHARD

ROBERT PAIGE
HORACE McMAHON
AND THE
MISS UNIVERSE CONTEST BEAUTIES

A UNIVERSAL INTERNATIONAL PICTURE

David S. Horsley; Art Directors: Alexander Golitzen, Robert Boyle; Set Decorators: R. A. Gausman, Julia Heron; Costumes: Leah Rhodes; Makeup: Bud Westmore; Assistant Director: William Holland; Running Time: 77 minutes.

Bud Abbott, Lou Costello, Robert Paige, Mari Blanchard, Martha Hyer, Horace McMahon, Jack Kruschen, Anita Ekberg, Jackie Loughery, Jean Willes, Joe Kirk, Herold Goodwin, Hal Forrest, Jack Tesler, James Flavin, Sid Saylor, Russ Conway, Paul Newlan, Tim Graham, Ken Christy, Grace Lenard, Billy Newell, Harry Lang, Milt Bronson, Robert Forrest, Dudley Dickerson, Rex Lease, Frank Marlowe, Bobby Barber, Miss Universe Contestants.

Abbott and Costello Meet Dr. Jekyll and Mr. Hyde (Universal; August 10, 1953)

Director: Charles Lamont; Producer: Howard Christie; Screenplay: Lee Loeb, John Grant; Original Story: Sid Fields, Grant Garrett; Director of Photography: George Robinson; Musical Director: Joseph Gershenson; Dance Director: Kenny Williams; Film Editor: Russell Schoengarth; Special Effects: David S. Horsley; Dialogue Director: Milt Bronson; Art Directors: Bernard Herzbrun, Eric Orbom; Set Decorators: R. A. Gausman, John Austin; Sound Directors: Leslie I. Carey, Robert Pritchard; Costumes: Rosemary Odell; Makeup: Bud Westmore; Assistant Director: William Holland; Running Time: 76 minutes.

Bud Abbott, Lou Costello, Boris Karloff, Craig Stevens, Helen Westcott, Reginald Denny, John Dierkes, Patti McKaye, Lucille Lamarr, Carmen de Lavallade, Henry Corden, Marjorie Bennett, Harry Cording, Arthur Gould-Porter, Clyde Cook, John Rogers, Herbert Deans, Judith Brian, Gil Perkins, Hilda Plowright, Keith Hitchcock, Donald Kerr, Clive Morgan, Tony Marshe, Michael Hadlow.

Abbott and Costello Meet the Keystone Kops (Universal; January 31, 1955)

Director: Charles Lamont; Producer: Howard Christie; Screenplay: John Grant; Original Story: Lee Loeb; Director of Photography: Reggie Lanning; Music Supervision: Joseph Gershenson; Film Editor: Edward Curtiss; Art Directors: Alexander Golitzen, Bill Newberry; Set Decorators: R. A. Gausman, Julia Heron; Sound Directors: Leslie I. Carey, William Hedgcock; Costumes: Jay A. Morley, Jr.; Makeup: Bud Westmore; Assistant Director: William Holland; Running Time: 79 minutes.

Bud Abbott, Lou Costello, Fred Clark, Lynn Bari, Maxie Rosenbloom, Frank Wilcox, Herold Goodwin, Mack Sennett, Roscoe Ates, Paul Dubov, Joe Besser, Harry Tyler, Henry Kulky, Joe Devlin, William Haade, Jack Daly, Byron Keith, Houseley Stevens, Murray Leonard, Marjorie Bennett, Charles Dorety, Donald Kerr, Heinie Conklin, Forrest Burns, Don House, Jack Stoney, Carole Costello, Hank Mann.

Abbott and Costello Meet the Mummy (Universal; May 23, 1955)

Director: Charles Lamont; Producer: Howard Christie; Screenplay: John Grant; Original Story: Lee Loeb; Director of Photography: George Robinson; Musical Direction: Joseph Gershenson; Film Editor: Russell Schoengarth; Art Directors: Alexander Golitzen, Bill Newberry; Set Decorators: R. A. Gausman, James M. Walters; Sound Director: Leslie I. Carey; Gowns: Rosemary Odell; Makeup: Bud Westmore; Script Supervisor: Betty Abbott; Dialogue Director: Milt Bronson; Running Time: 79 minutes.

Bud Abbott, Lou Costello, Marie Windsor, Michael Ansara, Dan Seymour, Kurt Katch, Richard Karlan, Richard Deacon, Mel Welles, Peggy King, Mazzone-Abbott Dancers, The Chandra-Kaly and Hi Dancers, George Khoury, Eddie Parker, Jan Arvan, Ted Hecht, Michael Vallon, Kem Dibbs, Mitchell Kowal, Ken Alton, Lee Sharon, Hank Mann, Donald Kerr, Harry Medoza, Jean Hartelle, Mitchell Kowal, Kam Tong, Robin Morse, Lee Sharon, Carole Costello, John Powell.

Opposite, top: Abbott and Costello Meet the Mummy (1955). **Unidentified, Bud with the accursed medallion, and Lou.** *Bottom: Dance with Me, Henry* (1956). **Ron Hargrave, Bud, Lou, Gigi Perreau (original lobby card).**

BUD **ABBOTT** and LOU **COSTELLO** **Dance WITH ME, henry!**

Featuring GIGI PERREAU · RUSTY HAMER · MARY WICKES · TED DE CORSIA · RON HARGRAVE
Screenplay by DEVERY FREEMAN · Produced by BOB GOLDSTEIN · Directed by CHARLES BARTON · UNITED ARTISTS

Dance with Me, Henry (United Artists; December 14, 1956)

Director: Charles T. Barton; Producer: Bob Goldstein; Screenplay: Devery Freeman; Original Story: William Kozlenko, Leslie Kardos; Director of Photography: George Robinson; Musical Score: Paul Dunlap; Orchestrations: Frank Comstock; Film Editor: Robert Golden; Assistant Director: Herb Mendelson; Art Director: Leslie Thomas; Set Decorator: Morris Hoffman; Makeup: Abe Haberman; Wardrobe: Albert Deano; Special Effects: Herbert Townsky; Sound Director: Early Snyder; Running Time: 79 minutes.

Bud Abbott, Lou Costello, Gigi Perreau, Rusty Hamer, Mary Wickes, Ted de Corsia, Ron Hargrave, Sherry Alberoni, Frank Wilcox, Richard Reeves, Paul Sorenson, Robert Shayne, John Cliff, Phil Garris, Walter Reed, Eddie Marr, David McMahon, Gil Rankin, Rod Williams.

The 30 Foot Bride of Candy Rock (Columbia; August 6, 1959)

Director: Sidney Miller; Producer: Lewis J. Rachmil; Screenplay: Rowland Barber, Arthur Ross; Original Story: Lawrence J. Goldman; Story Idea: Jack Rabin, Irving Block; Director of Photography: Frank G. Carson (Mattascope); Musical Direction: Raoul Kraushaar; Film Editor: Al Clark; Art Director: William Flannery; Set Decorator: James A. Crowe; Assistant Director: William Dorfman; Makeup: Clay Campbell; Recording Supervisor: John Livadary; Sound Director: George Cooper; Running Time: 75 minutes.

Lou Costello, Dorothy Provine, Gale Gordon, Jimmy Conlin, Charles Lane, Robert Burton, Will Wright, Lenny Kent, Ruth Perrott, Peter Leeds, Bobby Barber, Joey Faye, Doodles Weaver, Jack Rice, Russell Trent, Joe Greene, Robert Nichols, Veola Vonn, Jack Straw, Arthur Walsh, Michael Hagen, Mark Scott, James Bryce.

The World of Abbott and Costello (Universal; April 8, 1965)

Producers: Max J. Rosenberg, Milton Subotsky; Associate Producer: Norman E. Gluck; Editorial Director: Sidney Meyer; Narration written by Gene Wood; Narrator: Jack Leonard; Musical Supervision: Joseph Gershenson; Running Time: 75 minutes.

CHAPTER NOTES

Preface

1. Chris Costello, letter to Scott Allen Nollen, 1996.

Introduction

1. Stephen Cox and John Lofflin, *The Abbott and Costello Story* (Nashville, Tenn.: Cumberland House, 1997), pp. 15–17.
2. Cox and Lofflin, pp. 19–20.
3. Chris Costello, with Raymond Strait, *Lou's on First* (New York: St. Martin's Griffin, 1981), p. 66.

Chapter 1

1. Chris Costello, *Lou's on First*, p. 48.
2. Chris Costello, *Lou's on First*, p. 51.

Chapter 2

1. *New York Times*, 14 February 1941.
2. Maxene Andrews, with Bill Gilbert, *Over Here, Over There: The Andrews Sisters and the USO in World War II* (New York: Kensington Publishing Corp., 1993), pp. 17–18.
3. Chris Costello, *Lou's on First*, p. 57.
4. Chris Costello, *Lou's on First*, p. 176.
5. Chris Costello, *Lou's on First*, p. 57.
6. Chris Costello, *Lou's on First*, p. 61.
7. Bob Furmanek and Ron Palumbo, *Abbott and Costello in Hollywood* (New York: Perigee Books, 1991), p. 45.
8. Maxene Andrews, p. 3.
9. Bosley Crowther, "Low Comedy of a High Order," *New York Times*, 15 June 1941.

Chapter 3

1. Furmanek and Palumbo, p. 59.
2. Stephen Cox and John Loufflin, *The Abbott and Costello Story* (Nashville, Tenn.: Cumberland House, 1997), p. 49.
3. Maxene Andrews, p. 36.

Chapter 4

1. Frank S. Nugent, "Loco Boys Make Good," *New York Times*, 24 August 1941.

2. Nugent.
3. Chris Costello, *Lou's on First*, p. 71.
4. Bob Furmanek and Ron Palumbo, p. 64.

Chapter 5

1. Chris Costello, *Lou's on First*, p. 76.
2. Chris Costello, *Lou's on First*, p. 79.
3. Mulholland, p. 80.

Chapter 6

1. Bob Furmanek and Ron Palumbo, p. 80.

Chapter 7

1. *Pardon My Sarong* pressbook (Universal Pictures, 1942).
2. "Boy's Red Cross Circus Stars Abbott, Costello," *New York Times*, 1 August 1942.

Chapter 8

1. Furmanek and Palumbo, p. 96.

Chapter 9

1. Chris Costello, *Lou's on First*, p. 102.
2. Fred Stanley, "Hollywood Flash: Studios Scrap Many War StoriesThe Horror Boys ConveneOther News," *New York Times*, 16 April 1944.
3. Stanley.

Chapter 10

1. Paul P. Kennedy, "Abbott-Costello, Inc.: Question Is How Long Can the Comedians Get Away with the Same Old Routines," *New York Times*, 20 August 1944.

Chapter 11

1. *New York Herald-Tribune*, July 1945.
2. Paddy Costello, *The Abbott and Costello Show: 100th Anniversary Collection*. Season One, Disc Five (Passport International Entertainment, 2006).

Chapter 12

1. Furmanek and Palumbo, p. 129.
2. A.H. Weiler, "Comics' Crisis and Other Items," *New York Times*, 29 July 1945.

Chapter 13

1. Chris Costello, *Lou's on First*, 90.
2. *Abbott and Costello on Tour* (New York: Popular Programs, Inc., 1946), p. 2.
3. *Abbott and Costello on Tour*, p. 2.
4. *Abbott and Costello on Tour*, p. 4.
5. *Abbott and Costello on Tour*, p. 4.
6. *Abbott and Costello on Tour*, p. 20.

Chapter 14

1. *Buck Privates Come Home* pressbook (Universal-International Pictures, 1947), p. 2.
2. Paddy Costello, *The Abbott and Costello Show: 100th Anniversary Collection*. Season Two, Disc Five (Passport International Entertainment, 2006).
3. *Buck Privates Come Home*, p. 4.
4. *Buck Privates Come Home*, p. 4.

5. *Buck Privates Come Home*, p. 4.
6. *Buck Privates Come Home*, p. 4.
7. Stephen Cox and John Loufflin, p. 118.
8. *Buck Privates Come Home*, p. 6.
9. *Buck Privates Come Home*, p. 7.
10. Mulholland, p. 135.

Chapter 15

1. Stephen Cox and John Lofflin, p. 68
2. Stephen Cox and John Lofflin, p. 68
3. Bosley Crowther, "The Screen," *New York Times*, 24 July 1947.
4. Chris Costello, *Lou's on First*, , 187.
5. Paddy Costello, Season One, Disc Five.
6. Chris Costello, *Lou's on First*, p. 193.
7. Chris Costello, *Lou's on First*, p. 208.
8. Chris Costello, *Lou's on First*, p. 212.
9. Chris Costello, *Lou's on First*, p. 196.
10. Chris Costello, *Lou's on First*, p. 197.
11. Chris Costello, *Lou's on First*, p. 247.
12. Chris Costello, *Lou's on First*, p. 237.
13. Maxene Andrews, p. 231.
14. Paddy Costello, Season Two, Disc Five.

BIBLIOGRAPHY

Interviews

Costello, Paddy, and Chris Costello. *The Abbott and Costello Show: 100th Anniversary Collection*. Season One, Disc Five, and Season Two, Disc Five. Passport International Entertainment, 2006.

Letters

Costello, Chris. Letters to Scott Allen Nollen, 1996.
Costello, Chris. Letters to Scott Allen Nollen, 2007–2008.

Periodicals

New York Herald-Tribune, 1940–1959.
New York Times, 1940–1959.
Variety, 1940–1959.

Publicity Programs and Pressbooks

Abbott and Costello on Tour. New York: Popular Programs, Inc., 1946.
Buck Privates Come Home. Universal-International Pictures, 1947.
Pardon My Sarong. Universal Pictures Corporation, 1942.

Memoirs

Andrews, Maxene, with Bill Gilbert. *Over Here, Over There: The Andrews Sisters and the USO in World War II*. New York: Kensington Publishing Corp., 1993.

Books about Abbott and Costello

Costello, Chris, with Raymond Strait. *Lou's on First*. New York: St. Martin's Griffin, 1981.
Cox, Stephen, and John Lofflin. *The Abbott and Costello Story*. Nashville, Tenn.: Cumberland House, 1997.
Furmanek, Bob, and Ron Palumbo. *Abbott and Costello in Hollywood*. New York: Perigee Books, 1991.
Mulholland, Jim. *The Abbott and Costello Book*. New York: Popular Library, 1975.

Books about Film

Nollen, Scott Allen. *The Boys: The Cinematic World of Laurel and Hardy*. Jefferson, North Carolina: McFarland and Company, Inc., 1989.
Sforza, John. *Swing It! The Andrews Sisters Story*. Lexington: The University Press of Kentucky, 1999.

INDEX

Numbers in **_bold italics_** indicate pages with photographs